C++ Math Class Library

Permutations, Partitions, Calculators, and Gaming

erard

JOHN WILEY & SONS, INC.
New York   Chichester   Brisbane   Toronto   Singapore

Associate Publisher: Katherine Schowalter
Editor: Diane Cerra
Managing Editor: Frank Grazioli
Editorial Production & Design: Lachina Publishing Services

This text is printed on acid-free paper.

Library of Congress Cataloging-in-Publication Data:

Gerard, Scott N., 1956-
    C++ math class library : permutations, partitions, calculators &
gaming / by Scott N. Gerard.
      p. cm.
    Includes bibliographical references and index.
    ISBN 0-471-59243-9 (acid-free)
    1. C++ (Computer program language) 2. Mathematics—Data
processing. I. Title. II. Title: C plus plus math class library.
QA76.73.C153G47 1994
510 ′ .285 ′ 5133—dc20   93-29732
                                      CIP

Printed in the United States of America
10 9 8 7 6 5 4 3 2 1

To Walt and Alice
my loving and supportive parents

CONTENTS

v

P A R T   T H R E E   **Games** _____ **53**

10   Functions   177

FIGURES

PREFACE

This book is for programmers who are interested in mathematics and familiar with C++. It is for programmers who are tired of reinventing code that acts "kinda-like" an existing, well-known concept. It is a book for programmers who know that mathematics is full of well-known and useful concepts and who want to tap into these concepts and their power. It is a book for programmers who want to pick up existing code, plug it into their applications, and increase their productivity.

One of the best ways to be more productive is to *stop* writing code and reuse existing programs, particularly for well-defined problems that can be, or have been, solved once and for all. We need libraries of ready-to-run routines.

All of us have written many subroutines in the past. Why not just take all of those routines and tie them up with a pretty bow and call it a library? If only things were that easy. Most subroutines are written with too many assumptions and hooks into their main program. There is a natural tendency to do this. But all those dependencies force us to spend time duplicating their environment or tweaking the code.

Writing general-purpose code is more difficult than writing single-purpose code. Instead of having the exact details of the main program in front of us, we must try to anticipate any and all possible clients. Instead of providing only the function and options required for the specific task at hand, we must provide all relevant operations.

I believe object-oriented (OO) programming makes it easier to write general-purpose code than in non-OO paradigms. Instead of focusing on some hypothetical client and trying to figure out all of its needs, OO focuses on specific objects and asks what operations make sense for that object. OO is not PP (panacea-programming). But although OO has been "overhyped" recently, it does encourage a way of thinking about problems that I believe will be as much a part of future languages as strong data typing has become. Simply put, OO is a good idea and it helps organize programming.

My goals for this book are to

- provide C++ source code for ready-to-run classes,
- leverage the power of mathematical concepts that have stood the test of time,
- give you some ideas where you might apply these concepts in programming applications, and
- teach you some interesting mathematics along the way.

For those of you who like to know the "why" as well as the "what," some proofs are included. But the proofs are clearly marked and can be skipped.

Mid-level Functions

What kinds of routines should be in a programmer's library? A library should not contain programs for entire applications. Complete applications are usually too specific to be heavily reused. And the number of distinct applications is far too large for any reasonable library. Complete applications are just too large for inclusion in a library.

Many books have been published with titles like "A Zillion Little Programs for Your PC." These books are filled with routines to turn on and off the PC speaker, switch video display modes, and so on. These routines fill a certain niche, but are usually not portable to other machines. Primitive functions are needed to write more complex programs, but they do not provide very much function by themselves. They will account for only a small percentage of code in your applications. Therefore, they are too small to greatly increase your productivity because you still have a lot of code to write.

The library routines we're looking for should be not too small and not too big. A library should be made up of medium-sized routines in terms of both size and complexity. Library routines should be complex enough that they can completely take over all processing in one area of an application. And this suggests writing library routines as objects that know how to maintain themselves.

Unusual Classes

In almost every new programming book—regardless of language—the authors present the ever-popular stacks and queues. Stacks and queues are good examples to illustrate the concepts of data hiding, abstraction, and encapsulation. They are small enough that they can be presented without going through a lot of code, and they are truly useful. However, I will assume you already have a number of these books and therefore do not need yet another version.

Instead, I intend to provide other useful data types that are "above" these basic types, that is, data types that are more complex and provide richer function. These routines are portable (or nearly so) to any machine with a C++ compiler. Some of the classes (in particular, the calculator classes) depend on the lists and sets in Borland's class library. If you want to compile my classes on a machine without Borland's classes, you will need to do some reworking.

This book provides a collection of data types that are out of the ordinary, and are intermediate in both size and complexity. There are no stacks or queues, and no sorting routines. All classes are related, in one way or another, to mathematics. This book contains the following classes:

Functions   In programming, functions are useful as lookup tables, and for representing finite state machines.

Perm Permutations have many uses. Besides being a fundamental abstraction of one-to-one and onto functions, they can model card games and other modern puzzles like Rubik's Cube.

Part Partitions are ideal for representing the concepts of equality and connection.

Polya This handles unusual types of enumeration problems, like the number of distinct ways to paint the faces of a cube, or the number of distinct bracelets.

Calculator These classes make it easy to create calculators for your data types.

Region A region is a mapping between points on a plane, or in a space, and the integers. The region classes support rectangular, triangular, and trapezoidal regions in two dimensions as well as cubical, tetrahedral, pyramidal, and other types of regions in three dimensions.

Xform These are classes for transforming points including translations, transformations by a group, and general linear transformations.

Hexgrid These routines manipulate grids of hexagons, which are commonly used in simulation and fantasy games.

Enum IO These routines read and write enumerations by name.

Hashing This class combines data into a hash value.

Binomial In addition to computing binomial coefficients, these routines convert between binary integers and "cogets" (see Chapter 3) in the binomial numbering system.

C++

All the code in this book is in C++ because C++ is the mostly widely used object-oriented language today. This book does *not* cover the basics of the C++ language. There are many good books on C++; for example, see Stroustrup (1991), Lippman (1989), and Meyers (1992).

I will not mount a major defense of the merits of object-oriented programming in C++. If you are reading this book, you probably already agree that C++ is useful, productive, and just plain fun. I will say that I think it is easier to consider all the operations a specific object can reasonably support, than to try and imagine all possible requests from some hypothetical client. This gives me greater confidence that my classes are complete.

Trademarks

All Borland products are trademarks or registered trademarks of Borland International, Inc. Rubik's Cube is a trademark of Ideal Toy Corporation.

Acknowledgments

There are a great many people I want to thank for their help and support of this project. Nancy Hankins, Dave Borrillo, and Craig Orcutt deserve special thanks. They helped get me started, checked my results, and kept me going. I'd also like to thank Joe and Sue Cahill, Joe Collette, Auther Eberiel, Diane Gerard, Paul Gunsch, Charles and Christian Hankins, Tim Hamel, Jim Herring, Eric Johnson, Steve Knight, Mike Moore, A. Carolyn Neal, Jeff Palm, Curt Rose, Dave and Karen Scudiero, Abolfaz Sirjani, Mike Smith, Francine Stenzel, and Tom Turner.

PART ONE

Introduction

1

Getting Started

Minimum Requirements

All the programs in this book compile using Borland's C++ compiler, version 3.1. Most programs will *not* compile with Borland's Turbo C++ because it does not support templates.

The executable files on the diskette require an 80286 processor running DOS 4.0 or higher. The source and executable files require about 2 Mbytes of storage on your hard disk. To make all the files requires 4 Mbytes of memory and an additional 500 Kbytes of hard disk for the object files.

With some additional work, you should be able to easily port many of these programs to other compilers. However, some of the classes are dependent on Borland's library. So while the function classes do not depend on Borland's library, the calculator classes do. Of course, you will have to rework those classes if you port to a different compiler.

Making a Backup Copy

Before you start to use the enclosed disk, I strongly recommend that you make a backup copy of the original. Remember, however, that a backup disk is for your personal use only. Any other use of the backup disk violates copyright law. Please take the time now to make a backup, using the instructions below (they assume your floppy diskette drive is A).

3

1. DISKCOPY A: A:.
2. Follow the DOS prompts for inserting the correct diskette at the correct time. The source diskette is the original MATHPP diskette; the target is your backup diskette.
3. Store the original MATHPP diskette in a safe place.

Installation

The diskette contains all the source and .EXE files for the programs described in this book. It also contains a makefile to compile and link all the programs, and a READ.ME file. Please read through READ.ME for any last minute changes.

Most of the files on the diskette are in compressed format, so you must use the installation program on the diskette.

1. Insert your backup copy of MATHPP into floppy drive A.
2. Enter A: to make A the default driver.
3. Enter INSTALL.
4. After the title screen appears, you will see a screen where you can set the installation options. By default, the source and executables are placed in subdirectory C:\MATHPP. To select an option, type the highlighted letter or use the arrow keys to move the menu bar to the desired option. Press Enter to change the option.
5. To start the installation, select the Start Installation option and press Enter.

When the installation is complete, remove your diskette and store it in a safe place.

Throughout the book, I will use "C>" as the DOS prompt even though it is very unlikely you will actually be working in the root directory of your hard disk. It is meant to suggest that you are entering commands to the DOS command processor.

Makefile

The executables on the disk were compiled to run on an 80286 without a floating point processor to satisfy the widest possible audience. You can make the executables with different compiler options using the makefile on the diskette. To change the compiler and linker options, edit the bottom part of the makefile where the configuration files are created. The makefile also supports the following macro variables:

BCPATH   This is the drive and directory that contains the Borland C++ compiler and libraries. The default path is C:\BC.

MDL   This is the memory model (t, s, c, m, l, or h). The value must be a lowercase letter. Some programs are too big to compile under some memory models. All programs compile with the default memory model m (medium memory model).

You must have already compiled the Borland class library for the memory model you select.

FP87   Use hardware floating point instructions rather than the floating point emulator (the default).

For example, if you installed the Borland compiler in D:\BC31, and you want to compile all programs using the large memory model, you would enter

```
make -DBCPATH=D:\BC31 -DMDL=1
```

The makefile contains make "targets" for groups of programs:

allcfg   Makes new configuration files and *all* programs. It is the first target in the make file, so it is used if you do not specify a target.

cfg   Makes the compiler and linker configuration files.

allexe   Makes all programs. It is the same as allcfg except that it does not make the cfg configuration files.

region   Makes all the region and board programs.

calc   Makes all the calculator programs.

User Assistance and Information

John Wiley & Sons, Inc., is pleased to provide assistance to users of this software package. Should you have questions regarding the use of this package, please call our technical support number at (212) 850-6194 weekdays between 9 A.M. and 4 P.M. Eastern Time.

To place additional orders or to request information about other Wiley products, please call (800) 879-4539.

2

Conventions and Notations

OO Diagrams

I use a modified version of Grady Booch's (1992a, b) notation to illustrate class and object relationships (see Figure 2.1). I have had to modify it slightly because his notation seems to defy any graphics program that is not specifically written to handle its symbology. I will also use only a subset of his notation. Subsets are sometimes called "Booch Lite."

Classes and objects are rectangles rather than Booch's famous "blobs" or "clouds." However, classes are still outlined with dashed lines and objects are still outlined with solid lines.

A great deal of information can be represented in "Classic" Booch diagrams. Only three relationships concern us here.

A derived class "inherits" from, or "is" a specialized kind of its base class. That is, every method of a base class makes sense for a derived class. Public inheritance in C++ models the inherits relation. A solid-line arrow points from a derived class to its base class. I also use inherits to show that an object instance "is" an instance of a class.

Instead of Booch's double-lined notation for "uses" relation, I use a single-line notation. The circled end of the relationship marks the "using" class; the plain end marks the "used" class. A solid circle means the using class "contains," or is the only object that has a pointer to the used class. Classes "own" their contents and are responsible for cleaning up after them. An open circle means the using class does not contain or own the used class. A few of the diagrams add numbers to show how many times the relationship applies, for example, how many copies are contained.

Figure 2.2 is an example of this notation. Class Scope is the base class for all the derived scope classes. Scope uses, but does not own, Identifier instances. Scope also

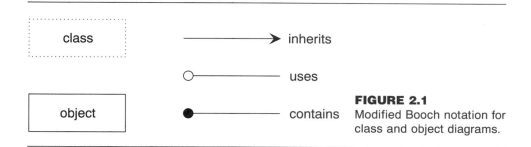

FIGURE 2.1
Modified Booch notation for class and object diagrams.

contains a Dictionary class, although Dictionaries do not show up in Scope's public interface. The Dictionary object is used only internally in Scope's implementation.

Both the OrderedScope and SortedScope classes are directly derived from Scope (inheritance), and both contain a DoubleList class in their implementation. ValueScope is derived from OrderedScope and it contains a SetOfList class in its implementation.

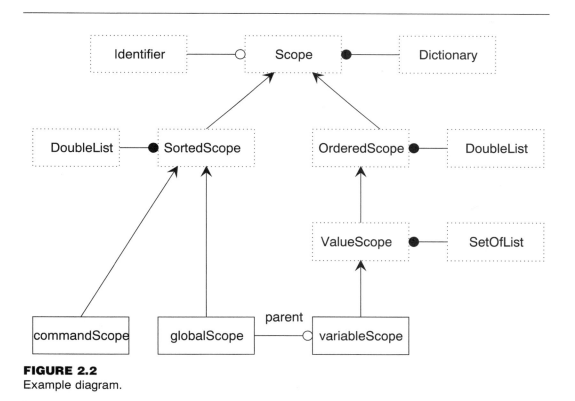

FIGURE 2.2
Example diagram.

The last three boxes are objects rather than classes. Both commandScope and globalScope are object instances of class SortedScope. variableScope is an instance of class ValueScope and it uses (sends messages to) its parent globalScope.

These diagrams are not necessarily complete. For example, class Scope is actually derived from Borland's TShouldDelete class, and Scope also uses classes String and Variable (a class derived from Identifier). These diagrams are intended only to give you the big picture of how the classes fit together. Adding every class would needlessly complicate the diagram without clarifying anything.

Coding Conventions

Rather than forcing you to discover the patterns I have used in writing the programs, this section describes some of them.

Naming Conventions

Classes with an "Imp" suffix are not intended to be used directly by clients. In some cases, Imp classes are used to collect functions into a common place (PartImp); in some cases, Imp classes are the internal, hidden body classes that hold the implementation for external, visible handle classes (see Chapter 5, "Handles and Bodies").

C++ has no built-in mechanism for extracting the name of the current class or the name of the base class. But these concepts are useful for both clarity and maintenance, so many classes contain typedefs ThisClass, BaseClass and RootClass. ThisClass is the current class. BaseClass is the one and only base class. None of these classes use multiple inheritance, so a single name is not a problem. RootClass is intended to be the basemost class; that is, it is the base class of the base class of the . . . . In the C++ language accepted by Borland's v3.1 compiler, a member function in a derived class must return *exactly* the same type as the member function it is overriding in the base class. Since the base class itself may be derived from another class, these member functions need to return a value of type RootClass. In new versions of C++, overriding functions in derived classes can return ThisClass rather than RootClass.

Consistency Checks

Many classes have a member function valid(). It checks whether an object instance is in a valid state. In formal terms, it tests the class's invariant. valid() should *always* return TRUE. While valid() can be called directly by the programmer, its primary use is so that methods can execute the statement

```
assert( valid() );
```

If the object fails this check, the program halts. This run-time checking can be turned off by defining NDEBUG and recompiling with the program.

In theory, every method should run valid() before it begins and after it finishes. However, even during development, all this checking can cause the program to run very slowly. I tend to check valid() only at the beginning of "important" methods.

I also arrange for valid() to check a condition that is established in the constructor, and broken by the destructor. That is, I ensure that a destructed object will fail valid(). I had a terrible time debugging some classes during initial development. The problem was that two different routines thought they owned the same object, and they both decided to delete it when they were finished. With the valid() checks, any method calls on objects that had been destroyed would die instantly. Destructors should "stomp all over" the bytes that *used* to hold the object. It makes valid()'s job that much easier and makes it less likely for any method to work properly on a destroyed object. Many classes have a pointer to storage they allocate from the heap. valid() should ensure it is not NULL, and the destructor should zap it back to NULL.

Related Operators

By convention, operators like == and != have a specific relationship to each other. If a class does not maintain those relationships, clients will probably fail. One way to ensure these relationships are always true is to write one operator in terms of the other.

I often use member function compare() to test two objects for equality. Operators == and != are inline, global functions that invoke compare(). Placing the class-specific equality checks in the single compare functions ensures that either operator == or operator != is always true. Making the operators global functions allows C++ to automatically convert both operands in the comparison. If they were member functions, only the second operand could be converted. *this is never converted.

Operators like + and += should also maintain a certain relationship to each other. This can be done by writing one in terms of the other. But which one is primitive and which one is derived? It depends on the class. If addition can be done in place, then += should be the primitive operation. Then operator + can be written as

```
T operator + (const T& a, const T& b) {
    T result = a;                // or T result = a.copy();
    return result += b;
};
```

Note that operator + returns a T, not a T&. Operator + creates a new object (result). It is wrong to return a reference to result because result will be destructed as the return completes. Figure 2.3 shows the two operators and how variables flow into an operator on the left and the results are returned on the right.

If addition cannot be done in place, then operator + is primitive, and operator += can be written as

```
T& operator += (const T& b) {
    T temp = *this;
    return *this = temp + b;
};
```

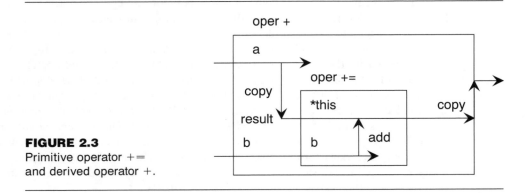

FIGURE 2.3
Primitive operator +=
and derived operator +.

Figure 2.4 shows how the original value of *this is copy constructed into a temporary before addition starts.

Templates

Many of these classes are templates. I like the template feature very much. I believe the reason so many people *talk* about stacks rather than shipping *code* for stacks is that the stack concept is too variable for a single piece of nontemplate code with fixed data types, fixed precisions, and fixed operations. To a compiler, a stack of integers is quite

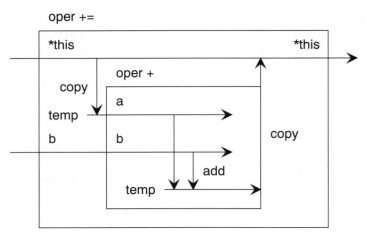

FIGURE 2.4
Primitive operator + and how operator += uses it.

different from a stack of pointers to integers. User-defined typedefs don't solve the problem either because they are limited to just one kind of stack per application—an unreasonable restriction. I think templates (with the possible exception of Ada's generics) are the minimum amount of machinery needed to capture the variability of concepts like "stack." I use templates so you can alter the precision of internal variables (e.g., short integers versus long integers), and to tailor a class to a user-defined class.

Function bodies (in .cpp files) are normally compiled separately from the application that uses them. However, function bodies for template classes and template functions cannot be compiled until the template arguments are known. Only an application knows the arguments it uses. To reduce the number of files on the diskette, each application main program includes the .cpp files for the template classes it needs. This means all template function bodies are recompiled whenever the application is recompiled.

Another way to handle this problem is to create an additional .cpp file that does nothing but instantiate the template using the template arguments. For example, since application P2Board uses class template Reg2Rect instantiated with class Point2, create a file named P2BRect.cpp with the following contents:

```
#include "Point2.hpp"
#include "Reg2Rect.cpp"

#pragma option -Jgd
typedef Reg2Rect<Point2> fake;
```

The -Jgd pragma option causes the compiler to generate public definitions for all template instances. The typedef fake causes the template Reg2Rect to be instantiated and compiled using class Point2, but has no other use in the program. P2BRect.cpp can be compiled like any other file and linked with the main object file for P2Board. Since P2Board uses many other templates, you will need a similar file for every other template.

The total number of compiled lines in an application is quite a bit larger using this approach since common include files must be processed multiple times. In the P2Board example, a change to Point2.hpp will cause essentially all the instantiation files to be recompiled. But during development, incremental changes that affect a small number of files may require fewer lines to be recompiled.

Ranking

There are times when you want an array of values indexed by a data type. The compiler inherently supports this operation only if the data type is an integer. To solve this problem, many of the classes support methods rank() and unrank() that convert an instance of the class back and forth to unique integers between 0 and $n - 1$ where n is the total number of possible data type instances. For example, there are $n!$ permutations of n elements. Permutation's rank() method converts any permutation to a number in the range $[0..n! - 1]$. unrank() is the reverse operation of rank() and converts a number in the range $[0..n! - 1]$ to a permutation. If d is some date type value, then $d = $ unrank(rank(d)) for all d.

For example, I had an application that was supposed to generate all possible permutations in different orders (see Chapter 13, "Change Ringing"). To make sure I never generated the same permutation twice, I used rank() to generate a rank value for each new permutation. I used that value to index into a bit array to see if I had already generated that permutation.

The `randomDist` calculator command uses the data type's rank() to convert random data values to an index into an array of counters.

The random() method can always be written as the unrank() of a random integer. However, there are usually more efficient ways to write random(). And sometimes a special random() routine can generate random data values whose rank is larger than the long unsigned integer (the maximum rank value). For example, Permutation's random() will happily generate random permutations with a hundred elements, but unrank() can handle only permutations with 12 or fewer elements because 13! is too big for a long unsigned.

unrank() can be used to iterate over all values of the data type:

```
Type t;

for (long i = 0; i < numTValues; ++i) {   // iterate over Type
    t.unrank(i);                           // set t to the i-th value
    // process t
};
```

Virtual Copy Constructors

Suppose D is a derived class of B, and that D adds data members so that the size of D is larger than the size of B. Any application that creates objects of class D and then uses them as instances of class B is going to have problems whenever it tries to make a copy of an object. The reason is B's copy constructor knows nothing about D's additional data members. Virtual copy constructors are a way around this.

```
class B {

    typedef B BaseClass;
    typedef B ThisClass;

protected:
    typedef B RootClass;

public:
    ThisClass* copy () const { return (ThisClass*) _copy(); };

protected:
    virtual RootClass* _copy () const { return new ThisClass(*this); };
};

class D: public B {
```

```
    typedef B BaseClass;
    typedef D ThisClass;

public:
    ThisClass* copy () const { return (ThisClass*) _copy(); };

protected:
    virtual RootClass* _copy () const { return new ThisClass(*this); };
};
```

Virtual member function _copy() creates a copy of *this and returns a pointer to the copy. Every derived class D must override _copy to call its own copy constructor. Note that the code for _copy is always written in terms of ThisClass, but ThisClass is different for every class. Now the application can call b._copy() and get a faithful copy of b regardless of b's actual type (B or D). Because of the language Borland v3.1 accepts, _copy() must always return exactly the same type. The only useful type for B::_copy() to return is a B*. Therefore, _copy() in every derived class must also return a B*. Generically, this is the basemost class in the hierarchy, which is the value of RootClass.

However, an application may want to create a copy of D without downcasting the type from D to B. Nonvirtual member copy() handles that. It casts the results of _copy() to ThisClass, which is always type safe. Users need access only to copy(), so _copy() is protected.

Future versions of C++ will relax the restriction on returned parameters. By that time, _copy() can be eliminated and its body moved into copy().

PART TWO

Foundation Modules

3

Binomials

Binomial Coefficients

Binomial coefficients show up in counting problems, statistics, and in the ranking and unranking of partitions (see Chapter 14). Routine binomial() computes the binomial coefficient of two integers n and k

$$binomial(n,k) = \binom{n}{k} = \frac{n!}{k!\,(n-k)!} \qquad [1]$$

where $k!$ is the factorial of k. Binomial coefficients can be defined for negative n using the formula

$$binomial(n,k) = \frac{n(n-1)\ldots(n-k+1)}{k(k-1)\ldots 1}$$

for $k \geq 0$ and 0 when $k < 0$.

One of the reasons binomial coefficients are important is because they are the coefficients in the expansion

$$(x + y)^n = \sum_{k=0}^{n} \binom{n}{k} x^k y^{n-k}$$

Binomial Iterator

The computation of binomial() is necessarily iterative. However, there are applications that need to generate many binomial coefficients that differ by one unit in either n or k. Equation [1] shows there is a lot of similar computation in these cases.

$$\binom{n+1}{k} = \frac{(n+1)n(n-1)\ldots(n-k+2)}{k(k-1)\ldots 1}$$

$$= \frac{n+1}{n-k-1}\binom{n}{k}$$

This equation holds except when $n - k - 1 = 0$. Similar formulas hold for decrementing n, and incrementing and decrementing k. Since these calculations are much cheaper than computing binomial() from scratch, it is worthwhile encapsulating this knowledge into a class.

BinIter is a class that contains a binomial coefficient. BinIter's constructor requires values for n and k and computes that binomial coefficient using binomial(). It knows how to increment and decrement the current value of either n or k and how to adjust the binomial coefficient.

```
#include "Binomial.hpp"
BinIter   binIter(5,3);          // = binomial(5,3) = 10

cout << binIter.bin();           // prints 10

binIter.incN();                  // = binomial(6,3) = 20
binIter.decK();                  // = binomial(6,2) = 15

cout << binIter.n() << binIter.k();  // prints 6 and 2
```

Binomial Number System

We are all familiar with the decimal and binary numbering systems. There is also a binomial numbering system (Knuth, 1968b:72; Gimpel, 1976:329). The binomial numbering system is used in class Part (see Chapter 14) to rank and unrank partitions.

Given a positive integer n (called the "nome") every number m can be written as

$$m = \binom{c_1}{1} + \binom{c_2}{2} + \cdots + \binom{c_n}{n}$$

The numbers $c_1, c_2, \ldots, c_n$ are called "cogets" (as opposed to digits). The number of cogets is the nome. There is a unique representation when

$$0 \leq c_1 < c_2 < \cdots < c_n \qquad\qquad [2]$$

Routines numToCogets and cogetsToNum() convert between a number and its representation as cogets with nome *n*. cogetsToNum() does not assume the cogets are in increasing order. numToCogets() always selects the unique representation implied by that ordering.

```
#include "Binomial.hpp"

int    nome=3;
long   coget[nome];

// fill the first three slots of coget with the binomial
// representation of 14 using nome=3.
numToCogets( 14, cogets, nome);

cout << coget[0] << coget[1] << coget[2];
```

This prints the numbers 1, 3 and 5. As a check, binomial(1,1) = 1, binomial(3,2) = 3 and binomial(5,3) = 10, which is 1 + 3 + 10 = 14.

Implementation Comments

binomial() computes coefficients using integer multiplication and division and the formula

$$binomial(n,k) = \frac{n}{1}\,\frac{n-1}{2}\cdots\frac{n-k+1}{k}$$

Every division will always have a zero remainder if the multiplication is done first. The division by 2 will be exact because either *n* or *n* − 1 must be even. The division by 3 will be exact because one of *n*, *n* − 1, or *n* − 2 must be a multiple of 3. The division by 4 is exact because *n*, *n* − 1, *n* − 2, and *n* − 3 must contain one factor of 4 and another even number, for 3 factors of 2. One factor of 2 was removed by the division by 2; the other two factors of 2 can be safely removed by the division by 4.

Similar analysis shows that the BinIter routines will also never round during integer divide.

Possible Improvements

Internal routine findCoget() returns the largest coget (the number on top) for a binomial coefficient with a given *k*, that is less than or equal to a user-specified number. It is called by numToCoget(). findCoget() increments a BinIter object until it finds a binomial coefficient that equals or exceeds the number. It would be nice to speed up this linear search. The performance of a few special cases could be improved. If $k = 1$, then findCoget() can return the number as the coget. If $k = 2$, findCoget() might perform faster using a formula involving an integer square root (although this is not certain). However, there doesn't seem to be any way to speed up the search for larger values of k. Even a binary search may not improve things because it is more expensive to compute "isolated" binomial coefficients than it is to step through them with a BinIter.

Multinomial coefficients, a generalization of binomial coefficients, can be defined as

$$\binom{k_1 + k_2 + \cdots + k_m}{k_1, k_2, \ldots, k_m} = \binom{k_1}{k_1}\binom{k_1 + k_2}{k_2}\cdots\binom{k_1 + k_2 + \cdots + k_m}{k_m}$$

$$= \frac{(k_1 + k_2 + \cdots + k_m)!}{k_1!\,k_2!\ldots k_m!}$$

The k_i values on the bottom completely define the multinomial coefficient because the top number must be the sum of the bottom numbers. Therefore, a multinomial() routine needs only an array containing the bottom numbers as input. The binomial coefficient is just a multinomial coefficient with the two bottom values k and $n - k$.

A MultiIter class could also be defined. Instead of incN(), decN(), incK() and decK(), MultiIter would use inc(i) and dec(i) to increment and decrement the ith bottom value.

Multinomial coefficients are important because they are the coefficients in the expansion

$$(x_1 + x_2 + \cdots + x_m)^n = \sum_{k_1 + k_2 + \cdots + k_m = n} \binom{n}{k_1, k_2, \ldots, k_m} x_1^{k_1} x_2^{k_2} \ldots x_m^{k_m}$$

Source Code

File BinIter.hpp

```
#ifndef _BINITER_HPP
#define _BINITER_HPP
//************************************************************************
// TITLE: BinIter -- Iterator for Binomial coefficients
//
// AUTHOR: Scott N Gerard, Rochester, MN
// LANGUAGE: C++
//
// FUNCTION:
//    Given one binomial coefficient Bin(n,k), it is easy to compute
//    the binomial coefficient for n+1, n-1, k+1, and k-1.
//
```

```
// IMPLEMENTATION:
//    The binomial coefficient Bin(n,k) is equal to
//    n * (n-1) * ... * (n-k+1) / ( k * (k-1) * ... * 1 ).
//    The inc and dec functions follow directly from this expression.
//
// CHANGE LOG:
//    28Aug92 - Initial coding.  SN Gerard
//    09Dec92 - Make into a template, and fix a few bugs.  SN Gerard
//**********************************************************************
#include "Binomial.hpp"

template <class T>
class BinIter {

private:
    T  nn, kk, bbin;                    // bbin = Binomial(nn,kk)

public:
    BinIter(T n, T k): nn(n), kk(k), bbin(binomial(nn,kk)) {};

    // use default copy constructor
    // use default assignment
    // use default destructor

    // reset to a specific (n,k)
    void set(T n, T k) {
        nn = n;
        kk = k;
        bbin = binomial(nn,kk);
    };

    //**********************************************************************
    // Accessors
    //**********************************************************************
    T n()   const { return nn;   };      // return current n
    T k()   const { return kk;   };      // return current k
    T bin() const { return bbin; };      // return binomail(n,k)

    //**********************************************************************
    // Increment and decrement routines.
    // The multiplication is done before the division.  This way the
    // division will never have a non-zero remainder.
    //**********************************************************************
    BinIter& incN () {
        if (nn-kk+1 != 0)
            bbin = bbin * (nn+1) / (nn-kk+1);
        else if (kk >= 0)
            bbin = 1;
        else
            bbin = 0;
        ++nn;
```

(continued)

File BinIter.hpp   *(continued)*

```
      return *this;
   };

   BinIter& decN () {
      if (nn != 0)
         bbin = bbin * (nn-kk) / nn;
      else if (kk >= 0)
         // bbin is 1 if kk is even; -1 if kk is odd
         bbin = (long(kk) & 1) ? -1: 1;
      else
         bbin = 0;
      --nn;
      return *this;
   };

   BinIter& incK () {
      if (kk >= 0)
         bbin = bbin * (nn-kk) / (kk+1);
      else if (kk == -1)
         bbin = 1;
      else
         bbin = 0;
      ++kk;
      return *this;
   };

   BinIter& decK () {
      if (nn-kk+1 != 0)
         bbin = bbin * kk / (nn-kk+1);
      else if (kk > 0)
         bbin = 1;
      else
         bbin = 0;
      --kk;
      return *this;
   };

};
#endif
```

File Binomial.hpp

```
#ifndef _BINOMIAL_HPP
#define _BINOMIAL_HPP
//*********************************************************************
// TITLE: Binomial -- binomial operations
//
// AUTHOR: Scott N Gerard, Rochester, MN
// LANGUAGE: C++
//
```

```
// FUNCTION:
//    Computes binomial coefficients.
//
// CHANGE LOG:
//    05Dec91 - Initial coding.  SN Gerard
//    29Aug92 - Convert to C++.  SN Gerard
//**********************************************************************

//**********************************************************************
// Return the number of combinations of n things taken k at a time
//**********************************************************************
long binomial (long n, long k);

//**********************************************************************
// Binomial Number System
//
// Given an integer n (called the "nome") every number m can be written
// as
//
//     m = bin(c1,1) + bin(c2,2) + bin(c3,3) + ... + bin(cn,n)
//
// The numbers (c1, c2, c3, ..., cn) are called "cogets" (as opposed to
// digits).  The number of cogets is the nome.  This coget
// representation is unique when the following criterion is also applied
//
//    0 <= c1 < c2 < c3 < ... < cn
//
// NumToCogets and CogetsToNum convert between a number and its
// representation as cogets with nome n. CogetsToNum does not assume
// the cogets are increasing order; NumToCogets always selects the
// unique representation implied by that ordering.
//
// For more info on the "binomial number system" see Kunth, Vol 1,
// "Fundamental Algorithms", section 1.2.6, exercise 56, and also James
// F. Gimpel, "Algorithms in Snobol4", John Wiley & Sons, p329, 1976.
//
//**********************************************************************

//**********************************************************************
// Return the value of a number described by the cogets.
// (This routine does not depend on the cogets being ordered).
//**********************************************************************
long cogetsToNum (const long* coget, const long nome);

//**********************************************************************
// Convert a number to its unique coget representation
//**********************************************************************
void numToCogets (const long num,
   long* coget,
   const unsigned nome);

#endif
```

File Binomial.cpp

```cpp
//*********************************************************************
// TITLE: Binomial -- binomial operations
//
// AUTHOR: Scott N Gerard, Rochester, MN
// LANGUAGE: C++
//
// FUNCTION:
//    Computes binomial coefficients.
//
// CHANGE LOG:
//    05Dec91 - Initial coding.  SN Gerard
//*********************************************************************
#include "Binomial.hpp"

//*********************************************************************
// Return the number of combinations of n things taken k at a time
//*********************************************************************
long binomial (long n, long k) {

    if (n >= 0)                      .      // n is positive
        // bin(n,k) = bin(n,n-k).  Optimize loop by picking smaller k
        if (2*k > n)                        // set k = min( k, n-k)
            k = n-k;                        // bin(n,k) = bin(n,n-k)

    // no way to optimize computation when n is negative

    if (k < 0)                              // make sure k is positive
        return 0;

    //*********************************************************************
    // binomial(n,k) = n/1 * (n-1)/2 * (n-2)/3 * (n-3)/4 * ...
    // The divisions will always have a zero remainder if the
    // multiplication is done first.
    //*********************************************************************
    long numer = n;                  // = n-i
    long denom = 1;                  // = i
    long value = 1;                  // val = bin(n,0);

    for (long i = 1; i <= k; ++i)
        value = value * numer-- / denom++;     // val = val * (n-i) / i

    return value;
};

//*********************************************************************
// Internal Routine:
// Return the largest coget such that binomial(coget,k) <= num.
// Also decrement num by binomial(coget,k) in preparation for next call.
//*********************************************************************
unsigned findCoget( long& num, const unsigned k) {

    unsigned    coget = k;                   // the returned value
```

```
long            binCK = 1;                      // = binomial(coget,k)
long            prvBinCK = 0;                   // = binomial(coget-1,k)

//***********************************************************************
// Find the largest coget such that binomial(coget,k) <= num.
// Use binomial(n,k) = n/(n-k) * binomial(n-1,k)
//***********************************************************************
for (;;) {
    if (binCK < num) {
        // binCK is too small.  increase coget
        prvBinCK = binCK;
        ++coget;
        binCK = binCK * coget / (coget-k);
                                // adjust bin(coget,i) for coget+1

    } else if (binCK == num) {
        // coget is the correct value, and binCK = binomial(coget,k)
        break;

    } else {
        // we went too far.  Back up cog
        --coget;
        binCK = prvBinCK;
        break;
    };
};

num -= binCK;
return coget;
};

//***********************************************************************
// Return the value of a number described by the cogets.
// (This routine does not depend on the cogets being ordered).
//***********************************************************************
long cogetsToNum (const long* cogets, const long nome) {

    long number = 0;
    for (unsigned i = 0; i < nome; ++i)
        number += binomial( cogets[i], i+1);

    return number;
};

//***********************************************************************
// Convert a number to its unique coget representation
//***********************************************************************
void numToCogets (const long num, long* coget, const unsigned nome) {

    long number = num;
    // Find the cogets from high to low.
    for (unsigned i = nome; i >= 1; --i)
        coget[i-1] = findCoget(number, i);

};
```

4

Compare

Many applications (e.g., binary searching) require a three-way branch to separately handle the $a < b$, $a = b$, and $a > b$ cases. But relational operators are either TRUE or FALSE. To fully categorize the relationships between two values requires multiple relational operations. FORTRAN is superior in this respect with its three-way branching IF statement. Sakkinen (1987) argues for three-way comparison values in addition to the boolean relational operators. The types in this chapter define systemwide, multivalued comparison types.

The Algol family of languages (Algol, Pascal, Modula-2, Ada) all define a boolean type. And by doing so they assert that the boolean type is distinct from the integer type. C and C++ have glossed over the issue by merging boolean into integer. While this works for booleans, it begins to break down for types similar to boolean. But even many C programmers introduce a boolean type to make their programs easier to understand and more maintainable. In this chapter, I present types for representing the result of a comparison.

C and C++ use the convention that 0 is FALSE and anything else is TRUE. strcmp() uses that convention that -1 means the first argument is less than the second, 0 means the two are equal, and $+1$ means the first argument is greater than the second. While these conventions are simple and reasonable, the values are not very mnemonic. And there is no obvious way to extend these values when there are more than three possible results (e.g., unordered). While it is easy to store these values in integer subrange variables, programmers all too often neglect this extra level of checking. In short, TRUE has more meaning than 1 (or 10 or 937) and GreaterThan is more meaningful than $+1$.

The types in this chapter provide a common way to support comparisons. Instead of using special integer values, an enumeration type provides mnemonics like LT (less than), EQ (equal to), and GT (greater than). Comparing sets can result in five natural conditions: SetIN (included in), SetEQ (equal to), SetCO (contains), SetOV (overlap), and SetDJ (disjoint).

It is important to have these identifiers declared in a separate, common enumeration so all comparison routines can use exactly the same type. Otherwise the "EQ" used in one module would be different from the "EQ" used in other modules. This would cause a lot of confusion, and many needless type errors.

Testing a BOOLEAN relational operator is done with an IF statement. Testing a multivalued comparison value is done with a CASE statement. This chapter contains five compare modules.

BOOL	This enumeration is for types that are either equal or not equal. ($a < b$ has no meaning.) Permutations are a good example.
TotalCompare	This enumeration is for "totally ordered" types. Integers, characters, enumerations, character strings, and arrays in lexicographical order are examples of totally ordered types. This module is *not* a superset of all compare values.
PartCompare	This enumeration is for "partially ordered" values. The IEEE definition for standard binary floating-point arithmetic is an example of such a data type.
SetCompare	This enumeration provides five values necessary for set comparison.
SigCompare	This enumeration provides an extended set of comparison values for comparing floating points with a certain range of significance as is often found in numerical applications.

You might wonder why we don't just put all values into a single "super" compare module. We don't do it because set comparison values make absolutely no sense for the partially ordered REAL type, and vice versa. We know exactly one of $a < b$, $a = b$ and $a > b$ is true for totally ordered types. But this is not true for partially ordered types. These enumerations are distinct.

Common Features of the Comparisons

All five enumerations define a comparison type. The values of the enumeration are exhaustive and mutually exclusive. compare(a,b), where a and b are of some type T, always results in exactly one of these enumerated comparison values.

Routine reverse() switches the direction of a comparison. (A comp B) is the same as (B reverse(comp) A). If the comparison of two values of type T is expensive, reverse() is cheaper than recomparing the two values. A switch statement is the best way to fully classify the result of a comparison. T is a partially ordered type.

```
#include "PartCompare.hpp"

PartCompare  comp;
T  a, b;                        // T is a partially ordered type
```

```
comp = compare(a,b);              // compare a and b

switch (comp) {
case PartLT:    ... // a < b
case PartEQ:    ... // a = b
case PartGT:    ... // a > b
case PartUN:    ... // a and b are unordered
};
```

How does a programmer test for $a \neq b$ or $a \leq b$ or any other relationship that is satisfied by a set of comparison values? Each comparison defines a number of bit sets that represent sets of comparison values. Each bit of the set corresponds to one comparison value. For example, PartCompare defines the set PartLESet, which has two on bits: one for PartLT and one for PartEQ. Routine inSet() tests whether a comparison value is a member of a bit set.

```
#include "PartCompare.hpp"

PartCompare  comp;
T  a, b;                          // T is a partially ordered type

template <classSet, class Compare>
inline BOOL inSet(Compare comp, Set set)
   { return BOOL(set & (1 << comp)); };

comp = compare(a,b);            // compare a and b
if ( inSet(comp,PartLESet) )    // is comp in PartLESet ?
   // a <= b
else
   // a > b or they are unordered
```

Each file defines a number of sets that correspond to interesting combinations of comparison values. One of these is AllSet. It has all possible comparison values.

There is a temptation to write boolean procedures for these tests, and eliminate the sets altogether:

```
BOOL isGE( PartCompare: comp) {
    switch (comp) {
    case PartEQ:
    case PartGT:
      return TRUE;

    case PartLT:
    case PartUN:
      return FALSE;
    };
};
```

A client code would use the procedure like this:

```
if ( isGE( compare(A,B) )
   // do something
```

But the set representation is preferred for two reasons:

- Sets expose their members for further processing. We can combine multiple sets into a single relation and still get the same fast performance for tests. There is no equivalent operation on the members hidden inside a subroutine. There is nothing wrong with letting the client use its computational powers.
- The bit representation compresses the information into the smallest possible space. Subroutines are much larger.

Total Compare

Enumeration TotalCompare is for data types that are totally ordered. A type is "totally ordered" if for *all* values A and B exactly one of the following conditions is true:

LT   A < B (less than)
EQ   A = B (equal to)
GT   A > B (greater than)

This is the most common situation. It is used for comparing integers, characters, enumerations, and strings of characters.

The order of the three comparison values is natural: "LessThan" < "EqualTo" < "GreaterThan." Therefore, we can use operators like <= on comparison values.

```
if ( comparison <= EQ )
   // comparison is LT or EQ
else
   // comparison is GT
```

Note that sets for the three-valued TotalCompare are not as important as they are for comparisons with more values, since checking for any two values can be done by testing for not equal to the third.

It would be tempting to change the standard procedure strcmp() to return a TotalCompare. It would make the resulting code easier to read. But there is too much code already written assuming it returns −1, 0, or +1.

Partial Compare

For **partially ordered** types, exactly one of the following is true:

PartLT   A < B (less than)
PartEQ   A = B (equal to)
PartGT   A > B (greater than)
PartUN   A U B (A and B are unordered)

The IEEE binary floating point standard (1981) for floating point numbers defines "NaN" values (Not-a-Number). They usually represent error conditions like the square root of a negative number. A NaN is equal to itself, but unordered with every other real value and every other NaN. PartUN is also the proper result when comparing two quantities with different physical dimensions: 6 meters and 10 kilograms are unordered.

PartCompare does not have to apply to a data type as a whole. Suppose we write a routine to determine whether one integer evenly divides another. PartCompare is ideally suited as the return value.

```
PartCompare divides(int a, int b) {
    if       ( a == b )        return PartEQ;
    else if ( a % b == 0 ) return PartLT;
    else if ( b % a == 0 ) return PartGT;
    else                       return PartUN;
};
```

Set Compare

When comparing two sets we could return a PartCompare with PartEQ for set equality, PartLT for subset, PartGT for superset, and PartUN for all other pairs of sets. But a further classification is more useful. Following Sakkinen (1987), we will use the following values for the comparison of two sets:

SetIN   The left set is a proper subset of the right set. Every member of the left set is in the right set, but there are more members in the right set.

SetEQ   The two sets contain exactly the same members.

SetCO   The left set is a proper superset of the right set. Every member in the right set is in the left set, but there are more members in the left set.

SetOV   The two sets have members in common (a nonempty intersection), but they each contain members that are not in the other.

Sets {1,2} and {2,3} are overlapping.

SetDJ   Neither set is empty, but they have no members in common.

Sets {1,2} and {4,5} are disjoint.

An empty set is always considered a proper subset of any nonempty set. If both sets are empty, they are "SetEQ."

The ordering of set comparison values cannot be used in general. It is meaningless to code

```
if ( comp >= SetCO )      // meaningless comparison
    // do something
```

The bit sets SetPSubSet and SetISubSet provide tests for proper and improper subsets. SetPSupSet and SetISupSet provide tests for proper and improper supersets.

Routine classifySetCompare() returns a SetCompare value given three boolean parameters. When comparing bit sets, the inputs are easily computed as $a\&b$, $a\&(^{\wedge}b)$, and $b\&(^{\wedge}a)$.

Compare for Numerical Analysis

In numerical applications there is a need for comparison within some "significance" amount between two floating point values. The significance amount is a parameter to the compare routine. The following are the comparison values for compare(float A, float B, float sig):

SigSLT A is significantly less than B ($A <= B - sig$).

SigILT A is insignificantly less than B ($B - sig < A < B$). A is numerically less than B, but it is not enough of a difference to be meaningful to the application.

SigEEQ A is exactly equal to B.

SigIGT A is insignificantly greater than B ($B < A < B + sig$). A is numerically greater than B, but it is not enough of a difference to be meaningful to the application.

SigSGT A is significantly greater than B ($B + sig <= A$).

SigUN A and B cannot be compared. This occurs only with NaNs and infinities.

As an example, the Newton-Raphson method can be used to find an approximate root of an equation. The method works by starting with an initial guess for the root, and then successively improving it. The method stops when the change in the root is no longer significant. So, to find the root accurate to 10^{-6} we might reasonably set the significance to 10^{-7}. The code might look like this:

```
sig = 1.0E-7;
curroot = ...initial guess...;
for (;;) {
   prevroot = curroot;
   curroot  = NewtonRaphson( curroot );

   SigCompare comp = compare( prevroot, curroot, sig);
   if ( inSet(comp,SigAESet) )   // approximately equal
      break;
};
```

Source Code

File Bool.hpp

```
#ifndef _BOOL
#define _BOOL
```

(continued)

File Bool.hpp *(continued)*

```
// define a boolean data type
enum BOOL {FALSE, TRUE};

#endif
```

File TotalCompare.hpp

```
#ifndef _TOTALCOMP_H
#define _TOTALCOMP_H
//*************************************************************************
// TITLE:  TotalCompare -- Comparison values for totally ordered types
//
// AUTHOR: Scott N Gerard, Rochester, MN
// LANGUAGE: C++
//
// FUNCTION:
//     Two partially ordered values maybe LessThan, EqualTo, or
//     GreaterThan one another.
//
// CHANGE LOG:
//     31Aug87 - Initial coding. Scott N Gerard
//     07Feb88 - Add Reverse function. Scott N Gerard
//     30Dec89 - Rename from Compare to TotalCompare. SN Gerard
//     26Jun93 - Convert to C++.  SN Gerard
//*************************************************************************

enum TotalCompare {LT, EQ, GT};

typedef unsigned char TotalCompSet;

const TotalCompSet LTSet  = 1 << LT;
const TotalCompSet EQSet  = 1 << EQ;
const TotalCompSet GTSet  = 1 << GT;

const TotalCompSet LESet  =  LTSet + EQSet;
const TotalCompSet GESet  =          EQSet + GTSet;

const TotalCompSet AllSet =  LTSet + EQSet + GTSet;

//*************************************************************************
// A comp B  ==  B reverse(comp) A
//*************************************************************************
TotalCompare reverse(TotalCompare comp);

#endif
```

File TotalCompare.cpp

```
//*************************************************************************
// TITLE:  TotalCompare -- Comparison values for totally ordered types
//
```

```
// AUTHOR: Scott N Gerard, Rochester, MN
// LANGUAGE: C++
//
// FUNCTION:
//    Two partially ordered values maybe LessThan, EqualTo, or
//    GreaterThan one another.  They may also be UnOrdered.
//
// CHANGE LOG:
//    31Aug87 - Initial coding. Scott N Gerard
//    07Feb88 - Add Reverse function. Scott N Gerard
//    30Dec89 - Rename from Compare to TotalCompare. SN Gerard
//    26Jun93 - Convert to C++.  SN Gerard
//*********************************************************************
#include "TotalCompare.hpp"


//*********************************************************************
// A comp B  ==  B reverse(comp) A
//*********************************************************************
TotalCompare reverse(TotalCompare comp) {
    switch (comp) {
    case LT:  return GT;
    case EQ:  return EQ;
    case GT:  return LT;
    };
};
```

File PartCompare.hpp

```
#ifndef _PARTCOMP_H
#define _PARTCOMP_H
//*********************************************************************
// TITLE:  PartCompare -- Comparison values for partially ordered types
//
// AUTHOR: Scott N Gerard, Rochester, MN
// LANGUAGE: C++
//
// FUNCTION:
//    Two partially ordered values maybe LessThan, EqualTo, or
//    GreaterThan one another.  They may also be UnOrdered.
//
// CHANGE LOG:
//    31Dec89 - Initial coding. Scott N Gerard
//    26Apr92 - Convert to C++.  Scott N Gerard
//*********************************************************************

enum PartCompare {PartLT, PartEQ, PartGT, PartUN};

// define a set of PartCompare values
typedef unsigned char PartCompareSet;

const PartCompareSet
    PartLTSet = 1 << PartLT,
    PartEQSet = 1 << PartEQ,
```

(continued)

File PartCompare.hpp   *(continued)*

```
    PartGTSet = 1 << PartGT,
    PartUNSet = 1 << PartUN;

const PartCompareSet
// PartLTSet  = PartLTSet,
   PartLESet  = PartLTSet+PartEQSet,
// PartEQSet  =           PartEQSet,
   PartGESet  =           PartEQSet+PartGTSet,
// PartGTSet  =                     PartGTSet,
   PartNESet  = PartLTSet+          PartGTSet+PartUNSet, // not equal
// PartUNSet  =                               PartUnSet, // unordered

   PartAllSet = PartLTSet+PartEQSet+PartGTSet+PartUNSet;

//*********************************************************************
// A comp B  ==  B reverse(comp) A
//*********************************************************************
PartCompare reverse(PartCompare comp);

#endif
```

File PartCompare.cpp

```
//*********************************************************************
// TITLE:  PartCompare -- Comparison values for partially ordered types
//
// AUTHOR: Scott N Gerard, Rochester, MN
// LANGUAGE: C++
//
// FUNCTION:
//    Two partially ordered values maybe LessThan, EqualTo, or
//    GreaterThan one another.  They may also be UnOrdered.
//
// CHANGE LOG:
//    31Dec89 - Initial coding. Scott N Gerard
//    26Apr92 - Conversion from Modula-2 to C++.  Scott N Gerard
//*********************************************************************
#include "PartCompare.hpp"

//*********************************************************************
// A comp B  ==  B reverse(comp) A
//*********************************************************************
PartCompare reverse(PartCompare comp) {
   switch (comp) {
   case PartLT:  return PartGT;
   case PartEQ:  return PartEQ;
   case PartGT:  return PartLT;
   case PartUN:  return PartUN;
   };
};
```

5

Utility Classes

UnInit Class

Let D be a derived class of B. B, as a self-contained entity, should only provide public constructors that put all of its instances in a known, initialized state. D should do likewise. D's constructors will always call some constructor of B.

A performance problem can arise if D's constructors must undo or write over a significant part of the work done in B's constructors. What we need is an additional, protected constructor for B that does not perform the work we know will have to be redone by D. In some cases this uninitializing constructor naturally has an argument list with a unique set of types; sometimes not. To distinguish the uninitializing constructor from all other constructors, we can add a special, unique type such as class UnInit.

The UnInit class has no data and no member functions. In fact, the value of an UnInit instance is irrelevant. Only its type is important. Class UnInit unambiguously distinguishes the uninitializing constructor.

The Function classes use class UnInit.

Ident

Routine getIdent() reads an identifier from an input stream, and returns the first n characters in the user's buffer. If the identifier is longer than n characters, the excess is discarded. This means the routine will read long identifiers, but truncates them to n characters.

Following the rules for many languages, an identifier may contain letters, numbers, underscores, and the national characters ("@", "#" or "$"). An identifier may not begin with a number. The acceptable characters are defined by character classifying routines like those in ctype.h. isIdent1() tests whether a character is valid as the first character of an identifier. isIdent() tests whether a character is valid inside an identifier.

```
#include "Ident.hpp"

char id[20];

getIdent( cin, id, 20);
```

The national characters are included for use by the calculators.

EnumIO

C++ does not provide a nice, built-in way to read and write values of an enumeration. If you write an enumeration, its integer value is written. EnumIO reads and writes enumeration values by name.

After you define the enumeration type, define an array of character strings, one string for each enumeration value. Add a final empty string to mark the end of the array. The names in the array must be valid identifiers as read by getIdent() above.

Macro enumIORead() defines an iostream operator >> to read an enumeration value by name, and macro enumIOWrite() defines an iostream operator << to write the name for an enumeration. As a convenience, macro enumIO() invokes both macros. All three macros require the enumeration type, and the array of names. Now you can read and write enumerations just like any other types.

```
#include "EnumIO.hpp"

enum Fruit {Apple, Banana, Cantaloupe, Date, Grape};

char* FruitNames[] =
    { "Apple", "Banana", "Cantaloupe", "Date", "Grape", "" };

enumIO(Fruit,FruitNames);         // define operators  << and >>

Fruit f = Apple;

cout << f;                        // writes "Apple"
cin  >> f;                        // read a fruit name
```

If the enumeration values are not consecutive integers, you must place a nonnull string in the names array. "?" would be a good choice.

There are a number of ways to extend this idea.

- The current read routine is case sensitive. It might be useful to provide a read routine that ignores the case of input strings.

- These routines work best for enumerations that have consecutive integer values. An enumeration whose values are 1, 2, 4, 8, 16, 32 and 64 would require many dummy names.
- A linear search is used to find an input name. For large enumerations, it would be faster to put the names in a Dictionary that uses a hash table.

IntMath

Greatest Common Divisor

Routine gcd() computes the greatest common divisor of two integers using Euclid's famous algorithm. However, instead of limiting its input to positive integers, this gcd() accepts all integers. gcd(a,b) returns a positive number that evenly divides both a and b and minimizes abs(a/gcd) and abs(b/gcd). Zero does not constrain gcd since every integer evenly divides zero. gcd(n,0) = gcd(0,n) = n implies 0/gcd = 0 and n/gcd = 1. As a special case, gcd(0,0) = 1 even though every integer evenly divides zero. The inputs can be negative because gcd(n,m) divides both $-n$ and $-m$.

Least Common Multiple

Routine lcm() computes the least common multiple of two numbers. It is defined in terms of gcd(). lcm() is computed in such a way that the result will not cause integer overflow unless the lcm() itself is too large to fit in a long integer.

Square Root

Routine sqrt() computes the square root of its first parameter, a long unsigned integer. If its second parameter is FALSE, it returns the square root of the number rounded to the next smallest integer (floor of $\sqrt{n}$). If its second parameter is TRUE, it returns the square root rounded up to the next largest integer (ceil of $\sqrt{x}$). For the details of the algorithm see "Square Root Algorithm," later in this chapter.

Hashing

Method rank() is a one-to-one mapping between the values of a data type and the integers. But rank() cannot be written for data types that have more than 2^{32} possible data values.

Method hash() slams the internal contents of a data value instance together and produces a **hash value.** The hash value is hopefully an essentially random integer that represents the value of the data. hash() is a *function* of the data value; a data value always returns exactly the same hash value. Hopefully, different data values give different data values. This is only a hope or a desire, and cannot be guareenteed. If there are

$2^{32} + 1$ different data values, there has to be at least one "collision" (when two distinct data values have the same hash value they "collide" with each other). In practice, collisions are much more common.

Hash values are most often used to index hash tables. To add a data value to a hash table, compute its hash value i and add the data value to the ith list of the hash table. To see if a data value is already in the hash table, recompute its hash value, which returns the same i, and search just the ith list. There is no need to search any other list of the hash table. A different data value with hash value j will be in the jth list, not in the ith list.

In almost all real applications, there are multiple data values that have the same hash value. These colliding data values are part of the same hash table list. A good hash function evenly distributes the data values so each list has about the same number of data values. If the hash table has 101 lists (hash tables work best with a prime number of lists), then, on average, only 1 percent of the total entries in the hash table must be examined to find any particular data value. Searching a single list is 100 times faster than searching through all the values in the hash table.

SimpHasher Class

Two classes are provided for hashing. Class Hasher is an abstract class for hashing routines. It defines operator $<<$ methods to add different data types to the hash value. These are all routed to method put() that hashes n bytes of memory. Adding values to a hash object looks like writing values to an output stream.

Class SimpHasher is a concrete class with a simple hash function. It is similar to the method suggested by G. D. Knott (Knuth, 1973c:512). Where Knott suggested left shifting, SimpHasher uses left rotation so bits are not shifted off the left end and completely lost.

Hasher and SimpHasher are template classes. The template parameter must be an integer type, and controls the size of the hash value.

```
#include "SimpHasher.hpp"

SimpHasher<int>  hasher;

hasher << 13 << 26 << 39;
hasher << "This is a char string";
hasher << 9.15;

int index = hasher.result(HASH_TABLE_SIZE);
// index hash table using index.
```

A Person class would use SimpHasher like this

```
#include "SimpHasher.hpp"

class Person {
```

```
    char*   name;
    int     age;

    unsigned long hash() {
        SimpHasher<int> h;
        h << name << age;
        return h.result();
    };
};
```

Handles and Bodies

Assume we have a base class B with derived classes D1 and D2, and suppose the derived classes each add their own data to the class. (For a specific example, see Chapter 10.) How can a user work with the derived classes generically by assuming they are just instances of class B?

The size of each derived class is larger than the size of the base class. And variables of class B are too small to hold the contents of any derived class. Therefore, the user cannot work directly with variables of type B.

Can the user work with variables of type B* (pointer to B)? This means the storage for the derived classes must be allocated from the heap, and giving our user a pointer to the storage means we are also giving her responsibility for releasing that storage. But we want to allow big expressions of many B objects like arithmetic expressions with parentheses, and subexpressions. Temporary instances of B will be created and deleted within a single statement, and our user will never even see the pointers for intermediate results. So letting her work directly with pointers (B* variables) cannot work either.

The way around this problem is the **handle/body** framework (Coplien, 1992:133). Each original class is split into two classes: a handle class and a body class. The initial single hierarchy of classes splits into two "parallel" class hierarchies: a handle hierarchy and a body hierarchy.

Client programs *only* use handle classes. Body classes are hidden implementation details. So we give the handle classes the nice application names B, D1, and D2. The hidden body classes are renamed to something like BImp, D1Imp, and D2Imp. Each handle class is a "smart pointer" to its body, and a handle "delegates" all its requests to its body. The bodies are where the real work happens. Handles (or handlers) manage their bodies. A handle's destructor deletes its body object (when necessary). Since C++ guarantees destructors are always run—even on intermediate, temporary objects—the compiler will automatically do the necessary housecleaning for intermediate expressions, regardless of their complexity.

There are different strategies for memory management. The Handle and RefCount classes here use "reference counting." All bodies are derived from class RefCount. Each Refcount instance keeps a count of the number of handles that reference it. The handle destructor decrements the count and deletes the body when the count drops to zero. This also gives us some saving in storage since two handles may share the same body.

Handles have two methods to access their bodies. readRef() returns a read-only reference. writeRef() returns a reference to a changeable body. Multiple handles can reference the same body (this happens when handles are copied). As long as all handles use read-only references they can share the same body. But when a handle asks for a writeRef() to a shared body, the handle gets its own copy of the body.

Implementation Comments

Square Root Algorithm

Many square root routines are based on the well-known Newton-Raphson method, which requires floating point operations. This section derives the classical square root algorithm for integers, which has not received its fair share of notoriety. Variants of this approach are suitable for implementation in hardware as primitive machine instructions.

Let n (the radicand) be the number whose square root is to be found and x (the radical) the approximate square root of n. If n can be stored as a $2w$-bit binary number, then x can be stored in w bits. We are looking for an algorithm that will compute x and r where

$$n = x^2 + r \qquad [3]$$

where x is the largest number whose square is less than or equal to n and $0 \leq r$ is the remainder.

We solve the problem iteratively, determining one bit of x during each pass. First we determine the most significant bit (bit w), then the next most significant bit (bit $w - 1$), down to bit 1. Let y_i be the ith bit in the binary representaion of x,

$$x = \sum_{i=1}^{w} y_i 2^i$$

where y_i is either 0 or 1. Let x_i be the ith estimate of x. Given x_i, the next approximation of x is

$$x_{i-1} = x_i + y_i 2^i \qquad [4]$$

Rewrite Equation [3] in terms of the approximate root x_i and the corresponding remainder r_i

$$r_i = n - x_i^2$$

Substitute $i \mapsto i - 1$ in this equation and use Equation [4] to substitute x_{i-1}.

$$r_{i-1} = n - x_{i-1}^2$$
$$= n - x_i^2 - y_i x_i 2^{i+1} - y_i^2 2^{2i} \qquad [5]$$
$$= r_i - y_i(x_i 2^{i+1} + 2^{2i})$$

Now define the quantities

$$s_i = x_i 2^{i+1}$$
$$t_i = 2^{2i}$$

Substituting $i \mapsto i - 1$ in s_i

$$s_{i-1} = x_{i-1} 2^i$$
$$= (x_i + y_i 2^i) 2^i$$
$$= \frac{1}{2}(x_i 2^{i+1}) + y_i 2^{2i} \qquad [6]$$
$$= \frac{1}{2} s_i + y_i t_i$$

Substituting $i \mapsto i - 1$ in t_i

$$t_{i-1} = 2^{2(i-1)}$$
$$= \frac{1}{4} t_i \qquad [7]$$

The remainder r must not be negative. Therefore every r_i must be positive. If $y_i = 1$ in Equation [5] makes r_{i-1} negative, then y_i must equal 0.

With this information, we can write the code for the algorithm. The then and else statements come from Equations [5], [6], and [7].

```
long w = 16;               // assume 32 bit input; 16 bit output
// long i = w;
// long xi = 0;
long ri = n;               // = n - 0 ** 2
long si = 0;               // = 2 ** 17 * xi = 0
long ti = x40000000;       // = 2 ** (2*i-2) = 2**30

for ( i = w; i > 0; --i ) {
    if ( ri - si - ti < 0 ) {     // would yi=1 make new ri negative?
        // yi = 0;
        ri = ri;
        si = si / 2;
        ti = ti / 4;
```

```
  } else {                       // can increase x, so do it
     // yi = 1;
     ri = ri - si - ti;
     si = si / 2 + ti;
     ti = ti / 4;
  };
};
xi = si / 2;
```

The C++ code for sqrt() moves some of these computations around to locally optimize the code, but is otherwise the same. Of course, it would be easy to modify this routine to return the remainder rather than performing the rounding directly.

Source Code

File EnumIO.hpp

```cpp
#ifndef _ENUMIO_HPP
#define _ENUMIO_HPP
//***********************************************************************
// TITLE: EnumIO --   IO for enumerations
//
// AUTHOR: Scott N Gerard, Rochester, MN
// LANGUAGE: C++
//
// FUNCTION:
//     Functions to read and write enumeration types as character strings.
//
// CHANGE LOG:
//     11Mar93 - Initial coding.  SN Gerard
//***********************************************************************
#include <assert.h>
#include <string.h>
#include "Ident.hpp"


//***********************************************************************
// readName reads a name from the stream and looks up the name in the
// name table.
//***********************************************************************
istream& readName (istream& is, unsigned& i, char** names);

//***********************************************************************
// writeName writes the i-th name in array names onto the stream.
//***********************************************************************
ostream& writeName (ostream& os, unsigned i, char** names);


//***********************************************************************
// Define macros to create stream operators to read and write an
```

```
// enumerated type T using readName and writeName.  Using template
// functions for these routines would mean every undefined type T would
// try to use these functions.  Using macros may not be the "correct"
// way to define these functions, but it is safer.
//*********************************************************************
#define enumIORead(T,names) \
istream& operator >> (istream& is, T& t) {  \
   unsigned i;                 \
   readName(is, i, names);     \
   t = T(i);                   \
   return is;                  \
};

#define enumIOWrite(T,names) \
ostream& operator << (ostream& os, const T t) \
   { return writeName(os, unsigned(t), names); };

// spit out both
#define enumIO(T,names) enumIORead(T,names) enumIOWrite(T,names)

#endif
```

File EnumIO.cpp

```
//*********************************************************************
// TITLE: EnumIO --  IO for enumerations
//
// AUTHOR: Scott N Gerard, Rochester, MN
// LANGUAGE: C++
//
// FUNCTION:
//    Functions to read and write enumeration types as character strings.
//
// CHANGE LOG:
//    11Mar93 - Initial coding.  SN Gerard
//    29Jun93 - Add MAX_ENUM_LEN constant. SN Gerard
//*********************************************************************
#include <assert.h>
#include <string.h>
#include "EnumIO.hpp"

const int MAX_ENUM_LEN = 20;

//*********************************************************************
// readName reads a name from the stream and looks up the name in the
// name table.
//*********************************************************************
istream& readName (istream& is, unsigned& i, char** names) {
   char ident[MAX_ENUM_LEN];
   getIdent(is, ident, sizeof(ident));
   for (i = 0; 0 != names[i]; ++i)
```

(continued)

File EnumIO.cpp   *(continued)*

```
      if (0 == strcmp(ident, names[i]) ) {
         return is;
      };
   i = -1;                            // could not find a match
   is.setf(ios::failbit);            // stream is in error
   return is;
};

//***********************************************************************
// writeName writes the i-th name in array names onto the stream.
//***********************************************************************
ostream& writeName (ostream& os, unsigned i, char** names) {
   #ifndef NDEBUG
      for (unsigned j=0; j <= i;  ++j)
         { assert( names[j] != 0 ); };
   #endif
   return os << names[i];
};
```

File IntMath.hpp

```
#ifndef _INTMATH_HPP
#define _INTMATH_HPP
//***********************************************************************
// TITLE: IntMath -- Math routines on INTEGERs and CARDINALs
//
// AUTHOR: Scott N Gerard, Rochester, MN
// LANGUAGE: C++
//
// CHANGE LOG:
//    24Apr88 - Initial coding.  SN Gerard
//    21Feb92 - Convert to C++.  SN Gerard
//***********************************************************************
#include "Bool.hpp"


//***********************************************************************
// Compute the square root of u.  If u is not a perfect square
// then round the actual square root down to the next integral value
//***********************************************************************
unsigned long sqrt (unsigned long u, const BOOL roundup);


//***********************************************************************
// Compute the greatest common denominator.
//***********************************************************************
long gcd (long a, long b);


//***********************************************************************
// Compute the least common multiple of a and b
//***********************************************************************
```

```
long lcm (long a, long b);

//*********************************************************************
// Maximum and minimum
//*********************************************************************
template <class T>
inline T min (T a, T b) {
   return a<b ? a : b;
};

template <class T>
inline T max (T a, T b) {
   return a>b ? a : b;
};

#endif
```

File IntMath.cpp

```
//*********************************************************************
// TITLE: IntMath -- integer math routines
//
// AUTHOR: Scott N Gerard, Rochester, MN
// LANGUAGE: C++
//
// CHANGE LOG:
//    24Apr88 - Initial coding.  SN Gerard
//    21Feb92 - Convert to C++.  SN Gerard
//*********************************************************************
#include <math.h>
#include "IntMath.hpp"


//*********************************************************************
// Compute the integer square root of n.  If n is not a perfect square
// then round the actual square root down to the next lower integer if
// roundup=FALSE.
//*********************************************************************
unsigned long sqrt (unsigned long n, const BOOL roundup) {

   unsigned long rem, s, t, temp;

   rem = n;
   s = 0;
   t = 0x40000000;
   do {
      temp = s + t;
      s = s >> 1;
      if (rem >= temp) {          // would remainder go negative ?
         rem -= temp;
         s += t;
      };
```

(continued)

File IntMath.cpp   *(continued)*

```
      t = t >> 2;                    // divide by 4
   } while (t != 0);

   if (roundup && (rem != 0))
      s++;
   return s;
};

//**********************************************************************
// Compute the greatest common denominator.  Returns a positive integer
// that minimizes abs(a/gcd) and abs(b/gcd).
//**********************************************************************
long gcd (long a, long b) {

   a = abs(a);
   b = abs(b);

   if ( a == 0 ) {
      if ( b == 0 )
         return 1;
      else
         return b;
   } else if ( b == 0 )
      return a;

   while (1) {
      if (a == b)
         break;
      else if (a > b)
         a = a - b;
      else
         b = b - a;
   };
   return b;
};


//**********************************************************************
// Compute the least common multiple of a and b.  By dividing first,
// integer overflow is avoided unless overflow is inevitable.
//**********************************************************************
long lcm (long a, long b) {
   return (a / gcd(a,b) ) * b;
};
```

File Hasher.hpp

```
#ifndef _HASHER_HPP
#define _HASHER_HPP
//**********************************************************************
// TITLE: Hasher -- calculate hash values
```

```
//
// AUTHOR: Scott N Gerard, Rochester, MN
// LANGUAGE: C++
//
// FUNCTION:
//    Abstract base class to hash bytes.
//
// CHANGE LOG:
//    29Dec90 - Initial coding.  SN Gerard
//    04Jun92 - Convert from Modula-2 to C++.  SN Gerard
//*********************************************************************
#include <string.h>
#include "Bool.hpp"


//*********************************************************************
// Include a single byte in an existing signiture.
//*********************************************************************
template <class T>
class Hasher {

    typedef Hasher<T> ThisClass;

protected:
    // Can't create instances of this abstract class
    Hasher() {};
    Hasher(const Hasher&) {};                     // no copy ctor
    void operator = (const Hasher&) {};           // no assignment

public:
    virtual Hasher() {};

    //*****************************************************************
    // Insert a block of bytes.
    //*****************************************************************
    virtual Hasher& put (
       const void*    mem,                 // address of first byte
       const unsigned len)                 // number of bytes
    = 0;

    //*****************************************************************
    // Insert a bit to the hasher.  The added bit is (bit != 0).
    //*****************************************************************
    virtual ThisClass& operator << (const BOOL bit)
       { return put(&bit, sizeof bit); };

    //*****************************************************************
    // Insert a byte.
    //*****************************************************************
    virtual ThisClass& operator << (const char byte)
       { return put(&byte, sizeof byte); };
```

(continued)

File Hasher.hpp   *(continued)*

```cpp
//********************************************************************
// Insert null terminate string.  The null byte is included to
// distinguish separately adding two strings, and adding one
// concatenated string.
//********************************************************************
virtual ThisClass& operator << (const char*  str)
   { return put(str, strlen(str)+1 ); };


//********************************************************************
// Insert different types of data to the hash object.
//********************************************************************
virtual ThisClass& operator << (const int    x  )
   { return put(&x, sizeof x ); };

virtual ThisClass& operator << (const float  x  )
   { return put(&x, sizeof x ); };

virtual ThisClass& operator << (const double x  )
   { return put(&x, sizeof x ); };


//********************************************************************
// Be careful adding pointer values to a hash value.  It adds the
// IDENTITY of a variable to the hash value rather than its VALUE.
//********************************************************************
virtual ThisClass& operator << (const void * ptr)
   { return put(&ptr, sizeof ptr ); };


//********************************************************************
// reset a hash object.
//********************************************************************
virtual ThisClass&  reset () = 0;


//********************************************************************
// Return the hashed value.  Return a value 0 <= x < mod.  If mod=0
// then return 0 <= x <= MAX(T).
//********************************************************************
virtual T result (const T mod = 0) const = 0;


//********************************************************************
// Compare hash values.  These operators compare the current value,
// but not the algorithm.  So a==b does NOT imply (a+x) == (b+x).
// Note: operators < and > are not meaningful on hash values.
//********************************************************************
friend BOOL operator == (const ThisClass& a, const ThisClass& b)
   { return BOOL( a.result() == b.result() ); };
friend BOOL operator != (const ThisClass& a, const ThisClass& b)
   { return BOOL( a.result() != b.result() ); };

};
#endif
```

File Handle.hpp

```
#ifndef _HANDLE_HPP
#define _HANDLE_HPP
//**********************************************************************
// TITLE: Handle --  a pointer that cleans up after itself
//
// AUTHOR: Scott N Gerard
// LANGUAGE: C++
//
// FUNCTION:
//    A Handle controls access to its referent (the thing it
//    points at) using reference counting.  The referent is of type T.
//    T must inherit from class RefCount.  Multiple Handle objects can
//    reference the same object.  When the last Handle's destructor is
//    called, the reference count drops to zero and the referent is
//    deleted.
//
//    All referents must be allocated from the heap (since delete will
//    be called).
//
//    A Handle object always points to a valid T or is null.  Method
//    _readRef and _writeRef against a null Ptr will allocate a new
//    object so the call never sees a null referent.
//
// CHANGE LOG:
//    07Feb93 - Initial coding.  SN Gerard
//**********************************************************************

#include "Bool.hpp"

//**********************************************************************
// When Handle<T> objects are declared, class T must include class
// RefCount as an ancestor class.
//**********************************************************************
class RefCount {
public:
    // use a long name so that name collisions will be unlikely when this
    // class is used as a base class of other objects.
    unsigned referenceCount;

    RefCount (): referenceCount(0) {};
    ~RefCount () { assert(referenceCount == 0); };
    virtual BOOL valid() const {
        // this is a reasonableness check.
        if (referenceCount > 100)
            cerr << "RefCount::valid Warning: more than 100 references\n";
        return TRUE;
    };
};

//**********************************************************************
```

(continued)

File Handle.hpp *(continued)*

```
// Class Handle<T> holds a reference to an object of class T which must
// have RefCount as a direct or indirect base class.  Multiple Handles
// can reference the same T at the same time.  When the number of Handles
// pointing to a RefCount drops to zero, the last Handle<T> destroys T.
//************************************************************************
template <class T>
class Handle {

    typedef Handle<T> ThisClass;
    typedef RefCount RefClass;

protected:
    T*  p;                          // pointer to referent or NULL

public:
    //********************************************************************
    // Constructors and destructor
    //********************************************************************
    Handle(): p(0) {};                          // a null pointer
    Handle(T* t): p(t) { attach(); };
    Handle(const Handle& copy);
    ~Handle() { release(); };

    //********************************************************************
    // Assignment operator
    //********************************************************************
    Handle& operator = (const Handle& copy) { return operator=(copy.p);};
    Handle& operator = (T* t);

    //********************************************************************
    // Check validity.
    //********************************************************************
    virtual BOOL valid () const;

protected:
    //********************************************************************
    // Extract referent.  Use _readRef for a read-only reference, use
    // _writeRef for a changable reference.  A _readRef shares the
    // referent with other Handle variables.  A _writeRef insures only
    // this Handle can access the referent (ie that the
    // referenceCount==1).
    //********************************************************************
    const T& _readRef () const;
    T& _writeRef() const;

    //********************************************************************
    // Attach and Release operations
    //********************************************************************
    void attach  () const;
    void release () const;
```

```
//************************************************************
// Allow derived classes to override allocation, copy and deletion.
// These need to be overriden to actually manipulate storage.
//************************************************************
virtual T* allocRef () const = 0;
virtual T* copyRef  () const = 0;
virtual void delRef () { delete p; };

};

#endif
```

File Handle.cpp

```
//************************************************************
// TITLE: Handle --  a pointer that cleans up after itself
//
// AUTHOR: Scott N Gerard
// LANGUAGE: C++
//
// FUNCTION:
//    A Handle object controls access to its referent object of class
//    T.
//
// CHANGE LOG:
//    07Feb93 - Initial coding.  SN Gerard
//************************************************************

#include "Handle.hpp"

//************************************************************
// Constructors and destructor
//************************************************************
template <class T>
Handle<T>::Handle(const Handle<T>& copy): p(copy.p) {
   assert( copy.valid() );
   attach();
};

//************************************************************
// Assignment operator
//************************************************************
template <class T>
Handle<T>& Handle<T>::operator = (T* t) {
   if ( p == t)                      // if setting p==t do nothing
      return *this;
   release();                        // release old referent
   p = t;
   attach();                         // attach new referent
   return *this;
};
```

(continued)

File Handle.cpp   *(continued)*

```cpp
//*********************************************************************
// Extract referent
//*********************************************************************
template <class T>
const T& Handle<T>::_readRef() const {
   assert( valid() );
   if ( p == 0 ) {                  // alloc T so user doesn't see null
      (T*) p = allocRef();
      attach();
   };
   return *p;
};

template <class T>
T& Handle<T>::_writeRef() const {
   assert( valid() );
   if ( p == 0 ) {                  // alloc T so user doesn't see null
      (T*) p = allocRef();
      attach();
   } else if (p->referenceCount != 1 ) {
      // copy T so we have exclusive use of the T
      release();
      (T*) p = copyRef();
      attach();
   };
   return *p;
};

//*********************************************************************
// Attach and Release operations
//*********************************************************************
template <class T>
void Handle<T>::attach  () const {
   if ( p != 0 )
      ++(p->referenceCount);
};

template <class T>
void Handle<T>::release () const {
   if ( p != 0 && --(p->referenceCount)==0 ) {
      ((Handle*)this)->delRef();            // drop const attribute
      (T*) p = 0;
   };
};

//*********************************************************************
// Check validity.
//*********************************************************************
template <class T>
BOOL Handle<T>::valid () const
   { return (p==0) ? TRUE : p->valid(); };
```

PART THREE

Games

6

Regions

Arrays are a great way to organize data. They create the illusion of two-dimensional memory where every pair of (x, y) points has its own storage location. The compiler converts the two-dimensional illusion into a single, linear address.

In the next three chapters, I develop a number of Region classes that are conceptually similar to common arrays. One of the classes, Reg2Rect (a 2D, rectangular region), duplicates the function of C++ arrays. This familiar example should help you understand regions in general, and allow your programs to use both simple and complex arrays within a single framework.

A **region** is a one-to-one and onto function between the integers in the range 0..n and a collection of points on a plane (2D) or in a space (3D). Member function rank() converts a point to an integer (cleverly called the rank value of the point), and unrank() converts the integer back to the point. The points of a region are usually adjacent to each other and a region usually has a specific shape (e.g., rectangle, triangle, trapezoid).

Regions can be used for scientific applications that need upper-triangular or lower-triangular matrices, or various kinds of band matrices. Regions can also be used to allocate storage for game boards. Chapter 8 defines a number of regions for games played on "hexagonal grids" that are popular in some simulation and fantasy games. Three-dimensional regions are also available: 3D rectangular arrays and 3D trapezoidal volumes. Extensions to more dimensions are clearly possible.

P2BOARD

The diskette includes three programs so you can experiment with regions. P2BOARD handles two-dimensional regions on the plane; P3BOARD handles three-dimensional regions in space; and H2BOARD handles two-dimensional regions of a hexgrid.

Start P2BOARD from any DOS command line.

C>P2BOARD

You are prompted for a type of region. Enter a single-letter character (any case). The capitalized letters in the prompt text indicate the valid options. We will spend the next three chapters covering all the different types of regions. But to show you a little of where we are headed, enter "h" for a hexagonal region. The next prompt asks for the size of the edge. Enter "3".

You will now see a picture of the *xy*-plane (dashes mark the *x*-axis, and vertical bars mark the *y*-axis) containing the numbers 0..36 arranged in a hexagonal shape.[1] Remember, a region is a one-to-one and onto function between points and integers. In this display, the contents of each point contain its rank value. This hexagonal region assigns point (0,0) a rank of 18, and assigns point (3, 3) a rank of 36. Points that are not part of the hexagonal region are displayed as dots.

```
Region (Rect, Trap, UpTri, DownTri, Hex, Chinese, xForm, X, Y): h
   edge: 3
Number of cells = 37
Enclosing Box: (-4,-4)-(4,4)


      .    .    .    .    |    .    .    .    .
      .    .    .    . 33 34   35   36    .
      .    .    . 28 29   30   31   32    .
      .    . 22 23   24   25   26   27    .
  ---- 15   16   17   18   19   20   21----
      . 9  10   11   12   13   14    .    .
      . 4   5    6    7    8    .    .    .
      . 0   1    2    3    .    .    .    .
      .    .    .    .    |    .    .    .    .
```

The next prompt asks whether you want to block all the points on the boundary of the hexagon. Enter "y" for yes. You get another copy of the display with each point on the edge of the hexagon filled with an asterisk (*). Unblocked points continue to show their rank.

```
Block all boundaries (y|n): y
Enclosing Box: (-4,-4)-(4,4)


      .    .    .    .    |    .    .    .    .
      .    .    .    .    *    *    *    *    .
      .    .    .    * 29   30   31    *    .
      .    . * 23   24   25   26    *    .
  ---- *   16   17   18   19   20    *----
      . * 10   11   12   13    *    .    .
      . *  5    6    7    *    .    .    .
      . *  *    *    *    .    .    .    .
      .    .    .    .    |    .    .    .    .
```

---

1. The hexagon is a little skewed. H2BOARD improves the display of the hexagon by displaying it on the hexgrid.

The last prompt is the number of additional points you would like to block, and a list of the points to block. Block the origin by entering "1 (0,0)". The hexagon is redisplayed with the origin blocked. You can continue to block more and more points. When you're done, enter "0".

```
Number and list of blockages: 1 (0,0)
Enclosing Box: (-4,-4)-(4,4)

    .    .    .    .    |    .    .    .    .
    .    .    .    .    *    *    *    *    .
    .    .    .    *   29   30   31    *    .
    .    .    *   23   24   25   26    *    .
----      *   16   17    *   19   20    *----
    .      *   10   11   12   13    *    .    .
    .      *    5    6    7    *    .    .    .
    .      *    *    *    *    .    .    .    .
    .    .    .    .    |    .    .    .    .
Number and list of blockages: 0
```

You can pass all these parameters to P2BOARD on the command line by enclosing them in quotes.

```
C>P2BOARD "h 3 y 1 (0,0) 0"
```

As a further example, build a rectangular region that maps points in a column-major order,

```
C>P2BOARD "r 4 5 y 0"
```

and build a Chinese checkers board

```
C>P2BOARD "c 3 n 0"
```

Point2 Class

Region classes are based on a point type. The region classes in P2BOARD are based on the class Point2. A Point2 instance is a point with x and y coordinates.

The interface and implementation of Point2 is quite simple and obvious (isn't it nice that *some* classes are simple and obvious?). The Point2 constructor takes two values that are assigned to x and y respectively. Point2's can be added with operators + and +=, subtracted with operators (binary) − and −=, and the coordinates can be negated using the (unary) −. Operators == and != compare two Point2's. The dist() member function computes the minimum distance between two points. The min(), max(), minValue(), and maxValue() member functions are used to compute minimum enclosing rectangles.

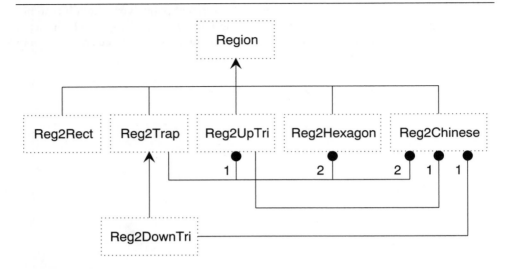

FIGURE 6.1
Two-dimensional Region classes.

Point2's are read and written to streams using the format "(x, y)":

```
#incude "Point2.hpp"

void main () {
    Point2   origin(0,0);
    Point2   p, q;

    cin >> p >> q;
    cout << "Distance between " << p << " and " << q << " = "
        << p.dist(q) << "\n";

    Point2 difference = p - q;
};
```

Region Class

Region is the abstract base class for all region classes (see Figures 6.1 and 6.2). It is a template class parameterized by a point type. Regions can be based on class Point2 (2D points), Point3 (3D points), or HexPoint (2D point on a hexgrid).

The two most important member functions of a region are rank() and unrank(). rank() converts a value of the point template class to a unique integer in the range 0..size() − 1. rank() corresponds to the indexing operator [] for normal C++ arrays. unrank() converts an integer in the range 0..size() − 1 to a point. rank() and unrank() are inverse operations. size() returns the number of points in the region.

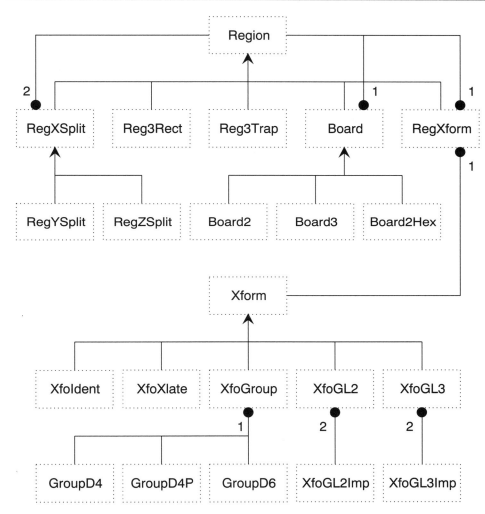

FIGURE 6.2
Three-dimensional and other region classes.

```
Point2          p;
Reg2Rect<Point2> reg(....)        // or any other region class

cin >> p;
int    r = reg.rank(p);          // rank value of point p
Point2 q = reg.unrank(r);
if ( p != q ) { ... error ... };
```

Member function bounds() returns whether or not a point is in the region. It returns a value of the enumeration type BOUNDS.

```
enum BOUNDS {OutBound, OnBound, InBound};
```

If bounds() returns OnBound, the point is on the border of the region. OutBound means the point is definitely outside the borders of the region. InBound points are part of the region, but not on the border. OnBound and InBound points are part of the region; OutBound points are not. Member onBoard() calls bounds() and returns TRUE if the point is OnBound or InBound.

```
cin >> p;
switch ( reg.bounds(p) ) {
case OutBound:
    cout << "Point is off the board";
    break;
case OnBound:
    cout << "Can only step in some directions";
    break;
case InBound:
    cout << "Steps in any direction are possible";
    break;
};
```

Some regions do not cover all the points within their borders, for example, a rectangular region where every other row and every other column are skipped. To handle these cases, there are versions of rank() and bounds() called rankEx() and boundsEx(). They return an "exact" flag that is FALSE if the point was rounded at any point during the conversion. rankEx() returns the integer of an adjacent point even if exact = FALSE. In some cases you want to consider a point valid even if it was rounded (exact = FALSE), and in other cases you don't want to consider rounded points. rankEx() performs the real work. rank() calls rankEx() and throws away the exact flag.

checkBounds() returns the current checking state for a region. When checking is enabled, calling rank() with a point that is not part of the region, or calling unrank() with an integer outside the range 0..size() − 1 results in a fatal error. Note that setCheckBounds() is a constant member function. Even though it does in fact change the state of the region, this change is not considered "significant" by the interface.

The last method is enclosure(). It returns the lower-left and upper-right corners of the minimum rectangle that encloses all points of the region. This rectangle is the minimum rectangle that must be displayed to show all points in the region. It is used by the display routines.

Reg2Rect Class

The only derived class in Figure 6.1 we will cover in this chapter is Reg2Rect. All the other classes are derived from, or depend on, Reg2Trap, which is covered in Chapter 7.

Reg2Rect is a two-dimensional, rectangular region. It maps storage in column-major order: rank values usually increment as the *x*-coordinate increments. Note that C++ lays out its arrays in row-major order. Rank value 0 always maps to the origin. It can map the 64 cells of an 8 × 8 chess board.

```
C>P2BOARD "r 8 8 n 0"
```

Game Boards

Except for the Board classes, regions do not allocate storage for the points in their region. They simply convert between points and integers using rank() and unrank(). Board is a template class with two template arguments: a point class and a class of the information to be kept for each cell of the board. Class Board and it derivatives, Board2, Board3, and Board2Hex, dynamically allocate an array of these cells from the heap; one cell for each point on the board. The board constructors require a Region instance that controls the size and shape of the board.

Boards also know how to display themselves. They do this by displaying a background and asking each cell to display() itself in the proper order. Rather than depending on system-dependent graphic primitives, the three board classes derived from Board in Figure 6.2 write themselves using typewriter-like output. While not as pleasant to look at, they are more portable. It should be quite easy to create new board and cell classes that generate nicer output.

Board2 is based on Point2 and creates a two-dimensional output with *x*- and *y*-axes. Board3, based on Point3, produces a three-dimensional output by outputting a series of two-dimensional slices, one slice for each value of *z*. Board2Hex, based on HexPoint, creates a two-dimensional output on a hexgrid (see Chapter 8 for more details). Its has *u*-, *v*-, and *w*-axes, marked by "-", "\", and "/" respectively.

The cell class contains all the information about each cell on the board. The exact list of cell information is very dependent on the game, but it might include:

- Is the cell on the edge (boundary) of the board?
- Is a cell blocked or can a player occupy the cell?
- What is the dominant terrain of the cell: road, forest, lake, building?
- Are there any special objects located in the cell?
- Which piece is currently occupying the cell? Which opponent does it belong to? What type of piece is it (e.g., an F-16 or the white king)?
- Which steps ($+u$, $-u$, $+v$, $-v$, $+w$, $-w$) are legal? Are there walls or hedges between this cell and any adjacent cell? This type of information allows you to block movement without blocking out an entire cell.

Operator[]() allows you to index into the board array using either a point or a rank value. Passing points is most intuitive, but you get faster performance using rank values because this eliminates the call to rank().

RegXform Class

Reg2Rect does not support coordinate translation, so it always numbers the x and y coordinates in the chess board example above as 0..7 rather than as 1..8. It is tempting to add a translation factor directly into the Reg2Rect class. However, it is not hard to imagine other transformations that would be useful in some applications. Should all these different transformations also be added to Reg2Rect? No. There is a better way.

Class RegXform is a region that transforms other regions. It contains (has) two subobjects: an instance of Xform and an instance of Region. It uses the Xform object to transform coordinates, and then passes the transformed coordinates to the region object.

Class Xform is a transformation of all the points on the plane. Every Xform also has both a "forward" transformation map() and a "backward" transformation mapInv() that is the inverse of the forward transformation. When I build a RegXform instance, conceptually I find it most natural to first build a subregion located at $(0, 0)$, and then build a transformation that moves the subregion from $(0, 0)$ to its final location. This means RegXform::unrank() uses the forward transformation of the Xform, and RegXform::rank() uses the backward transformation.

We can now build a rectangular region that has coordinates 1..8. We need an instance of Reg2Rect that determines the shape and size of the region, and we need an instance of XfoXlate (coordinate translation) that adds $(1, 1)$ to each point it is given (this is the forward transformation; the backward transformation subtracts $(1, 1)$ from every point).

To display this shifted board with P2BOARD, start out by entering "f" to build a RegXform at the first prompt. You then see the same prompt again, indented. The second prompt is for the subregion that is part of RegXform. In this case, the subregion is the 8×8 Reg2Rect. So enter "r" and fill in the data about the rectangle. The next prompt is for an instance of class Xform. Enter "x" for a translation (XfoXlate), and then enter the translation amount as "$(1, 1)$" The translation amount is enclosed in parentheses because XfoXlate accepts an instance of Point2. The complete set of inputs is

```
C>P2BOARD "f    r 8 8    x (1,1)    n 0"
```

Xform Class

Class Xform is a transformation of all points on the plane or in space. It has no boundary; it transforms all points. Like the Region class hierarchy, the Xform class hierarchy contains template classes where the template argument is a point (Point2, Point3, or HexPoint). Its two most important methods are map() and mapInv(): map() is the "forward" transformation, the one defined by the arguments to the constructor; mapInv() is the inverse transformation.

A transformation of integer coordinates will not always be exact, perhaps because integer division causes rounding. Xform provides mapEx() and mapInvEx() methods that return whether any rounding occurred.

Xforms know how to compute their own inverses. inverse() returns a new Xform whose map() and mapInv() are interchanged.

There are a number of classes derived from Xform.

Xfoldent Class

This is the identity transformation. map() and mapInv() return the point they were passed. You may be asking yourself, why in the world would this class be useful? Rather than building a RegXform with an XfoIdent transformation, just skip the RegXform altogether. While skipping the RegXform is certainly a faster solution, it may be more difficult to change the structure of a network of objects than it is to keep the same structure and "nop" some of the pieces. The speed lost by going through the extra RegXform and XfoIdent at run-time may be far less than the time it takes to change the program so the RegXform is optional. The reason for defining XfoIdent is the same as the reason for defining addition by 0.

This class is independent of the implementation of the point template class. It works as well for two-dimensional Point2's as for three-dimensional Point3's. It requires the point class support assignment and a copy constructor.

XfoXlate Class

This class **translates** all input points by the amount specified on the constructor. The forward transformation adds the point; the backward transformation subtracts the point. This class is also independent of the implementation of the point template class. It requires only the point class support addition and subtraction.

XfoGroup Class

This class transforms points in two steps:

1. Transforming the point by calling a group (like GroupD4 or GroupD6).
2. Translation.

The primary discussion of groups is in "VLSI Design" in Chapter 13. But the basic transformation is not terribly difficult to understand. GroupD4 can interchange the x and y axes. It can also flip the sign of either the x- or y-axes, or flip both. The collection of all such transformations is the same as (isomorphic to) the dihedral(4) group: the symmetries of the square. Specifically, GroupD4 can rotate the x- and y-axes by any multiple of 90° (R90, R180, and R270), it can flip the sign of the x or y axis (FlipX and FlipY), it can interchange the x and y axes (Diag1 and Diag2), or it can leave everything alone (Ident).

The second transformation, the translation, is not strictly necessary. It could equally well be provided by XfoXlate. But in practice, translation will be required for every application of XfoGroup, so I have included that function directly. Am I being inconsistent because Reg2Rect doesn't include a translation amount? Perhaps. I can imagine a number of uses for Reg2Rect that are fixed to $(0, 0)$; but I can't imagine using XfoGroup without also wanting translation (for example, in VLSI design). In any case, I invoke designer's prerogative and keep the translation.

GroupD4's Diag1 transformation converts a region from column-major order to row-major order:

```
C>P2BOARD "f      r 8 8     d Diag1 (0,0)     n 0"
```

General Linear Transformations

Classes XfoGL2 and XfoGL3 are **general linear transformations**. These classes are dependent on the number of coordinates in the point class. XfoGL2 is for two-dimensional points and XfoGL3 is for three-dimensional points. General linear transformations of n-dimensions, abbreviated GL(n), are the most general form of rigid, linear transformation and transform a point p to a point p'. Each transformed coordinate is a linear combination of the original coordinates. They are usually written in matrix notation as

$$p' = (D \times p + xlate)/denom \qquad [8]$$

where D is a matrix and xlate is the amount of translation. For these classes, all coefficients are integers and all operations are integer operations. Denom has been added to collect all rounding into a single place. Division by denom would not be necessary if all coefficients and operations were floating point.

XfoGL2 transforms instances of Point2 using

$$\begin{pmatrix} p'_x \\ p'_y \end{pmatrix} = \left[\begin{pmatrix} D_{xx} & D_{yx} \\ D_{xy} & D_{yy} \end{pmatrix} \begin{pmatrix} p_x \\ p_y \end{pmatrix} + \begin{pmatrix} xlate_x \\ xlate_y \end{pmatrix} \right] \Big/ denom \qquad [9]$$

Its constructor takes three Point2 values. The first Point2, xStep, specifies the difference between the transformed location of point $(1, 0)$ minus the transformed location of $(0, 0)$. That is, a step of $(1, 0)$ in the original coordinates corresponds to a step of xStep in the transformed coordinates. Looking at the equation, the coordinates of xStep are the first column of the D matrix (D_{xx} and D_{xy}). Similarly, a step of $(0, 1)$ in the original coordinates corresponds to a step of yStep in the transformed coordinates. The coordinates of yStep are the second column of the D matrix (D_{yx} and D_{yy}). The third Point2 is the translation vector.

The final value on the constructor is denom. If you need a transformation that involves any fractional coefficients, collect the denominators into denom (i.e., set denom to the least common multiple of all coefficient denominators).

As an example, let's transform the chessboard. Set xStep to $(2, 0)$ to skip every other column, and set yStep to $(1, 1)$ to skew the y axis to a 45° line. Then set the translation to $(-5, -3)$ just for fun. Since none of the coefficients are fractional, denom is 1.

```
C>P2BOARD "f   r 8 8   g (2,0)(1,1)(-5,-3) 1   n 0"
```

The GL(n) transformation is the most general of all the transformations listed in this book. Every other transformation can be converted to a GL(n) transformation. However, a GL(2) transformation requires four multiplications, four additions, and two divisions. A GL(3) transformation requires nine multiplications, nine additions, and three divisions. Some applications do not require the flexibility of a GL(n) transformation and should not have to pay for the extra function.

XfoGL2 contains two instances of XfoGL2Imp: one for its forward transformation and one for its backward transformation. XfoGL2Imp is a single, one-way, GL(2) transformation—it has no backward transformation. Creating the separate XfoGL2Imp class simplified the coding for XfoGL2. Similarly, XfoGL3 contains two instances of XfoGL3Imp. It is quite probable XfoGL2Imp and XfoGL3Imp will have other uses.

Three-Dimensional Regions

Extending the existing classes to three-dimensional regions is simple. First, we need a three-dimensional point. Point3 is the same as Point2, with the addition of another coordinate z. Point3 objects can be added, subtracted, compared, and so forth, just like Point2 objects. Of course, they are read from and written to a stream as "(x, y, z)".

We also need a new class to map 3D rectangular regions and a new class for 3D trapezoidal regions. These are the Reg3Rect and Reg3Trap in Figure 6.2.

Many of the region template classes can be instantiated using Point3 as the template argument. For example, RegXform still requires an Xform object and a subregion object. Since RegXform itself makes no assumptions about the details of the point template class, it works equally well with Point3 objects. The Xform classes XfoIdent, XfoXlate, and XfoGroup are equally ignorant of their point class details. They can be instantiated with a Point3 template argument also.

P3BOARD is the same as P2BOARD except that it is based on Point3 rather than Point2. We can build a three-dimensional, rectangular region that is 5 × 4 × 3:

```
C>P3BOARD "r 5 4 3 n 0"
```

You will see a number of plane cross-sections of the three-dimensional region. As for P2BOARD, the rank value of each point is displayed, and points not in the region print as dots.

Quad Trees and Oct Trees

The region classes so far have produced a single shape. Those regions may have been transformed multiple times, but there has always been just one shape. The RegXSplit class creates a region that has two subregions. It divides the entire 2D plane (or 3D space) in half. All points with an x coordinate less than the "split point" are in the first subregion, and all points with an x coordinate greater than or equal to the split point are in the second subregion. Each subregion can be any class derived from Region. Classes RegYSplit and RegZSplit are similar except they divide points based on their y or z coordinates.

As a simple example, let's use a single RegXSplit object whose subregions are 3×3 Reg2Rects. At the first P2BOARD prompt enter "x" for a RegXSplit object. The next prompt is the same as the first, except indented. This prompt is asking for the type of the first subregion. Enter "r 3 3" for the first Reg2Rect.

The next prompt asks for RegXSplit's "split point." The plane is divided in half at the x coordinate of the split point. Since most regions cover $(0, 0)$, most instances of subregion 2 will also need to be translated; RegXSplit translates the points in subregion 2 by subtracting the split point. That is, once a point is known to be in subregion 2, the point is adjusted by subtracting the split point before passing it to subregion 2. In this example, enter a split point of $(4, -1)$ (the x coordinate of 4 is one larger than necessary, but visually separates the two subregions). All points with $x < 4$ are in subregion1, and all points in subregion 2 are translated by subtracting $(4, -1)$. So, the original point $(4, -1)$ is mapped to the origin of the subregion 2.

At the next prompt, enter another 3×3 instance of Reg2Rect for the second subregion of RegXSplit. And finally, enter the parameters for blockages. The full set of parameters is

```
C>P2BOARD "x    r 3 3    (4,-1)    r 3 3    n 0"
```

Since RegXSplit's subregions can be any class derived from Region, we have a lot of flexibility. One subregion may be a Reg2Rect while the other is a Reg2Chinese. Or one subregion may be a transformed region (RegXform) while the other is not or has a different transformation. But the most interesting case is when the subregions are instances of a splitting class.

Assume an instance of RegXSplit has subregions that are instances of RegYSplit. The RegXSplit instance divides the plane in half. Points in the left half of the plane are then passed to the first RegYSplit subregion, and points in the right half of the plane are passed to the second RegYSplit subregion. Each RegYSplit subregion further divides the plane in half. But since they already see only half the points, these three classes have divided the entire plane into four pieces. If each of the RegYSplit instances have rectangular subregions, this structure would map out four rectangles. Note that the two RegYSplit objects do not need to split at the same y coordinate.

```
C>P2BOARD "x y r 3 3 (0,5) r 3 3 (4,-1) y r 3 3 (0,4) r 3 3 n 0"
```

Using the principle, "if it worked once, do it over and over again," the RegYSplit instances can have subregions that are instances of RegXSplit, dividing the plane into eight subregions. Clearly, we can add more and more layers of splitting classes to divide the plane into as many subregions as necessary. What we have done is set up a two-dimensional, binary tree called a quad tree. Figure 6.3 shows how multiple layers of RegXSplit and RegYSplit divide the plane into small regions.

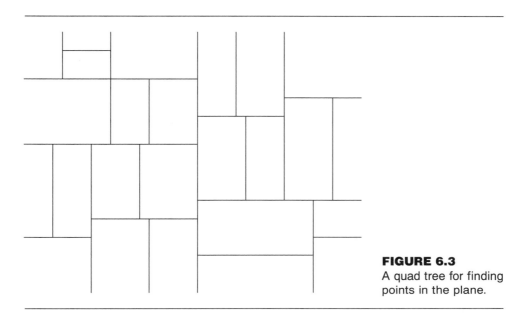

FIGURE 6.3
A quad tree for finding
points in the plane.

The term *quad tree* seems to cover many related data structures (Knuth, 1973c:555; Scott and Iyengar, 1986). In its classic form, each node of a quad tree is either a leaf node or has four children. In some forms, the subregions are squares whose edge is a power of 2. These splitting classes allow a more flexible structure. A **quad tree** is a recursive structure in which every node is either a leaf node (an instance of Region that is not a splitting class), or is a binary node that divides at an x- or y-coordinate. This structure is called a quad tree even though it contains only binary nodes because it achieves the same result as a classic quad tree with its four-way nodes. Each layer should divide the number of points approximately in half. Normally, if layer n of the quad tree splits on x coordinates, level $n + 1$ splits on y coordinates, but this is not required.

The same technique can be used in three-dimensions with the obvious extension to RegZSplit. In three dimensions, these structures are called **oct trees**.

When rank() of a splitting class is called, it checks the point's coordinates and calls rank() on one of its subregions. If the subregion is also a splitting class, the subregion checks a (usually different) coordinate and calls rank() on one of the sub-subregions. This continues until it finds a leaf region like Reg2Rect that can actually compute the rank of the point. As the rank value is returned up through the classes, each class adjusts the rank value of all points in the second subregion to skip over all points in the first subregion.

One of the problems with this approach is that the distinction between OnBound and InBound is not always correct for points on either side of the split line. The borders of each subregion are reported as OnBound even when the two subregions are adjacent.

This problem can be fixed by explicitly testing adjacent points that cross the split line. However, if bounds() returns OutBound, the point is indeed not part of the region.

With these classes you can construct a region for literally *any* collection of points. Just split the plane with splitting class instances until each point is in its own subregion. Then make a 1×1 Reg2Rect region for each point. If you plan to do this frequently, you should probably derive a RegPoint class from Region. RegPoint is a region of a single point. It would return 0 for its rank, and its bounds check would be a simple comparison.

Usage Notes for Games

To build a game board:

1. Select the region that matches the shape of the board. Decide on the size and whether or not you want run-time checking.
2. Define a class or struct for the information to be kept for each cell.
3. Declare a board using the cell class as a template argument. The region is a parameter to the constructor.
4. Indexing the board is done with operator[]().

To visit every cell on the board (for example, when initializing the board), loop over the rank values [0..size() − 1]. Use unrank() to convert an array index to a point. If a player wants to move right one unit, do the following:

1. Add $(1, 0)$ to his current position using operator + ().
2. Call inBounds() to see if the new position is on the board.
3. Call operator[]() to access that cell's information.
4. Check whether that cell can be occupied.

To move from cell A to cell B, compute the difference of B − A. Then extract the (x, y) coordinates and step along these coordinates in any order to find an open path. Each order is a shortest path from A to B.

Implementation Comments

Bounds Checking

Method bounds() must be able to return OutBound, OnBound, or InBound for any point. Since this check will be performed frequently in a real application, the test needs to be as fast as possible. This section derives a general method for any region.

Consider the directed line segment $\overrightarrow{rs}$ from point r to point s on a two-dimensional plane (see Figure 6.4). This line divides the plane into two half-planes. Given any point p, we need to quickly find which half-plane contains it. If we walk along the line from r to s, one of the half-planes will lie to the left. Now, rotate the vector $\overrightarrow{rs}$ 90° counter-

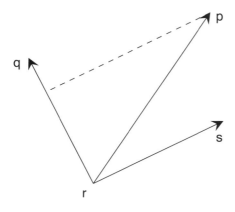

FIGURE 6.4
Two-dimensional boundary checking.

clockwise about r, and call the rotated vector $\vec{rq}$. $\vec{rq}$ is perpendicular to $\vec{rs}$ and it points into the left half-plane. The coordinates of $\vec{rq}$ are $(-(s_y - r_y), s_x - r_x)$. If the dot product of $\vec{rq}$ and $\vec{rp}$ is positive, then p is in the left half-plane; if it is negative, p is in the right half-plane; if it is zero, p lays on the line $\overline{rs}$. In terms of the coordinates, p lays in the left half-plane defined by $\vec{rs}$ if and only if:

$$0 \le (p_y - r_y)(s_x - r_x) - (p_x - r_x)(s_y - r_y) \qquad [10]$$

Neither the length of $\vec{rs}$ nor that of $\vec{rq}$ affects whether their dot product is positive or negative. Any vector with the same direction as $\vec{rs}$ is sufficient. In the bounds checking code, the entire edge of a region is used as $\vec{rs}$.

So, to determine if point p is inside an area, apply this formula once for each edge where $\vec{rs}$ is an edge of the region. p is inside if and only if all results (the minimum) are greater than or equal to zero. Most regions have edges with known slopes, so these equations can be simplified and combined to reduce the overall computation. Plugging in the edges for Reg2Rect gives the simplified checks we intuitively knew were correct.

r	s	boundary check
$(0, 0)$	$(3, 0)$	$0 \le p_y$
$(3, 0)$	$(3, 3)$	$p_x \le 3$
$(3, 3)$	$(0, 3)$	$3 \le p_y$
$(0, 3)$	$(0, 0)$	$0 \le p_x$

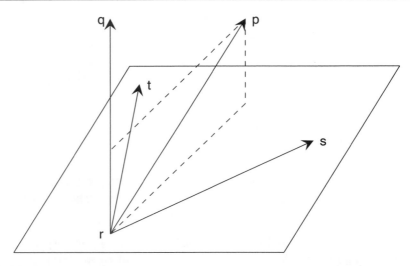

FIGURE 6.5
Three-dimensional boundary checking.

The boundary checks for the trapezoidal regions derived from Equation [10] are not so obvious.

Function int2Bounds() converts the sign of an integer (positive, negative, or zero) to a BOUNDS object. It is good for mapping the left-hand side of Equation [10] to a BOUNDS result.

A similar equation holds in three dimensions. Let points r, s, and t be three non-colinear points on a boundary plane of a solid region (see Figure 6.5). If, relative to r, s is to the right of t in the plane, then the cross-product of $\overrightarrow{rs}$ and $\overrightarrow{rt}$ is a vector $\overrightarrow{rq}$ that points "up." Given any point p, the dot product of $\overrightarrow{rp}$ and $\overrightarrow{rq}$ is positive if p is "above" the plane, negative if p is "below," and zero if p lies in the plane. That is, p is on or above the plane if and only if

$$0 \leq \det \begin{vmatrix} p_x - r_x & p_y - r_y & p_z - r_z \\ s_x - r_x & s_y - r_y & s_z - r_z \\ t_x - r_x & t_y - r_y & t_z - r_z \end{vmatrix} \quad [11]$$

To determine if a point p is inside a given volume, check it against all planes of the volume using Equation [11]. Tetrahedrons have four planes to check, triangular cylinders five planes, and parallelepipeds six planes.

Error Handling

Whenever a region detects an error it calls either rankError() or pointError() to report the problem. These methods print out the bad piece of input data. Unfortunately, the input value may not be the value the user entered due to any number of transformations that were called before a region detected the error. The nice way to handle this would use C++ exception handlers that reverse transform the bad values back to the user's input. For now, programmer beware!

Performance

The reason for these classes is to provide a function similar to C++'s native arrays which are quite fast. While it is probably impossible to match that performance, that should be the goal. For that reason, most classes use inlining for the ranking, unranking, and boundary checking code. Since the other methods will not be called as frequently, they are out-of-line calls.

Possible Extensions

You could write specialized iterators for certain common game chores:

- Visit all cells within d units of a particular cell. It should ignore cells that are off the board.
- Visit all cells along a straight line path between two cells. This is needed to determine if one cell has a clear "shot" at another cell. This could be implemented using Bresenham's line drawing algorithm.
- Visit all cells for which one cell has a clear view. This is the list of all cells that can be attacked.

There are many possibilities for additional Region and Xform classes:

- As mentioned in the section on the splitting classes, you might want a RegPoint class—the ultimate quad tree leaf node—that maps a single point.
- Add a Reg2Sym class for representing symmetric regions like symmetric matrices. While it appears to be a rectangular region, it is derived from a triangular region. It would fold all points (x, y) with $y > x$ to (y, x), so (x, y) and (y, x) have the same rank value.
- Add a RegSeq class that is a sequence of subregions. It would contain a list of subregions. Searching this class would be slower than a tree of splitting classes, but would allow regions that overlap (the splitting classes do not work with overlapping regions). For example, the red (or black) cells of a checkerboard could be built out of two 4×4 Reg2Rects, with origins $(0, 0)$, and $(1, 1)$, each of which is transformed using XfoGL2 to skip every other row and column.

- Regions can be transformed multiple times using multiple RegXform instances. But there is no means to combine tranformations without using RegXform. You might want to add an XfoPair class that has two Xforms. XfoPair would map a point first through the first sub-Xform, and then map the result through the second sub-Xform.
- Add an XfoSkew class with the transformation

$$\begin{pmatrix} x' \\ y' \end{pmatrix} = \begin{pmatrix} x + y \\ y \end{pmatrix}$$

This transformation is used in many of the trapezoidal classes for hexgrids. This would be a specialized version of XfoGL2 but it would be faster.
- Add an XfoScale class that multiplies all *x*-coordinates by one amount and all *y*-coordinates by another amount. The general linear transformation already does this, so it makes sense only if you do this a lot and want to save some performance.

Bounds checking (boundsEx()) currently returns two values: a BOUNDS value and an exact flag. It might be better to combine these two values into a single Bounds class. This would simplify the code since operators could be defined for the Bounds class.[2] However, the BOUNDS enumeration is still needed to represent OutBound, OnBound and InBound.

Region::enclosure() currently returns two points that are the opposite sides of the minimum enclosing rectangle. However, this code, which depends on min() and max(), implicitly assumes the desired rectangle has sides parallel to the *x*- and *y*-axes. This is not true for HexPoints, and causes problems for Board2Hex::setDisplaySizeToBox(). That method has to look at *every* point in the region, and compute an enclosure based on transformed points. A better way to handle this would be to add an Enclosure class. It would grow to enclose every point added to it. Class HexEnclosure, derived from Enclosure, would handle the transformations required for a hexgrid. If you do this, you will also have to change the enclosure() methods of every region to add every vertex on their *convex hull*.[3] So Reg2Rect and Reg2Trap would add their four corner points, Reg2Hexagon would add its six corner points, and Reg2Chinese (the only concave region defined here) would add the six points at the ends of its triangles. Enclosure should be a template class with a point class as template argument so it can be extended to three dimensions.

_____

2. Operators cannot be defined for enumerations in Borland's 3.1 compiler. Borland's OS/2 compiler does allow this.

3. A convex hull in two dimensions is a polygon that does not have any concave vertices. That is, every pair of adjacent edges has an angle less than 180°.

Source Code

File Bounds.hpp

```
#ifndef _BOUNDS
#define _BOUNDS
//*********************************************************************
// FUNCTION:
//    Define a data type to describe the relationship between a point
//    and a region defined by some number of boundaries.
//
// CHANGE LOG:
//    22Feb92 - Initial Coding.  SN Gerard
//*********************************************************************
enum BOUNDS {OutBound,        // outside the boundaries
             OnBound,         // on the boundary
             InBound};        // inside the boundaries

inline BOUNDS int2Bounds(int bnd) {
   if ( bnd < 0 )
      return OutBound;
   else if ( bnd == 0 )
      return OnBound;
   else // bnd > 0
      return InBound;
};
#endif
```

File Point2.hpp

```
#ifndef _POINT2_HPP
#define _POINT2_HPP
//*********************************************************************
// TITLE: Point2 -- two-dimensional point
//
// AUTHOR: Scott N Gerard, Rochester, MN
// LANGUAGE: C++
//
// FUNCTION:
//    A two-dimensional point with x and y coordinates.
//
//    This class is a leaf class -- it has no virtual functions.
//    Therefore instances to not contain a vtbl pointer that would
//    dramatically increase its size.
//
// CHANGE LOG:
//    18May93 - Initial coding.  SN Gerard
//    29Jun93 - Add hash().  SN Gerard
//*********************************************************************
#include <iostream.h>
```

(continued)

File Point2.hpp *(continued)*

```cpp
#include "Bool.hpp"

class Point2 {
public:
   //*********************************************************************
   // Constructors
   //*********************************************************************
   Point2 (int X=0, int Y=0): xx(X), yy(Y) {};

   //*********************************************************************
   // set and change coordinates
   //*********************************************************************
   int x () const    { return xx; };
   int y () const    { return yy; };

   Point2& x(const int X)  { xx = X;  return *this; }
   Point2& y(const int Y)  { yy = Y;  return *this; }

   //*********************************************************************
   // are the Points equal ?
   //*********************************************************************
   friend BOOL operator == (const Point2& p, const Point2& q)
      { return BOOL( (p.xx == q.xx) && (p.yy == q.yy) ); };

   friend BOOL operator != (const Point2& p, const Point2& q)
      { return BOOL( !(p == q) ); };

   //*********************************************************************
   // Add and subtract two Points
   //*********************************************************************
   friend Point2 operator + (const Point2& p, const Point2& q)
      { return Point2( p.xx+q.xx, p.yy+q.yy); };

   friend Point2 operator - (const Point2& p, const Point2& q)
      { return Point2( p.xx-q.xx, p.yy-q.yy); };

   Point2& operator += (const Point2& p) {
      xx += p.xx;
      yy += p.yy;
      return *this;
   };

   Point2& operator -= (const Point2& p) {
      xx -= p.xx;
      yy -= p.yy;
      return *this;
   };

   Point2& operator - () {                    // unary minus
      xx = -xx;
```

```
      yy = -yy;
      return *this;
   };

   //********************************************************************
   // Compute the minimum distance between two points
   //********************************************************************
   int dist (const Point2& hc) const;

   //********************************************************************
   // hash
   //********************************************************************
   long int hash () const;

   //********************************************************************
   // routines for minimums and maximums
   //********************************************************************
   Point2& minValue();
   Point2& maxValue();

   Point2& min (const Point2& p);
   Point2& max (const Point2& p);

   //********************************************************************
   // IO operations using external format "(x,y)"
   //********************************************************************
   friend istream& operator >> (istream&, Point2&);
   friend ostream& operator << (ostream&, const Point2&);

private:
   //********************************************************************
   // x and y coordinates.
   //********************************************************************
   int xx, yy;
};

#endif
```

File Point2.cpp

```
//********************************************************************
// TITLE: Point2 -- two-dimensional point
//
// AUTHOR: Scott N Gerard, Rochester, MN
// LANGUAGE: C++
//
// FUNCTION:
//    A two-dimensional point with x and y coordinates.
//
// CHANGE LOG:
//    18May93 - Initial coding.  SN Gerard
```

(continued)

File Point2.cpp *(continued)*

```
//    29Jun93 - Add hash().  SN Gerard
//***********************************************************************
#include <limits.h>
#include <stdlib.h>
#include "IntMath.hpp"
#include "Point2.hpp"
#include "SimpHasher.hpp"


//***********************************************************************
// Compute the minimum distance between two points
//***********************************************************************
int Point2::dist (const Point2& p) const {
   return abs(xx - p.xx) + abs(yy - p.yy);  // distance of shortest path
};


//***********************************************************************
// hash
//***********************************************************************
long int Point2::hash () const {
   SimpHasher<int> h;
   h << xx << yy;
   return h.result();
};


//***********************************************************************
// routines for minimums and maximums
//***********************************************************************
Point2& Point2::minValue() {
   xx = INT_MIN;
   yy = INT_MIN;
   return *this;
};


Point2& Point2::maxValue() {
   xx = INT_MAX;
   yy = INT_MAX;
   return *this;
};


Point2& Point2::min (const Point2& p) {
   xx = ::min(xx, 0+p.xx);               // NOTE: 0+p.xx is not const
   yy = ::min(yy, 0+p.yy);
   return *this;
};


Point2& Point2::max (const Point2& p) {
   xx = ::max(xx, 0+p.xx);
   yy = ::max(yy, 0+p.yy);
   return *this;
};
```

```
//**********************************************************************
// IO operations using external format "(x,y)"
//**********************************************************************
ostream& operator << (ostream& os, const Point2& p) {
   os << "(" << p.xx << "," << p.yy << ")";
   return os;
};

istream& operator >> (istream& is, Point2& p) {
   int inx, iny;
   char leftp, com, rightp;

   is >> leftp >> inx >> com >> iny >> rightp;

   if (is && leftp == '(' && com == ',' && rightp == ')' ) {
      p.xx = inx;
      p.yy = iny;
   }
   else {
      is.clear( ios::badbit  is.rdstate() );
   }
   return is;
};
```

File Region.hpp

```
#ifndef _REGION_HPP
#define _REGION_HPP
//**********************************************************************
// TITLE: Region -- region base class
//
// AUTHOR: Scott N Gerard, Rochester, MN
// LANGUAGE: C++
//
// FUNCTION:
//    This is the abstract class for all regions.
//
//    A region is a two or three dimensional area where every point in
//    the region is assigned a unique integer in the range 0..n.  rank()
//    converts a point to its integer, and unrank() converts an integer
//    to its point.
//
//    NOTE: the "const" attribute does not apply to setCheckBounds().
//    This attribute can be changed for any region.
//
// CHANGE LOG:
//    18May93 - Initial coding.  SN Gerard
//**********************************************************************
#include "Bool.hpp"
#include "Bounds.hpp"
```

(continued)

File Region.hpp   *(continued)*

```
template <class P>
class Region {

    typedef Region<P> ThisClass;

protected:

    typedef Region<P> RootClass;

    //*********************************************************************
    // constructor and destructor
    //*********************************************************************
    Region(BOOL checkBounds=TRUE): chkBounds(checkBounds)  {};
    virtual ~Region() {};

public:
    //*********************************************************************
    // make a copy
    //*********************************************************************
    ThisClass* copy() const { return (ThisClass*) _copy(); };

    //*********************************************************************
    // return the number of elements in the region
    //*********************************************************************
    int size() const { return elems; };

    //*********************************************************************
    // set/change bounds checking.  NOTE: the check value may be changed
    // even on const regions.  const refers to the region information.
    //*********************************************************************
    virtual BOOL checkBounds() const
        { return chkBounds; };

    virtual void setCheckBounds(BOOL checkBounds) const
        { ((Region<P>*)this)->chkBounds = checkBounds; };

    //*********************************************************************
    // Is coordinate {outside, on, inside} the boundary of the region ?
    //
    // This test is based on the following calculation:  Point (x,y) is on
    // the LEFT side of vector (x1,y1) -> (x2,y2) iff
    //
    //      (y-y1) * (x2-x1) - (x-x1) * (y2-y1) >= 0
    //
    // The sign of the expression reveals everything we need: positive
    // means inside (to the left of) the boundary, zero means on (collinear
    // with) the boundary, negative means outside (to the right of) the
    // boundary.
    //*********************************************************************
    virtual BOUNDS boundsEx (const P p, BOOL& exact) const = 0;
```

```
      virtual BOUNDS bounds    (const P p) const {
         BOOL exact;
         return boundsEx(p,exact);
      };

      //*******************************************************************
      // is the point on the region ?
      //*******************************************************************
      BOOL onBoard (const P p) const
         { return (BOOL) (bounds(p) != OutBound); };


      //*******************************************************************
      // return enclosing box
      //*******************************************************************
      virtual void enclosure (P& low, P& high) const;


      //*******************************************************************
      // Compute rank of p in the region.  If p is out of bounds of the
      // region and the description of the region specified checking then a
      // run-time error will be generated.
      //*******************************************************************
      virtual long rankEx (const P p, BOOL& exact) const = 0;
      virtual long rank   (const P p) const {
         BOOL exact;
         return rankEx(p,exact);
      };


      //*******************************************************************
      // Given a rank into a region, compute the Point that regions to it.
      // If rank is out of "bounds" of array and the description of region
      // specified checking then a run-time error will be generated.
      //*******************************************************************
      virtual P unrank (long rank) const = 0;


      //*******************************************************************
      // Error handlers
      //*******************************************************************
      void rankError   (int rank) const;   // rank out of bounds
      void pointError  (P p) const;         // Point out of bounds

protected:
      //*******************************************************************
      // data from constructor
      //*******************************************************************
      unsigned elems;                       // total elements in region
      BOOL     chkBounds;                   // perform subscript checking ?

      virtual RootClass* _copy() const = 0;
   };

#endif
```

File Region.cpp

```
//*********************************************************************
// TITLE: Region -- region base class
//
// AUTHOR: Scott N Gerard, Rochester, MN
// LANGUAGE: C++
//
// FUNCTION:
//     The abstract class for all regions.
//
//     A region is a two or three dimensional area where every point in
//     the region is assigned a unique integer in the range 0..n.  rank()
//     converts a point to its integer, and unrank() converts an integer
//     to its point.
//
// CHANGE LOG:
//     18May93 - Initial coding.  SN Gerard
//*********************************************************************
#include <stdlib.h>
#include "Region.hpp"


//*********************************************************************
// return enclosing box
//*********************************************************************
template <class P>
void Region<P>::enclosure (P& low, P& high) const {
   low.maxValue();
   high.minValue();

   // add EVERY point to the enclosure.  This is somewhat expensive,
   // but it is the only way if nothing more is known about the region.
   for (int i = 0; i < elems; ++i) {
      P p = unrank(i);
      low.min(p);
      high.max(p);
   };
};


//*********************************************************************
// Print an "out of bounds" error and halt.
//*********************************************************************
template <class P>
void Region<P>::rankError(long rank) const {
   cerr << "Region: rank value " << rank << " is too large." << endl;
   exit(EXIT_FAILURE);
};


//*********************************************************************
// Print an "out of bounds" error and halt.
//*********************************************************************
template <class P>
```

```
void Region<P>::pointError(P p) const {
    cerr << "Region: " << p << " is out of bounds." << endl;
    exit(EXIT_FAILURE);
};
```

File Reg2Rect.hpp

```
#ifndef _REG2RECT_HPP
#define _REG2RECT_HPP
//*********************************************************************
// TITLE: Reg2Rect -- 2D rectangular region
//
// AUTHOR: Scott N Gerard, Rochester, MN
// LANGUAGE: C++
//
// FUNCTION:
//    Map an rectangular region.  For example, defining a rectangle with
//    nx=6 and ny=4 gives the mapping
//
//            21    22    23    24    25    26    27
//            14    15    16    17    18    19    20
//             7     8     9    10    11    12    13
//             0     1     2     3     4     5     6
//
//
// CHANGE LOG:
//    18May93 - Initial coding.  SN Gerard
//*********************************************************************
#include "Region.hpp"

template <class P>
class Reg2Rect: public Region<P> {

    typedef Region<P> BaseClass;
    typedef Reg2Rect<P> ThisClass;

public:
    //*****************************************************************
    // constructor
    //*****************************************************************
    Reg2Rect (int nx, int ny, BOOL checkBounds=TRUE);

    //*****************************************************************
    // make a copy
    //*****************************************************************
    ThisClass* copy() const { return (ThisClass*) _copy(); };

    //*****************************************************************
    // where is Point?
    //*****************************************************************
    virtual BOUNDS boundsEx (const P p, BOOL& exact) const;
```

(continued)

File Reg2Rect.hpp *(continued)*

```
//**********************************************************************
// return enclosing box
//**********************************************************************
virtual void enclosure (P& low, P& high) const;

//**********************************************************************
// rank and unrank
//**********************************************************************
virtual long rankEx (const P p, BOOL& exact) const;
virtual P unrank (long rank) const;

protected:
//**********************************************************************
// constants of the transformation
//**********************************************************************
int nx;
int ny;

virtual RootClass* _copy() const { return new ThisClass(*this); };
};

#endif
```

File Reg2Rect.cpp

```
//**********************************************************************
// TITLE: Reg2Rect -- 2D rectangular region
//
// AUTHOR: Scott N Gerard, Rochester, MN
// LANGUAGE: C++
//
// FUNCTION:
//     Map an rectangular region.
//
// CHANGE LOG:
//     18May93 - Initial coding.  SN Gerard
//**********************************************************************
#include "Reg2Rect.hpp"
#include "IntMath.hpp"

//******************************************************************
// constructor
//******************************************************************
template <class P>
Reg2Rect<P>::Reg2Rect(int nX, int nY, BOOL checkBounds)
   :Region<P>(checkBounds), nx(nX), ny(nY)
   { elems = nx * ny; };

//******************************************************************
// is HexCoord {outside, on, inside} the "bounds" of region ?
//******************************************************************
```

```
template <class P>
BOUNDS Reg2Rect<P>::boundsEx (const P p, BOOL& exact) const {
   exact = TRUE;                        // always exact

   // use min to select OUTBOUND over ONBOUND, and ONBOUND over inBOUND
   return int2Bounds(
      min( min(0+p.x(), nx-p.x()-1), min(0+p.y(), ny-p.y()-1) ) );
};


//*******************************************************************
// return enclosing box
//*******************************************************************
template <class P>
void Reg2Rect<P>::enclosure (P& low, P& high) const {
   low = P(0,0);
   high = P(nx-1, ny-1);
};


//***********************************************************************
// rank
//***********************************************************************
template <class P>
long Reg2Rect<P>::rankEx (const P p, BOOL& exact) const {
   if (chkBounds && !onBoard(p))
      pointError(p);
   exact = TRUE;
   return p.y() * nx + p.x();
};


//***********************************************************************
// unrank
//***********************************************************************
template <class P>
P Reg2Rect<P>::unrank (long rank) const {
   if (chkBounds && (elems < rank))
      rankError(rank);
   return P(rank % nx, rank / nx);
};
```

File RegXSplit.hpp

```
#ifndef _REGXSPLIT_HPP
#define _REGXSPLIT_HPP
//***********************************************************************
// TITLE: RegXSplit -- region that divides at x-coordinate
//
// AUTHOR: Scott N Gerard, Rochester, MN
// LANGUAGE: C++
//
```

(continued)

File RegXSplit.hpp   *(continued)*

```
// FUNCTION:
//    This region divides space into two sub-regions.  All points
//    with an x-coordinate strictly less than the split point are routed
//    to the region 1.  All points with an x-coordinate >= the split
//    point are routed to region 2 after being translated by
//    split (while translation by split could be handled using RegXform
//    for the second region, this would be slower and it WILL be required
//    for every instance of this class since all simple regions start at
//    the origin.)
//
// CHANGE LOG:
//    26May93 - Initial coding.  SN Gerard
//************************************************************************
#include "Region.hpp"

template <class P>
class RegXSplit: public Region<P> {

    typedef Region<P> BaseClass;
    typedef RegXSplit<P> ThisClass;

public:
    //******************************************************************
    // constructor
    //******************************************************************
    RegXSplit (
        const Region<P>& Reg1,
        P Split,
        const Region<P>& Reg2,
        BOOL chkBounds=TRUE)

        :Region<P>(chkBounds),
        split(Split), size1(Reg1.size()),
        reg1(&Reg1), reg2(&Reg2)

        { elems = reg1->size() + reg2->size(); };

    //******************************************************************
    // make a copy
    //******************************************************************
    ThisClass* copy() const { return (ThisClass*) _copy(); };

    //******************************************************************
    // change checkBounds
    //******************************************************************
    virtual void setCheckBounds(BOOL checkBounds) const {
        BaseClass::setCheckBounds(checkBounds);
        reg1->setCheckBounds(checkBounds);
        reg2->setCheckBounds(checkBounds);
    };
```

```
//********************************************************************
// where is Point?
//********************************************************************
virtual BOUNDS boundsEx (const P p, BOOL& exact) const {
    if ( p.x() < split.x() )
        return reg1->boundsEx(p,exact);
    else
        return reg2->boundsEx(p-split,exact);
};

//********************************************************************
// return enclosing box
//********************************************************************
virtual void enclosure (P& low, P& high) const {
    P low2, high2;
    reg1->enclosure(low, high);
    reg2->enclosure(low2, high2);
    low2  += split;
    high2 += split;
    low.min(high).min(low2).min(high2);
    high.max(low).max(low2).max(high2);
};

//********************************************************************
// rank
//********************************************************************
virtual long rankEx (const P p, BOOL& exact) const {
    if ( p.x() < split.x() )
        return reg1->rankEx(p,exact);
    else
        return reg2->rankEx(p-split,exact) + size1;
};

//********************************************************************
// unrank
//********************************************************************
virtual P unrank (long rank) const {
    if ( rank < size1 )
        return reg1->unrank(rank);
    else
        return reg2->unrank(rank - size1) + split;
};

protected:
//********************************************************************
// data from constructor
//********************************************************************
P               split;          // if p.x < split.x, then use left else right
int             size1;          // number of elements in left

const Region<P>*  reg1;         // region below split point
const Region<P>*  reg2;         // region at, or above, split point
```

(continued)

File RegXSplit.hpp *(continued)*

```
    virtual RootClass* _copy() const { return new ThisClass(*this); };
};

#endif
```

File RegXform.hpp

```
#ifndef _REGXFORM_HPP
#define _REGXFORM_HPP
//**************************************************************************
// TITLE: RegXform -- Transformed region.
//
// AUTHOR: Scott N Gerard, Rochester, MN
// LANGUAGE: C++
//
// FUNCTION:
//     Transforms the coordinate and then maps a region.  Any class derived
//     from Xform is a suitable transformation.
//
// CHANGE LOG:
//     26Aug89 - Initial coding.  SN Gerard
//     20Oct89 - Split up Coeff routines.  SN Gerard
//     18May93 - Convert to C++.  SN Gerard
//**************************************************************************
#include "Region.hpp"
#include "Xform.hpp"

template <class P>
class RegXform: public Region<P> {

    typedef Region<P> BaseClass;
    typedef RegXform<P> ThisClass;

public:
    //*********************************************************************
    // constructor
    //*********************************************************************
    RegXform (Xform<P>& x, Region<P>& m, BOOL chkBounds=TRUE);

    //*********************************************************************
    // make a copy
    //*********************************************************************
    ThisClass* copy() const { return (ThisClass*) _copy(); };

    //*********************************************************************
    // change checkBounds
    //*********************************************************************
    virtual void setCheckBounds(BOOL checkBounds) const;
```

```
//*********************************************************************
// where is Point?
//*********************************************************************
virtual BOUNDS boundsEx (const P p, BOOL& exact) const;

//*********************************************************************
// return enclosing box
//*********************************************************************
virtual void enclosure (P& low, P& high) const;

//*********************************************************************
// rank
//*********************************************************************
virtual long rankEx (const P p, BOOL& exact) const;
virtual P unrank (long rank) const;

protected:
//*********************************************************************
// data from constructor
//*********************************************************************
virtual RootClass* _copy() const { return new ThisClass(*this); };

const Xform<P>*    xform;
const Region<P>*   reg;
};

#endif
```

File RegXform.cpp

```
//***********************************************************************
// TITLE: RegXform -- Transformed region.
//
// AUTHOR: Scott N Gerard, Rochester, MN
// LANGUAGE: C++
//
// FUNCTION:
//    Transforms the coordinate and then maps a region.  Any class derived
//    from Xform is a suitable transformation.
//
// CHANGE LOG:
//    26Aug89 - Initial coding.  SN Gerard
//    20Oct89 - Split up Coeff routines.  SN Gerard
//    18May93 - Convert to C++.  SN Gerard
//***********************************************************************
#include "RegXform.hpp"

//******************************************************************
// constructor
//******************************************************************
template <class P>
RegXform<P>::RegXform (Xform<P>& x, Region<P>& m, BOOL chkBounds=TRUE)
```
(continued)

File RegXform.cpp   *(continued)*

```
   :Region<P>(chkBounds), xform(&x), reg(&m)
   { elems = reg->size(); };

//*******************************************************************
// change checkBounds
//*******************************************************************
template <class P>
void RegXform<P>::setCheckBounds(BOOL checkBounds) const {
   BaseClass::setCheckBounds(checkBounds);
   reg->setCheckBounds(checkBounds);
};

//*******************************************************************
// where is Point?
//*******************************************************************
template <class P>
BOUNDS RegXform<P>::boundsEx (const P p, BOOL& exact) const {
   BOOL exact1, exact2;
   BOUNDS bnds = reg->boundsEx( xform->mapInvEx(p,exact1), exact2 );
   exact = BOOL( exact1 && exact2 );
   return bnds;
};

//*******************************************************************
// return enclosing box
//*******************************************************************
template <class P>
void RegXform<P>::enclosure (P& low, P& high) const {
   BOOL exact;
   P low1, high1;
   reg->enclosure( low1, high1);
   low1 = xform->mapEx(low1, exact);
   high1 = xform->mapEx(high1, exact);

   low = low1;
   high = high1;

   low.min(high1);              // low1 may be greater than high1
   high.max(low1);
};

//*******************************************************************
// rank
//*******************************************************************
template <class P>
long RegXform<P>::rankEx (const P p, BOOL& exact) const {
   BOOL exact1, exact2;
   int rnk = reg->rankEx( xform->mapInvEx(p, exact1), exact2 );
   exact = BOOL( exact1 && exact2 );
   return rnk;
};
```

```
//******************************************************************
// unrank
//******************************************************************
template <class P>
P RegXform<P>::unrank (long rank) const
    { return xform->map( reg->unrank( rank ) ); };
```

File Xform.hpp

```
#ifndef _XFORM_HPP
#define _XFORM_HPP
//**********************************************************************
// TITLE: Xform  -- abstract transformations
//
// AUTHOR: Scott N Gerard, Rochester, MN
// LANGUAGE: C++
//
// FUNCTION:
//    General, transformation.  It support both forward
//    and backward transformations (they are the inverse of each other).
//    The transformation may or may not be exact.  If there is any
//    rounding during conversion, the exact flag will be FALSE.
//
// CHANGE LOG:
//    19May93 - Initial coding.  SN Gerard
//**********************************************************************

template <class P>
class Xform {

    typedef Xform<P> ThisClass;

protected:
    typedef Xform<P> RootClass;

protected:
    //**********************************************************************
    // constructor is protected.  abstract class
    //**********************************************************************
    Xform () {};
    virtual ~Xform() {};

public:
    //**********************************************************************
    // make a copy
    //**********************************************************************
    ThisClass* copy() const { return (ThisClass*) _copy(); };

    //**********************************************************************
    // (Forward) map p to its new position.
    //**********************************************************************
```

(continued)

File Xform.hpp   *(continued)*

```
   virtual P mapEx (const P p, BOOL& exact) const = 0;

   virtual P map (const P p) const {
      BOOL exact;
      return mapEx(p, exact);                // ignore exact result
   };

   //********************************************************************
   // (Backward) map p to its new position.
   //********************************************************************
   virtual P mapInvEx (const P p, BOOL& exact) const = 0;

   virtual P mapInv (const P p) const {
      BOOL exact;
      return mapInvEx(p, exact);             // ignore exact result
   };

   //********************************************************************
   // The Xform inverts itself.
   //********************************************************************
   virtual RootClass& inverse () = 0;

protected:
   virtual RootClass* _copy() const = 0;
};

#endif
```

File XfoGroup.hpp

```
#ifndef _XFOGROUP_HPP
#define _XFOGROUP_HPP
//************************************************************************
// TITLE: XfoGroup -- group transformation + translation
//
// AUTHOR: Scott N Gerard, Rochester, MN
// LANGUAGE: C++
//
// FUNCTION:
//    Transform a point using a group, and then translate it.  The point
//    (x,y) is transformed to point (x',y')
//
//       ( x' ) = Group ( x ) + ( Ox )
//       ( y' )         ( y )   ( Oy )
//
//    where Group is conceptually a matrix.  If Group were really a
//    matrix, XfoGroup would be the same as XfoGLn.  However, Group is a
//    class which defines operations in its own, usually faster, way.
//
//    The group class must provide operations
```

```
//          groupMul:   multiplication of group elements
//          groupInv:   inverse of a group element
//          groupPoint: transform a point using a group element
//          operators << and >> for IO
//
// CHANGE LOG:
//    20May93 - Initial coding.  SN Gerard
//****************************************************************************
#include <iostream.h>
#include "Xform.hpp"

//****************************************************************************
// Transform coordinate points by flipping by an group P and then
// translating.
//****************************************************************************
template <class P, class G>
class XfoGroup: public Xform<P> {

    typedef Xform<P> BaseClass;
    typedef XfoGroup ThisClass;

public:
    //*********************************************************************
    // constructor
    // Specify the orientation and the new location of the origin.
    //*********************************************************************
    XfoGroup (G orient, const P origin=P() )
        :g(orient), xlate(origin) {};

    //*********************************************************************
    // make a copy
    //*********************************************************************
    ThisClass* copy() const { return (ThisClass*) _copy(); };

    //*********************************************************************
    // (Forward) map p to its new position.
    //*********************************************************************
    virtual P mapEx (const P p, BOOL& exact) const {
        exact = TRUE;
        return operPoint(g, p) + xlate;
    };

    //*********************************************************************
    // (Backward) map p to its new position.
    //*********************************************************************
    virtual P mapInvEx (const P p, BOOL& exact) const {
        exact = TRUE;
        return operPoint( operInv(g), p - xlate);
    };

    //*********************************************************************
    // invert the Xform
    //*********************************************************************
```

(continued)

File XfoGroup.hpp *(continued)*

```
   virtual RootClass& inverse ();

   //***********************************************************************
   // combine Xform b into *this.  If combine were "multiplication",
   // it would be "*=" rather than "*".
   //***********************************************************************
   ThisClass& combine (const ThisClass& b);

   //***********************************************************************
   // IO routines
   //***********************************************************************
   istream& readFrom (istream& is);
   ostream& printOn  (ostream& os) const;

protected:
   //***********************************************************************
   // constants of the transformation
   //***********************************************************************
   G   g;                          // group orientation
   P   xlate;                       // origin of transformation

   virtual RootClass* _copy() const { return new ThisClass(*this); };
};

#endif
```

File XfoGroup.cpp

```
//***************************************************************************
// TITLE: XfoGroup -- Group transformation + translation
//
// AUTHOR: Scott N Gerard, Rochester, MN
// LANGUAGE: C++
//
// FUNCTION:
//     Transform a point using a group, and then translate it.
//
// CHANGE LOG:
//     20May93 - Initial coding.  SN Gerard
//***************************************************************************
#include <string.h>
#include "XfoGroup.hpp"

//****************************************************************
// return the inverse transformation
//****************************************************************
template <class P, class G>
Xform<P>& XfoGroup<P,G>::inverse () {
   G gNew = operInv(g);
```

```
   P xlateNew = - operPoint( gNew, xlate);
   g = gNew;
   xlate = xlateNew;
   return *this;
};

//********************************************************************
// combine two transformations
//********************************************************************
template <class P, class G>
XfoGroup<P,G>& XfoGroup<P,G>::combine (const XfoGroup<P,G>& b) {
   G gNew = operMul( g, b.g);
   P xlateNew = operPoint( b.g, xlate) + b.xlate;
   g = gNew;
   xlate = xlateNew;
   return *this;
};

//********************************************************************
// IO routines
//********************************************************************
template <class P, class G>
istream& XfoGroup<P,G>::readFrom (istream& is) {
   char ch;
   is >> ch >> g >> ch >> xlate >> ch;
   return is;
};

template <class P, class G>
ostream& XfoGroup<P,G>::printOn (ostream& os) const {
   os << '{' << g << ' ' << xlate << ')';
   return os;
};
```

File GroupD4.hpp

```
#ifndef _GROUPD4_HPP
#define _GROUPD4_HPP
//********************************************************************
// TITLE: GroupD4 -- Group operations for dihedral(4)
//
// AUTHOR: Scott N Gerard, Rochester, MN
// LANGUAGE: C++
//
// FUNCTION:
//    The group Dihedral(4):  the group of symmetries of the square.
//    These transformations map the x- and y-axes to themselves in 8
//    different ways.
//
//        Ident: (x,y) => (+x,+y)    FlipX:  (x,y) => (-x,+y)
//        R90:   (x,y) => (-y,+x)    FlipY:  (x,y) => (+x,-y)
```

(continued)

File GroupD4.hpp   *(continued)*

```
//        R180:  (x,y) => (-x,-y)   Diag1:  (x,y) => (+y,+x)
//        R270:  (x,y) => (+y,-x)   Diag2:  (x,y) => (-y,-x)
//
//     Defines functions for group multiplication and inversion, and
//     for transforming Point2s.
//
// NOTE:
//     This class is specific for Point2 points.
//
// CHANGE LOG:
//     20May93 - Initial coding.  SN Gerard
//*************************************************************************
#include <iostream.h>
#include "Point2.hpp"


//*************************************************************************
// GroupD4 is an enumeration of the 8 different symmetries of the square.
//*************************************************************************
enum GroupD4 {Ident, R90, R180, R270, FlipX, FlipY, Diag1, Diag2};

Point2 operPoint (const GroupD4 a, const Point2 p);

GroupD4 operMul (const GroupD4 a, const GroupD4 b);
GroupD4 operInv (const GroupD4 a);

istream& operator >> (istream& is,       GroupD4& a);
ostream& operator << (ostream& os, const GroupD4 a);

#endif
```

File GroupD4.cpp

```
//*************************************************************************
// TITLE: GroupD4 -- Group operations for dihedral(4)
//
// AUTHOR: Scott N Gerard, Rochester, MN
// LANGUAGE: C++
//
// FUNCTION:
//     The group Dihedral(4):  the group of symmetries of the square.
//
// NOTE:
//     This class is specific for Point2 points.
//
// CHANGE LOG:
//     20May93 - Initial coding.  SN Gerard
//*************************************************************************
#include <assert.h>
#include "EnumIO.hpp"
#include "Point2.hpp"
```

```
#include "GroupD4.hpp"

//*******************************************************************
// transform point
//*******************************************************************
Point2 operPoint (const GroupD4 a, const Point2 p) {
    switch ( a ) {
    case Ident:   return Point2( +p.x(), +p.y());
    case R90:     return Point2( +p.y(), -p.x());
    case R180:    return Point2( -p.x(), -p.y());
    case R270:    return Point2( -p.y(), +p.x());
    case FlipX:   return Point2( -p.x(), +p.y());
    case FlipY:   return Point2( +p.x(), -p.y());
    case Diag1:   return Point2( +p.y(), +p.x());
    case Diag2:   return Point2( -p.y(), -p.x());
    };
    assert(0);                              // should never reach this point
    return Point2(0,0);
};

//***********************************************************************
// GroupD4 multiplication
//***********************************************************************
GroupD4 operMul (const GroupD4 a, const GroupD4 b) {
    static GroupD4 mulTable[8][8] = {
        Ident, R90,   R180,  R270,  FlipX, FlipY, Diag1, Diag2,
        R90,   R180,  R270,  Ident, Diag2, Diag1, FlipX, FlipY,
        R180,  R270,  Ident, R90,   FlipY, FlipX, Diag2, Diag1,
        R270,  Ident, R90,   R180,  Diag1, Diag2, FlipY, FlipX,
        FlipX, Diag1, FlipY, Diag2, Ident, R180,  R90,   R270,
        FlipY, Diag2, FlipX, Diag1, R180,  Ident, R270,  R90,
        Diag1, FlipY, Diag2, FlipX, R270,  R90,   Ident, R180,
        Diag2, FlipX, Diag1, FlipY, R90,   R270,  R180,  Ident };

    return mulTable[a][b];
};

//***********************************************************************
// GroupD4 inverse
//***********************************************************************
GroupD4 operInv (const GroupD4 a) {
    static GroupD4 inverse[8] = {
        Ident, R270,  R180,  R90,   FlipX, FlipY, Diag1, Diag2};

    return inverse[a];
};

//***********************************************************************
// GroupD4 IO routines
//***********************************************************************
char* GroupD4Names[] =
    {"Ident", "R90", "R180", "R270", "FlipX", "FlipY", "Diag1", "Diag2", ""};

enumIO(GroupD4,GroupD4Names);
```

File XfoGL2.hpp

```cpp
#ifndef _XFOGL2_HPP
#define _XFOGL2_HPP
//***********************************************************************
// TITLE: XfoGL2 -- 2D, general, linear transformation
//
// AUTHOR: Scott N Gerard, Rochester, MN
// LANGUAGE: C++
//
// FUNCTION:
//    Two-dimensional, general linear transformation GL(2,integer).  Point
//    (x,y) is transformed to point (x',y')
//
//        ( x' ) = [ ( Dxx  Dyx ) * ( x ) + ( Ox ) ] / denom
//        ( y' )   [ ( Dxy  Dyy )   ( y )   ( Oy ) ]
//
//    The D matrix and (Ox,Oy) coefficients are all divided by denom.
//
//    This class contains 2 copies of XfoGL2Imp.  One copy is the inverse
//    transformation of the other.
//
// NOTE:
//    This class should be used with 2D points.
//
// CHANGE LOG:
//    26Aug89 - Initial coding.  SN Gerard
//    20Oct89 - Split up Coeff routines.  SN Gerard
//    18May93 - Convert to C++.  SN Gerard
//***********************************************************************
#include "XfoGL2Imp.hpp"
#include "Xform.hpp"

template <class P>
class XfoGL2: public Xform<P> {

    typedef Xform<P> BaseClass;
    typedef XfoGL2<P> ThisClass;

public:
    //***********************************************************************
    // Constructor
    // Specify new locations of the origin (0,0) and the vectors for 1
    // step in the x direction (new(1,0) - new(0,0)) and for 1 step in the
    // y direction (new(0,1)-new(0,0)).
    //
    // All coordinates are divided by denom (which is normally = 1).
    //***********************************************************************
    XfoGL2 (
        P xStep =P(1,0),
        P yStep =P(0,1),
        P origin=P(0,0),
        int denom=1);
```

```
//*******************************************************************
// make a copy
//*******************************************************************
ThisClass* copy() const { return (ThisClass*) _copy(); };

//*******************************************************************
// (Forward) map p to its new position.
//*******************************************************************
virtual P mapEx (const P p, BOOL& exact) const
   { return coeff.mapEx(p,exact); };

//*******************************************************************
// (Backward) map p to its new position.
//*******************************************************************
virtual P mapInvEx (const P p, BOOL& exact) const
   { return coeffInv.mapEx(p,exact); };

//*******************************************************************
// invert the Xform
//*******************************************************************
virtual RootClass& inverse ();

//*******************************************************************
// combine Xform b into *this.  If combine were "multiplication",
// it would be "*=" rather than "*".
//*******************************************************************
ThisClass& combine (const ThisClass& b);

protected:
//*******************************************************************
// Use 2 XfoGL2Imp transformations; one for mapEx() and another for
// mapInvEx().
//*******************************************************************
XfoGL2Imp<P> coeff, coeffInv;

virtual RootClass* _copy() const { return new ThisClass(*this); };
};

#endif
```

File XfoGL2.cpp

```
//*******************************************************************
// TITLE: XfoGL2  -- 2D, general, linear transformation
//
// AUTHOR: Scott N Gerard, Rochester, MN
// LANGUAGE: C++
//
// FUNCTION:
//    Two-dimensional, general linear transformation GL(2,integer).
//
```

(continued)

File XfoGL2.cpp   *(continued)*

```cpp
// CHANGE LOG:
//    26Aug89 - Initial coding.  SN Gerard
//    20Oct89 - Split up Coeff routines.  SN Gerard
//    18May93 - Convert to C++.  SN Gerard
//*************************************************************************
#include <assert.h>
#include "XfoGL2.hpp"


//*************************************************************************
// constructor
//*************************************************************************
template <class P>
XfoGL2<P>::XfoGL2 (P xStep, P yStep, P origin, int denom)
   :coeff   (xStep, yStep, origin, denom),
    coeffInv(coeff.inverse())
    {};


//*************************************************************************
// Convert a XfoGL2 to its inverse
//*************************************************************************
template <class P>
Xform<P>& XfoGL2<P>::inverse () {

   XfoGL2Imp<P> temp = coeff;
   coeff = coeffInv;
   coeffInv = temp;
   return *this;
};


//*************************************************************************
// Combine two XfoGL2s
//
// 1/den' * D' = 1/(den1*den2) * D2 * D1
// O' = 1/den2 * D2 * O1 + O2
//*************************************************************************
template <class P>
XfoGL2<P>& XfoGL2<P>::combine (const XfoGL2<P>& b) {

   XfoGL2Imp<P> temp = coeff.combine(b.coeff);
   coeff = temp;
   coeffInv = coeff.inverse();
   return *this;
};
```

File XfoGL2Imp.hpp

```cpp
#ifndef _XFOGL2IMP_HPP
#define _XFOGL2IMP_HPP
//*************************************************************************
// TITLE: XfoGL2Imp -- 2D, general, linear transformation (one-way)
```

```
//
// AUTHOR: Scott N Gerard, Rochester, MN
// LANGUAGE: C++
//
// FUNCTION:
//    Two-dimensional, general, linear transformation GL(2,integer).
//    Point (x,y) is transformed to point (x',y')
//
//       ( x' ) = [ ( Dxx  Dyx ) * ( x ) + ( Ox ) ] / denom
//       ( y' )   [ ( Dxy  Dyy )   ( y )   ( Oy ) ]
//
//    The D matrix and (Ox,Oy) coefficients are all divided by denom.
//
// NOTE:
//    This class should be used with 2D points.
//
// CHANGE LOG:
//    21May83 - Initial coding.   SN Gerard
//*********************************************************************
#include "Xform.hpp"

template <class P>
class XfoGL2Imp {

    typedef XfoGL2Imp<P> BaseClass;
    typedef XfoGL2Imp<P> ThisClass;

public:
    //*****************************************************************
    // Constructor
    // Specify new locations of the origin (0,0) and the vectors for 1
    // step in the x direction (new(1,0) - new(0,0)) and for 1 step in the
    // y direction (new(0,1)-new(0,0)).
    //
    // All coordinates are divided by denom (which is normally = 1).
    //*****************************************************************
    XfoGL2Imp (
        const P xStep =P(1,0),
        const P yStep =P(0,1),
        const P origin=P(0,0),
        int denom=1);

    //*****************************************************************
    // Map p.   Inline for fast performance
    //*****************************************************************
    P mapEx (const P p, BOOL& exact) const {
        int x = p.x() * Dxx + p.y() * Dyx + Ox;
        int y = p.x() * Dxy + p.y() * Dyy + Oy;
        exact = BOOL( x % denom == 0 && y % denom == 0 );
        return P(x/denom, y/denom);   // round coordinates
    };
```

(continued)

File XfoGL2Imp.hpp   *(continued)*

```
P map (const P p) const {
  BOOL exact;
  return mapEx(p,exact);
};

//*********************************************************************
// return the inverse transformation
//*********************************************************************
ThisClass inverse () const;

//*********************************************************************
// combine two transformations
//*********************************************************************
ThisClass combine (const ThisClass& b) const;

protected:
//*********************************************************************
// constants of the transformation
//*********************************************************************
int Dxx, Dyx;                 // transformation matrix
int Dxy, Dyy;
int detD;                     // determinant of matrix D

int Ox, Oy;                   // origin of transformation * denom
int denom;                    // denominator
};

#endif
```

File XfoGL2Imp.cpp

```
//***********************************************************************
// TITLE: XfoGL2Imp -- 2D, general, linear transformation (one-way)
//
// AUTHOR: Scott N Gerard, Rochester, MN
// LANGUAGE: C++
//
// FUNCTION:
//    Two-dimensional, general, linear transformation GL(2,integer).
//
//       ( x' ) = [ ( Dxx  Dyx ) * ( x ) + ( Ox ) ] / denom
//       ( y' )   [ ( Dxy  Dyy )   ( y )   ( Oy ) ]
//
//    In the comments below adj(D) is the adjoint of D.  adj(D) is the
//    inverse of D times the determinant so that
//
//       D * adj(D) = detD * IdentityMatrix
//
// CHANGE LOG:
//    21May93 - Initial coding.  SN Gerard
//***********************************************************************
```

```
#include <assert.h>
#include "IntMath.hpp"
#include "XfoGL2Imp.hpp"

//************************************************************************
// constructor
//************************************************************************
template <class P>
XfoGL2Imp<P>::XfoGL2Imp (const P xStep,
   const P yStep,
   const P origin,
   int den)
   :Dxx(xStep.x()), Dxy(xStep.y()), Dyx(yStep.x()), Dyy(yStep.y()),
   Ox(origin.x()), Oy(origin.y()),
   denom(den)
{
   // remove redundant factors.
   int totGcd = gcd( gcd(gcd(Dxx,Dxy), gcd(Dyx,Dyy)), gcd(Ox,Oy) );

   Dxx   /= totGcd;
   Dxy   /= totGcd;
   Dyx   /= totGcd;
   Dyy   /= totGcd;
   Ox    /= totGcd;
   Oy    /= totGcd;
   denom /= totGcd;

   detD = Dxx * Dyy - Dxy * Dyx;          // determinant of D
};


//************************************************************************
// return the inverse transformation
//
// X = [ denom * adj(D) * X' - adj(D) * O ] / det(D)
//************************************************************************
template <class P>
XfoGL2Imp<P> XfoGL2Imp<P>::inverse () const {
   return XfoGL2Imp<P>(
      P(  Dyy * denom, -Dxy * denom),
      P( -Dyx * denom,  Dxx * denom),
      P( -(Ox * Dyy - Oy * Dyx), -(-Ox * Dxy + Oy * Dxx) ),
      detD);
};


//************************************************************************
// Combine two transformations
//************************************************************************
template <class P>
XfoGL2Imp<P> XfoGL2Imp<P>::combine (const XfoGL2Imp<P>& b) const {

   // unit is large enough that all coefficients will be integers
   int unit = lcm( detD, b.detD );
```

(continued)

File XfoGL.2Imp.cpp *(continued)*

```
    P origin = b.map( map( P(O,     O   ) ) );
    P xStep  = b.map( map( P(unit, O   ) ) );
    P yStep  = b.map( map( P(O,     unit) ) );

    return XfoGL2Imp<P>( xStep, yStep, origin, unit);
};
```

File P2Board.hpp

```
#include "Point2.hpp"
#include "cell.hpp"

typedef Point2 P;
```

File P2Board.cpp

```
//********************************************************************
// TITLE: P2Board -- Test Board template class
//
// AUTHOR: Scott N Gerard, Rochester, MN
// LANGUAGE: C++
//
// FUNCTION:
//    Two-dimensional boards.
//
// CHANGE LOG:
//    22Feb92 - Initial coding.  SN Gerard
//    31May983- Major rework.  SN Gerard
//********************************************************************
#include <string.h>
#include <iostream.h>
#include <strstream.h>
#include <conio.h>
#include <ctype.h>
#include <stdlib.h>

#pragma -Jgd
#include "SimpHasher.hpp"
#pragma -Jg

#include "P2Board.hpp"

#include "Reg2Rect.hpp"
#include "Reg2Trap.hpp"
#include "Reg2Hexagon.hpp"
#include "Reg2Chinese.hpp"
#include "RegXform.hpp"
#include "RegXSplit.hpp"
#include "RegYSplit.hpp"
```

```
#include "XfoIdent.hpp"
#include "XfoXlate.hpp"
#include "XfoGroup.hpp"
#include "GroupD4.hpp"
#include "GroupD4P.hpp"
#include "XfoGL2.hpp"

#include "Board.hpp"

//********************************************************************
// define a board of cells.  It will be initialized in buildboard.
//********************************************************************
Board<P, cell>*  board;

//********************************************************************
// For prompt indenting.  indent is backed-up thru indentString to give
// an increasingly longer string of blanks
//********************************************************************
char indentString[] = "                                    ";
char* indent = &indentString[ strlen(indentString) ];  // point to null
const int indentWidth = 2;

//********************************************************************
// read in a network of transformations
//********************************************************************
Xform<P>* readXform() {
    char        xformType;
    Xform<P>*   xform;
    Xform<P>*   xform1;
    Xform<P>*   xform2;
    GroupD4     or;
    GroupD4P    orPerm(IdentP);
    P           p;
    P           orig;
    P           xStep, yStep, origin;
    int         denom;

    do {
        cout << indent
            << "Xform (Ident, Xlate, D4, d4P, Gl2, inVerse):";
        cin >> xformType;
        indent -= indentWidth;

        switch ( toupper(xformType) ) {
        case 'I':
            xform = new XfoIdent<P>;
            break;
        case 'X':
            cout << indent << "translation:";
            cin >> p;
            xform = new XfoXlate<P>(p);
```

(continued)

File P2Board.cpp *(continued)*

```
            break;
        case 'D':
            cout << indent <<
                "Orient (Ident, R90, R180, R270, FlipX, FlipY, Diag1, Diag2):";
            cin >> or;
            cout << indent << "origin:";
            cin >> orig;
            xform = new XfoGroup<Point2,GroupD4>(or, orig);
            break;
        case 'P':
            cout << indent <<
                "Orient (e.g. \"(pX mX)(pY mY)!\") :";
            cin >> orPerm;
            cout << indent << "origin:";
            cin >> orig;
            xform = new XfoGroup<Point2,GroupD4P>(orPerm, orig);
            break;
        case 'G':
            cout << indent << "xStep, yStep, origin and denom:";
            cin >> xStep >> yStep >> origin >> denom;
            xform = new XfoGL2<P>(xStep, yStep, origin, denom);
            break;
        case 'V':
            xform = readXform();
            xform->inverse();
            break;
        default:
            cout << indent << "Invalid Xform type.\n";
        };
        if ( !cin ) {
            cerr << "Error in input.\n";
            exit(EXIT_FAILURE);
        };

        indent += indentWidth;
    } while  (xform == NULL);
    return xform;
};


//***********************************************************************
// read a split point.  Change any 99 coordinates to the region's
// high enclosure box + 1
//***********************************************************************
void adjustSplitPoint(
    const Region<P>* reg1,
    P split,
    const Region<P>* reg2)
{
    const int calc = 99;
    P low1, high1;
```

```
    P low2, high2;

    reg1->enclosure(low1, high1);
    reg2->enclosure(low2, high2);

    if (split.x() == calc)
        split.x( high1.x() - low2.x() + 1 );
    if (split.y() == calc)
        split.y( high1.y() - low2.y() + 1 );
};

//*********************************************************************
// read in a network of regions
//*********************************************************************
Region<P>* readReg() {
    char        regType;
    int         edge;
    Region<P>*  reg;
    Region<P>*  nestedReg;
    Region<P>*  sub1;
    Region<P>*  sub2;
    Xform<P>*   xform;
    P           split;
    int         nx, ny, delta;

    do {
        cout << indent <<
            "Region (Rect, Trap, UpTri, DownTri, Hex, Chinese, xForm, X, Y):";
        cin >> regType;
        indent -= indentWidth;

        switch ( toupper(regType) ) {
        case 'R':
            cout << indent << "nx and ny:";
            cin  >> nx >> ny;
            reg = new Reg2Rect<P>(nx, ny);
            break;
        case 'T':
            cout << indent << "nx, ny and delta:";
            cin  >> nx >> ny >> delta;
            reg = new Reg2Trap<P>(nx, ny, delta);
            break;
        case 'F':
            nestedReg = readReg();
            xform = readXform();
            reg = new RegXform<P>( *xform, *nestedReg);
            break;
        case 'U':            // up triangle
            cout << indent << "edge:";
            cin >> edge;
            reg = new Reg2UpTri<P>( edge );
            break;
```

(continued)

File P2Board.cpp *(continued)*

```
      case 'D':          // down triangle
         cout << indent << "edge:";
         cin >> edge;
         reg = new Reg2DownTri<P>( edge );
         break;
      case 'H':          // Hexagon
         cout << indent << "edge:";
         cin >> edge;
         reg = new Reg2Hexagon<P>( edge );
         break;
      case 'C':          // Chinese checkers
         cout << indent << "edge:";
         cin >> edge;
         reg = new Reg2Chinese<P>( edge );
         break;
      case 'X':
         sub1 = readReg();          // left
         cout << indent << "split point:";
         cin >> split;
         sub2 = readReg();          // right
         adjustSplitPoint(sub1, split, sub2);
         reg = new RegXSplit<P>( *sub1, split, *sub2, TRUE);
         break;
      case 'Y':
         sub1 = readReg();          // bottom
         cout << indent << "split point:";
         cin >> split;
         sub2 = readReg();          // top
         adjustSplitPoint(sub1, split, sub2);
         reg = new RegYSplit<P>( *sub1, split, *sub2, TRUE);
         break;
      default:
         cout << indent << "Invalid region type.\n";
      };
      if ( !cin ) {
         cerr << "Error in input.\n";
         exit(EXIT_FAILURE);
      };

      indent += indentWidth;
   } while  (reg == NULL);
   return reg;
};


//**********************************************************************
// build the board
//**********************************************************************
```

```
void buildBoard() {
    Region<P>* reg = readReg();
    board = new Board2<cell> ( *reg );
};

// include the template bodies
#include "Region.cpp"
#include "RegXform.cpp"
#include "Reg2Rect.cpp"
#include "Reg2Trap.cpp"
#include "Reg2Hexagon.cpp"
#include "Reg2Chinese.cpp"

#include "XfoGroup.cpp"
#include "XfoGL2.cpp"
#include "XfoGL2Imp.cpp"

#include "Perm.cpp"
#include "GroupD4P.cpp"
#include "SimpHasher.cpp"
#include "Board.cpp"

// include the board utilities and the main routine
#include "BoardUtilities.cpp"
```

7

Trapezoidal Regions

In this chapter, I develop a general algorithm to map two-dimensional triangular and trapezoidal regions, followed by the algorithm for three-dimensional trapezoidal regions. Rectangular regions are just a special case of the general algorithms. These algorithms can be used to lay out triangular and band matrices. In the next chapter, we will use them to lay out boards for Chinese checkers and other shapes on hexgrid game boards.

The formula to map multidimensional, rectangular arrays into memory is well known. For the three-dimensional array $a[l_1..h_1, l_2..h_2, l_3..h_3]$, the rank of $a[i, j, k]$ is (in row-major order):

$$rank(i, j, k) = ((i - l_1) \times \dim_2 + (j - l_2)) \times \dim_3 + (k - l_3)$$

where $\dim_i = h_i - l_i + 1$. Column-major order combines the index values in reverse order.

Two-Dimensional Algorithm

Rank

Figure 7.1 shows a trapezoid of points. Our goal is to construct a formula that will convert (x, y) coordinate pairs to the rank numbers shown in the figure. That is, we want a mapping that contains, in part, the following:

    (0, 0) to rank = 0
    (1, 0) to rank = 1

```
.  |  .   .   .   .   .   .   .   .   .   .   .   .   .
. 18 19 20 21 22 23 24 25 26 27 28 29  .
.  9 10 11 12 13 14 15 16 17  .   .   .   .
.  3  4  5  6  7  8  .   .   .   .   .   .   .
---0  1  2-------------------------------------
.  |  .   .   .   .   .   .   .   .   .   .   .   .
```

FIGURE 7.1
Trapezoidal mapping.

$$
\begin{aligned}
(\ 2, 0) \text{ to rank} &= 2 \\
(\ 0, 1) \text{ to rank} &= 3 \\
(\ 5, 1) \text{ to rank} &= 8 \\
(\ 0, 2) \text{ to rank} &= 9 \\
(\ 8, 2) \text{ to rank} &= 17 \\
(\ 0, 3) \text{ to rank} &= 18 \\
(11, 3) \text{ to rank} &= 29
\end{aligned}
$$

It will greatly simplify the next part to assume the trapezoid is "aligned" so that

- the rank of the origin is 0.
- elements with consecutive rank values are arranged in "sum-lines" parallel to the x-axis (column-major ordering).
- the first sum-line is $y = 0$ (the x-axis), followed by the sum-lines $y = 1$, $y = 2$, etc.
- the left edge of all sum-lines are vertically aligned at $x = 0$.

Trapezoids are more general than rectangles because the right edge of each sum-line changes. Let m_y be the x-coordinate of the right edge of sum-line y (there are $m_y + 1$ elements on sum-line y). A sum-line must contain whole points, so m_y must be an integer. The computation of the rank function is

$$
rank(x, y) = \sum_{j=0}^{y-1} \sum_{i=0}^{m_j} 1 + \sum_{i=0}^{x-1} 1 \tag{12}
$$

The first term sums over all points on all sum-lines less than y, and the second term sums over all points on sum-line y that are to the left of x.

If we are to have any chance at all of finding a general equation that does not involve lookup tables, m_y must be computable using a closed formula. For our purposes a linear formula will be sufficient (a similar derivation can be followed if higher-order polynomials are desired). Let $\delta = m_{y+1} - m_y$ be the difference in the number of points between adjacent sum-lines. Then

$$
m_y = m_0 + \delta \times y
$$

Inserting this into Equation [12] and expanding the sums, we get the general formula for converting a point to its rank value:

$$rank(x, y) = \frac{1}{2}\delta y^2 + \left(m_0 + 1 - \frac{1}{2}\delta\right)y + x \qquad [13]$$

This can also be written in a form similar to the one shown in Knuth (1973a:295–298). It shows clearly the contribution of the triangular part (the first term) and the rectangular part.

$$rank(x, y) = \delta\binom{y}{2} + (m_0 + 1)y + x \qquad [14]$$

All rectangular and triangular arrays are just special cases of Equation [13]. When $\delta = 0$, the y^2 term drops out, as does the last part of the y term, leaving the normal formula for column-major, rectangular arrays. Triangular arrays correspond to the case of $\delta = \pm 1$.

Number of Cells

The number of cells is just the rank of the last point plus one for the origin cell with rank $= 0$. The number of elements in sum-lines 0 through the nth complete sum-line is

$$elements(n) = rank(m_0 + \delta \times n, n) + 1 \qquad [15]$$

Expanding gives the result

$$elements(n) = \frac{1}{2}\delta n^2 + \left(m_0 + 1 + \frac{1}{2}\delta\right)n + m_0 + 1 \qquad [16]$$

Unrank

The previous discussion shows how rank() converts an (x, y) coordinate to a rank value. In this section, given a fixed rank value, we find the (x, y) pair.

If $\delta = 0$, we have the rectangular array case:

$$y = rank/(m_0 + 1)$$

$$x = rank\,\%\,(m_0 + 1) \qquad [17]$$

When $\delta \neq 0$, solve Equation [13] for y. Since $y \geq 0$ only the positive branch of the radical is meaningful:

$$y = \frac{1}{2\delta}\left[\sqrt{(2m_0 + 2 - \delta)^2 + 8\delta(rank(x,y) - x)} - (2m_0 + 2 - \delta)\right] \quad [18]$$

This is one equation in two unknowns: x and y. One must be eliminated. ($rank(x,y) - x$) is the rank value of the leftmost point on the sum-line; it is equal to $rank(0,y)$. In the rectangular array case we used integer division to remove x's contribution to rank. That will not work in the general case, but the approach is similar.

Let $ycoord(rank, x)$ be a function that converts a rank value integer and an x coordinate integer to a y coordinate by Equation [18]. We know

$$rank(0, y) \leq rank(x, y) < rank(0, y + 1)$$

Therefore

$$ycoord(rank(0,y), 0) \leq ycoord(rank(x,y), 0) < ycoord(rank(0, y + 1), 0)$$

$$y \leq ycoord(rank(x, y), 0) < y + 1$$

In the first and last expressions, $x = 0$ matches the rank value so $ycoord()$ returns exactly y and $y + 1$. Therefore, $ycoord(rank(x,y), 0)$ is a real number between y and $y + 1$. We can calculate y without knowing x by assuming $x = 0$ in Equation [18], and rounding y down by dropping any fractional part.

If $\delta > 0$ in Equation [18], as the rank increases the square root increases, the numerator increases, and y increases. To round y down, we must round down the square root and round down during division by 2δ. If $\delta < 0$, as the rank increases the square root decreases, the numerator decreases, and y increases. To round y down here, we must round up the square root and round down during division by 2δ.

We avoid any floating point operations by rounding as we go. Always round down when dividing by 2δ. Now all the operations are strictly on integers. Obviously division by 2δ must return an integer if y is to be correct. The square root extraction can also be rounded to an integer (as opposed to some multiple of $\frac{1}{2}$, $\frac{1}{3}$, etc.) since any fractional part would be eliminated by the division.

Once y is known, x can easily be calculated by finding $rank(0, y)$. Thus, in general, given a rank value,

$$y = [Round_\delta(\sqrt{(2m_0 + 2 - \delta)^2 + 8\,\delta rank(x,y)}) - (2m_0 + 2 - \delta)]/2\delta$$
$$[19a]$$

$$x = rank(x,y) - rank(0, y) \quad [19b]$$

where $Round_\delta$ rounds down for positive delta and rounds up for negative delta.

Reg2Trap Class

Reg2Trap maps any two-dimensional, trapezoidal region using Equations [13], [19a], and [19b] (see Figure 6.1 in Chapter 6). It is a template class that takes any two-dimensional point (Point2 or HexPoint) as its template argument. The region in Figure 7.1 is generated by

```
C>P2BOARD "t 2 3 3 n 0"
```

Triangle Classes

Reg2UpTri and Reg2DownTri are classes built using Reg2Trap. Both of their constructors require the size of the triangle's edge. Reg2DownTri is derived from Reg2Trap. Its constructor converts the edge size to Reg2Trap's constructor parameters.

Reg2UpTri *is* a Region that *has* a Reg2Trap. This is necessary because Reg2UpTri skews the *y*-coordinates so the triangle looks nicer on a hexgrid. The skewed region has a shape that Reg2Trap cannot map directly. If Reg2UpTri were derived from Reg2Trap, their bounds() and rank() functions would incompatibility disagree on the region's shape.

Of course, RegXform can transform trapezoidal regions into many strange orientations.

Row-, Column-, and Diagonal-Orders

Knuth (1973a:295–298) shows one way to compute the rank within a lower triangular matrix. But there are three ways to order the elements of a triangular matrix in memory: row-major order, where elements that are adjacent in memory form vertical lines in the two-dimensional array; column-major order, where adjacent memory elements form horizontal lines; and "diagonal-major" order, where adjacent memory elements form diagonal lines. Each order has different properties. The diagonal-major form is especially well suited for band-matrices where only elements on the main diagonal, and the first few diagonals adjacent to the main diagonal, are allocated.

Different clients reference elements in different sequences. Selecting a different order may improve a client's locality of reference. This is important for achieving maximum performance on systems with virtual memory. Or elements might be ordered so that each element depends only on elements with smaller rank values. Then the elements can be computed in rank order.

A triangular region in column-major order is

```
C>P2BOARD "t 4 4 -1   n 0"
```

RegXform changes the region to row-major order:

```
C>P2BOARD "f   t 4 4 -1 d Diag1 (0,0)   n 0"
```

A different RegXform changes it to diagonal-major order:

```
C>P2BOARD "f   t 4 4 -1   g (1,-1)(0,-1)(0,4) 1   n 0"
```

Three-Dimensional Algorithm

A similar derivation leads to the algorithm for three-dimensional regions.

Let m_{jk} be the x-coordinate of the last point on the sum-line with $y = j$ and $z = k$, and let n_k be the y-coordinate of the last sum-line in plane $z = k$. Assume m_{jk} and n_k are linear functions.

$$m_{jk} = m_{00} + \delta_{xy}j + \delta_{xz}k \qquad [20a]$$

$$n_k = n_0 + \delta_{yz}k \qquad [20b]$$

δ_{xy} is the change in x for a unit change in y, δ_{xz} is the change in x for a unit change in z, and δ_{yz} is the change in y for a unit change in z.

These conditions generate the shape shown in Figure 7.2. I do not know of a common, or even an uncommon, name for this shape.

The rank calculation is

$$rank(x, y, z) = \sum_{k=0}^{z-1} \sum_{j=0}^{n_k} \sum_{i=0}^{m_{jk}} 1 + \sum_{j=0}^{y-1} \sum_{i=0}^{m_{jz}} 1 + \sum_{i=0}^{x-1} 1 \qquad [21]$$

The first term is the sum of all points on all planes below z. The second term is the sum of all points on all sum-lines less than y on plane z. The third term is the number of points to the right of x on the sum-line with $y = j$ and $z = k$.

Expanding the sums is tedious, but gives the result

$$rank(x, y, z) = \frac{1}{12}[2c_2z^3 + 3(c_1 - c_2)z^2 + (c_2 - 3c_1 + 6c_0)z] + \delta_{xz}yz$$
$$+ \frac{1}{2}\delta_{xy}y^2 + \left[m_0 + 1 - \frac{1}{2}\delta_{xy}\right]y + x \qquad [22]$$

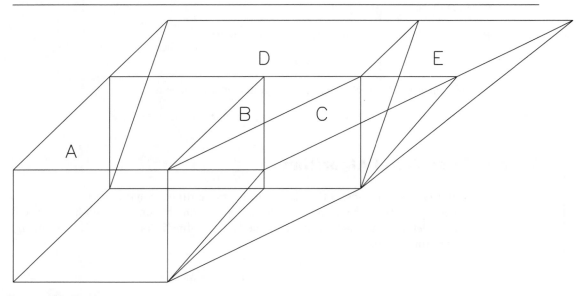

FIGURE 7.2
General form of the three-dimensional trapezoidal shape.

where

$$c_2 = \delta_{yz}(\delta_{xy}\,\delta_{yz} + 2\delta_{xz}) \qquad [22a]$$

$$c_1 = (2n_0 + 1)\,\delta_{xy}\,\delta_{yz} + 2(n_0 + 1)\,\delta_{xz} + 2(m_0 + 1)\,\delta_{yz} \qquad [22b]$$

$$c_0 = n_0(n_0 + 1)\,\delta_{xy} + 2(n_0 + 1)\,(m_0 + 1) \qquad [22c]$$

The two-dimensional case is readily recovered from this by setting z to zero. The three-dimensional, rectangular case is recovered by setting δ_{xy}, δ_{xz}, and δ_{yz} to zero.

Number of Cells

The number of cells is the rank value of the last point plus one for the origin cell with rank $= 0$. The number elements for p-complete sum-planes is

$$elements(p) = rank(m_{00} + \delta_{xy}(n_0 + \delta_{yz}p) + \delta_{xz}p, n_0 + \delta_{yz}p, p) + 1 \quad [23]$$

Unrank

To solve the three-dimensional case we first need to find the value for z in Equation [22]. Then plugging z into the formula gives a quadratic formula in y that can be solved. Finally, plugging both y and z into the formula gives x:

```
1. find z    rank(0,0,z) <= rank < rank(0,0,z+1)
2. find y    rank(0,y,z) <= rank < rank(0,y+1,z)
3. find x    = rank - rank(0,y,z)
```

However, we encounter problems in the first step trying to solve the third-degree polynomial for z. We might try to solve the three-dimensional case in the same way we solved the two-dimensional case. This would mean writing z as a function of x, y, and rank. Since this is a third-degree polynomial in z, we would use the cubic equation. When the determinant of the rank equation is negative, there are three real roots, and this does happen in practice. But the solution calls for the square root of the determinant. The only way around this is to break the equation up into its real and imaginary parts—effectively using complex numbers for the solution. Along with all the multiplications and additions required by this method, a closed formula is not very attractive.

The next method we might try, and the one normally used to solve cubic equations, is Newton-Raphson's iterative method. This method converges very quickly on the root (except in certain cases where it heads off for one of the two infinities). However, making an integer version of this algorithm is not easy. A division is used to calculate a correction to the current estimate of the root. When using floating points, there is no appreciable rounding and the Newton-Raphson works nicely. But there is no obvious way to control the rounding of the integer division to keep things under control. In short, an integral version of Newton-Raphson will not be used either.

The method we will use is the bisection method. It does not converge as fast as Newton-Raphson. But we can easily keep track of the rounding and get precisely the right result. As an overview, when solving for z, we know that $0 = \text{rank}(0,0,0) \leq \text{rank} < \text{rank}(0,0,nz+1)$ where nz is the maximum value of z. Thus $\text{rank}(0,0,z) - \text{rank}$ must have a zero somewhere in the range $[0..nz+1]$. By evaluating the sign of $\text{rank}(0,0,z) - \text{rank}$ at the midpoint of this range we can cut the range in half on each pass. This makes the algorithm $\log(n)$ where n is the number of planes in the region. For most cases, only a few iterations are required.

The bisection method is used again to bracket the zero of $\text{rank}(0,y,z) - \text{rank}$. We could use the closed formula from the two-dimensional case, but have chosen the bisection method for consistency. x is found by simple subtraction.

Implementation Comments

The programs are fairly straightforward implementations of the equations. The coefficients used internally in the implementation are slightly modified from the equations presented. This eliminates the need to use floating point operations or other special techniques for handling the results from integer divisions.

Source Code

File Reg2Trap.hpp

```
#ifndef _REG2TRAP_HPP
#define _REG2TRAP_HPP
//******************************************************************************
// TITLE: Reg2Trap -- 2D trapezoidal region
//
// AUTHOR: Scott N Gerard, Rochester, MN
// LANGUAGE: C++
//
// FUNCTION:
//     Map an trapezoidal region.  For example, defining a trapezoid with
//     nx=3, ny=3 and delta=+1 gives
//
//                  15    16    17    18    19    20    21
//                   9    10    11    12    13    14
//                   4     5     6     7     8
//                   0     1     2     3
//
// CHANGE LOG:
//     26Aug89 - Initial coding.  SN Gerard
//     20Oct89 - Split up Coeff routines.  SN Gerard
//     18May93 - Convert to C++.  SN Gerard
//******************************************************************************
#include "Region.hpp"

template <class P>
class Reg2Trap: public Region<P> {

    typedef Region<P> BaseClass;
    typedef Reg2Trap<P> ThisClass;

public:
    //**********************************************************************
    // constructor
    //**********************************************************************
    Reg2Trap(
        int  nX,                        // index of last x in first line
        int  nY,                        // index of last y line
        int  delta,                     // elem diff in adjacent lines
        BOOL checkBounds=TRUE);         // check bounds?

    //**********************************************************************
    // make a copy
    //**********************************************************************
    ThisClass* copy() const { return (ThisClass*) _copy(); };

    //**********************************************************************
    // where is Point?
    //**********************************************************************
```

```
    virtual BOUNDS boundsEx (const P p, BOOL& exact) const;

    //**********************************************************************
    // return enclosing box
    //**********************************************************************
    virtual void enclosure (P& low, P& high) const;

    //**********************************************************************
    // rank and unrank
    //**********************************************************************
    virtual long rankEx (const P p, BOOL& exact) const;
    virtual P unrank (long rank) const;

protected:
    //**********************************************************************
    // constants of the transformation
    //**********************************************************************
    int delta;
    int nx;
    int ny;

    virtual RootClass* _copy() const { return new ThisClass(*this); };

private:
    long ky;                            // y coeff in rank formula

    long kyky;                          // = ky * ky;
    long delta8;                        // = delta * 8;
    long delta2;                        // = delta * 2;
};

#endif
```

File Reg2Trap.cpp

```
//************************************************************************
// TITLE: Reg2Trap -- 2D trapezoidal region
//
// AUTHOR: Scott N Gerard, Rochester, MN
// LANGUAGE: C++
//
// FUNCTION:
//    Maps a trapezoidal region.
//
// CHANGE LOG:
//    26Aug89 - Initial coding.  SN Gerard
//    18May93 - Convert to C++.  SN Gerard
//************************************************************************ */
#include "IntMath.hpp"
#include "Reg2Trap.hpp"
```

(continued)

File Reg2Trap.cpp *(continued)*

```cpp
//******************************************************************
// constructor
//******************************************************************
template <class P>
Reg2Trap<P>::Reg2Trap(int nX, int nY, int del, BOOL checkBounds)
    :Region<P>(checkBounds), nx(nX), ny(nY), delta(del)
{
    // if ny is too large, reset ny so delta line never crosses y-axis
    if (nx + ny * delta < 0)
        ny = -nx / delta;

    ky = 2 * nx + 2 - delta;

    kyky = ky * ky;
    delta8 = delta * 8;
    delta2 = delta * 2;

    // return the number of elements in the array.  It equals rank
    // of last valid point + 1.
    int x2 = nx + delta * ny;
    int y2 = ny;
    elems = rank( P(x2,y2) ) + 1;
};


//******************************************************************
// where is Point?
//******************************************************************
template <class P>
BOUNDS Reg2Trap<P>::boundsEx (const P p, BOOL& exact) const {
    exact = TRUE;                    // always exact
    return int2Bounds( min(
        min(0+p.x(), nx+delta*p.y() - p.x()),
        min(0+p.y(), ny-p.y())
        ) );
};


//******************************************************************
// return enclosing box
//******************************************************************
template <class P>
void Reg2Trap<P>::enclosure (P& low, P& high) const {
    int del = ::max(0, 0+delta);      // NOTE: 0+delta is not const
    low = P(0,0);
    high.max( P(nx + del * ny, ny) );
};


//******************************************************************
// rank
//******************************************************************
template <class P>
long Reg2Trap<P>::rankEx (const P p, BOOL& exact) const {
```

```
   if ( checkBounds() && !onBoard(p) )
      pointError(p);

   exact = TRUE;
   int i = ((delta * p.y() + ky) * p.y()) / 2 + p.x();
   return i;
};


//**********************************************************************
// unrank
//**********************************************************************
template <class P>
P Reg2Trap<P>::unrank (long rnk) const {

   int x, y;

   if ( checkBounds() && (elems < rnk) )
      rankError(rnk);

   if ( delta == 0 ) {
      y = rnk / (nx + 1);
      x = rnk % (nx + 1);
   } else {
      y = (int(sqrt(kyky + delta8*rnk, BOOL(delta<0))) - ky) / delta2;
      x = rnk - rank( P(0,y) );
   };

   return P(x,y);
};
```

8

HexGrid

There are many computer games for playing chess and checkers. Throughout the game, they graphically display the 8×8 board and the current location of each piece. Internally, the program simply uses a square array to store the contents of the board. It is easy to convert between board coordinates and screen coordinates.

But computer games for playing some of the modern simulation or fantasy board games, or for playing Chinese checkers, are rare. Part of the reason may be a lack of routines for nonrectangular grids. This chapter describes classes of such routines. These classes make it easier to write nonrectangular games.

Overview

Some game boards are based on hexagons, and pieces are placed inside the hexagons. Other game boards are based on triangles, and pieces are placed in the corners of the triangles. Figure 8.1 shows how these two different boards are fundamentally the same. A layout where each cell is adjacent to six other cells is called a *hexagonal grid,* or **hexgrid** for short.

A game board is made up of a number of cells. Each cell may contain a player's piece. Players move their pieces from cell to cell. Pieces may be captured and removed from the board.

First, I describe a HexPoint class for working on an infinite hexgrid. The major task is assigning coordinates to each cell and selecting "natural" coordinates. Then we will look at moving around and finding the shortest path between two cells. Real games have finite boards with a definite shape. I describe the Reg2Hexagon and Reg2Chinese regions.

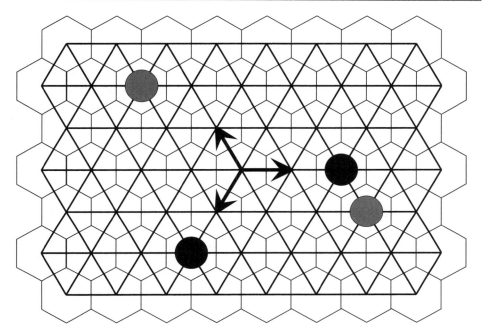

FIGURE 8.1
Hexgrid of hexagons overlaid with a hexgrid of triangles. The two layouts are
fundamentally the same. The center of every hexagon is the corner of a
triangle, and the center of every triangle is the corner of a hexagon.

Hexgrid Coordinates

Before we can do anything else, we must give each cell a name. Each cell of a rectangular board is named by its position on the x- and y-axes. Hexgrids have a natural
three-axis symmetry, so we will capitalize on that by using three axes instead of
two. Figure 8.1 shows a hexgrid with three unit vectors: $\hat{u}$, $\hat{v}$, and $\hat{w}$. The $\hat{u}$ unit vector
moves one cell to the right, $\hat{v}$ moves one cell to the upper left, and $\hat{w}$ moves one cell to
the lower left. The unit vectors $-\hat{u}$, $-\hat{v}$, and $-\hat{w}$ move in the opposite directions.

These three unit vectors name all the cells on the hexgrid using three coordinates
(u, v, w). Assign one cell (the origin cell) coordinates $(0, 0, 0)$. Give the cell to the right
of the origin coordinates $(1, 0, 0)$ since it is one $\hat{u}$ unit from the origin. Similarly, give
the cell one $\hat{v}$ unit from the origin coordinates $(0, 1, 0)$, and the cell one $\hat{w}$ unit from
the origin has coordinates $(0, 0, 1)$. To find the cell with coordinates (u, v, w), start at the
origin, and step u units in the $\hat{u}$ direction, v units in the $\hat{v}$ direction, and w units in the
$\hat{w}$ direction.

Natural Coordinates

Hexgrid coordinates are very similar to (x, y, z) coordinates in a three-dimensional space. However, there is one important difference: the coordinates for a cell are not unique! For example, the origin has coordinates $(0, 0, 0)$, but $(1, 1, 1)$ and $(2, 2, 2)$ are also coordinates for the origin. Each cell has multiple coordinate names because three independent values (u, v, and w) are used to specify a cell's locations, but a plane has only two independent directions. Because $1\hat{u} + 1\hat{v} + 1\hat{w} = 0$, adding $(1, 1, 1)$ to any cell (u, v, w) gives a new name for the same cell. Every cell has infinitely many coordinate names.

$$(u, v, w) = (u + k, v + k, w + k) \quad \text{for all } k \quad [24]$$

We could eliminate one of the coordinates, but that destroys the natural symmetry of the hexgrid. Instead, we will choose one of the many coordinate names as the "natural" one. Let $\text{MAX}(u, v, w)$ be the function that returns the largest of its three arguments. Also let $\text{MIN}(u, v, w)$ be the function that returns the smallest value, and $\text{MID}(u, v, w)$ be the function that returns the middle value. The **natural coordinates** of a cell are defined as the coordinates where $\text{MID}(u + k, v + k, w + k) = 0$. The natural form of a cell is easily generated by setting $k = -\text{MID}(u, v, w)$ in Equation [24]. The following table lists a few coordinates, their MAX, MID, and MIN values, and their natural form. Figure 8.2 shows the natural coordinates for each cell of a section of the hexgrid. Natural coordinates are easy to recognize; one value is positive (or zero), one value is zero, and one value is negative (or zero).

coordinates	MAX	MID	MIN	natural form
$(-1, 2, -4)$	2	-1	-4	$(0, 3, -3)$
$(-3, 5, -3)$	5	-3	-3	$(0, 8, 0)$
$(9, 9, 9)$	9	9	9	$(0, 0, 0)$
$(-1, 0, 3)$	3	0	-1	$(-1, 0, 3)$

HexPoint Class

Each instance of HexPoint is the coordinates for one point or cell of the hexgrid. Hex-Point has methods for setting and retrieving coordinates. HexPoint's constructor re-

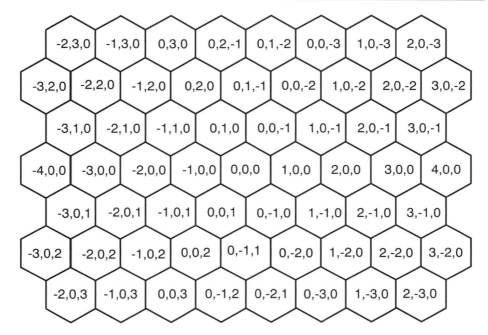

FIGURE 8.2
Hexgrid with natural coordinates. Each cell contains its natural coordinates.
Natural coordinates describe the shortest path from the origin to the cell.

quires (u, v, w) coordinate values, which may be defaulted to 0. Method set() assigns new coordinates to a HexPoint. It accepts both natural and unnatural coordinates, so you can specify coordinates any way you want. The get() method returns the (u, v, w) values in its parameters. get() always returns natural coordinates. set() followed by get() is a quick way to convert any (u, v, w) to natural coordinates.

```
#include  "HexPoint.hpp"
HexPoint  origin(0,0,0), dest;

dest.set(1,2,3);
dest.get(u,v,w);         // (u,v,w) = (-1,0,1) = natural form of (1,2,3)
```

Like Point2, HexPoints have all the normal and obvious point operations. Moving around the hexgrid is simple. To move one unit in the $\hat{u}$ direction from cell (u, v, w), add $(1, 0, 0)$ to get the new cell $(u + 1, v, w)$. Adding $(3, 0, -1)$ to a coordinates makes 3 $\hat{u}$ steps and -1 $\hat{w}$ steps. operator+() adds two HexPoints together. operator $-$() subtracts two HexPoints. Operators $+=$ and $-=$ are also defined.

```
HexPoint        curpos;
const HexPoint U(1,0,0), V(0,1,0), W(0,0,1);

curpos  = V + W;         // = (0,1,1).
curpos += U;             // move one step to the right
```

HexPoints are read from and written to streams using a "(u, v, w)" format.

For graphic display, getXY() and setXY() convert between HexPoint and Point2 instances with their two-dimensional (x, y) coordinates. The conversion from (u, v, w) coordinates to (x, y) coordinates is

$$(x, y) = (u \cos 0 + v \cos 120 + w \cos 240, u \sin 0 + v \sin 120 + w \sin 240)$$

$$(x, y) = \left(\frac{1}{2}(2u - v - w), \frac{\sqrt{3}}{2}(v - w) \right)$$

To keep (x,y) integers, getXY() and setXY() drop the conversion factors ½ and $\sqrt{3}/2$. Only half the (x, y) pairs convert exactly to valid HexPoints. The valid values form a checkerboard pattern. Method setXY() accepts Point2's with any (x, y) and selects the closest HexPoint.

```
HexPoint        curpos, userClick;
Point2          p;

p = curpos.getXY();      // convert HexPoint to Point2
gotoxy(p);               // new screen coordinates
cout << "X";             // show curpos on screen.
```

If you want your display to have the proper aspect ratio, call getXY() and then multiply x by ½ and y by $\sqrt{3}/2$. Divide by these values before calling setXY().

The current versions of getXY() and setXY() assume the $+u$ axis goes to the right (along the $+x$ axis). Define the macro variable VERT_U to switch getXY() and setXY() to make the $+u$ axis extend vertically (along the $+y$ axis). This alternate transformation is more useful for some games.

H2BOARD

The HexPoint routines are useful for general hexgrid computations on an infinite hexgrid plane, but any real game board has a specific shape with specific boundaries. The hexgrid region classes define regions with a specific shape and size.

H2BOARD is the same as P2BOARD, except that it uses HexPoints and the Board2Hex board class instead of Point2 and Board2. Board2Hex uses only every other x position to make the board look more like a hexgrid. The u-, v-, and w-axes are marked with "-", "\", and "/" respectively.

Reg2Hexagon Class

This class is a hexagonal region centered on the origin. This class has two subregions: one trapezoid for points below the *u*-axis, and one trapezoid for points on or above the *u*-axis. The constructor requires the size of the hexagon's edges.

```
C>H2BOARD
Region (Rect, Trap, Uptri, Downtri, Hex, Chinese, xForm): h
  edge: 3
Number of cells = 37
Enclosing Box: (-3,0,4)-(3,0,-4)
```

```
         .       \      .        .      `  .      /       .
    .       .         33      34      35      36       .       .
        .       28      29      30      31      32       .
    .       22      23      24      25      26      27       .
---- 15---- 16---- 17---- 18---- 19---- 20---- 21----
    .        9      10      11      12      13      14       .
        .        4       5       6       7       8       .
    .       .        0       1       2       3       .       .
         .       /      .        .      .        \       .
```

The Hexagon region that was skewed when displayed in P2BOARD looks straight in H2BOARD.

Reg2Chinese Class

This region is shaped like a Chinese checkers board centered on the origin. The constructor requires the size of the edges of the board (the size of the six triangles).

Reg2Chinese has four subregions: a Reg2DownTri for the bottom-most triangle, a trapezoid for all other points below the *u*-axis, a Reg2UpTri for the topmost triangle, and another trapezoid for all other points on or above the *u*-axis.

```
C>H2BOARD "c 3    n 0"
```

A normal Chinese checkers board has an edge of 4, but this is too large to display on an 80-column screen.

Shortest Path

Games must be able to compute the shortest distance and the shortest path between any two cells. This information is needed both to attack an opponent, and to defend against an opponent's attack.

There are usually many shortest paths between two cells. On a chessboard, there are many shortest paths between opposite corners. One path makes eight horizontal steps followed by eight vertical steps. Another shortest path makes eight vertical steps followed by eight horizontal steps. A zigzag of alternating horizontal and vertical paths is also a shortest path. We can describe all these shortest paths by the coordinates $(8, 8)$, which means any path that has eight vertical and eight horizontal steps in any order. If there are no other factors, any shortest path is just as good as another. However, on game boards, some paths may pass through blocked cells.

On a hexgrid, the shortest path between (u_1, v_1, w_1) and (u_2, v_2, w_2) is

$$shortest\_path = (\Delta u - MID)\hat{u} + (\Delta v - MID)\hat{v} + (\Delta w - MID)\hat{w}$$

where $\Delta u = u_2 - u_1$, $\Delta v = v_2 - v_1$, $\Delta w = w_2 - w_1$, and $MID = MID(\Delta u, \Delta v, \Delta w)$. That is, the shortest path between the two cells is the natural form of the difference $(\Delta u, \Delta v, \Delta w)$. This is why "natural" coordinates are so natural; they describe the shortest path between two cells, or from the origin to the cell. The length of this shortest path is

$$dist = MAX(\Delta u, \Delta v, \Delta w) - MIN(\Delta u, \Delta v, \Delta w)$$

The proof of these two results is given in "Shortest Path Proof," later in this chapter.

Let's look at two examples. What is the shortest path from any cell A to any cell B? In the simplest case, the path from A to B requires movement in just one direction. So the difference $(\Delta u, \Delta v, \Delta w)$ has one nonzero value. This is in natural form because all coordinates with one nonzero value are natural. For example, the shortest path from $(-2, 0, 3)$ to $(0, 2, -1)$ is $-6\hat{w}$. The natural form of their difference is

$$shortest\_path = (0, 2, -1) - (-2, 0, 3)$$
$$= (2, 2, -4)$$
$$= (0, 0, -6)$$

In all other cases, the path from A to B requires movement in just two directions. The path moves in one direction, turns 60° left or right, and moves in the second direction. Since the two movements are 60° apart, one movement is in a positive coordinate direction and the other is in a negative coordinate direction. Thus, $(\Delta u, \Delta v, \Delta w)$ has one positive value, one negative value, and one zero. Again, this is in natural form. For example, the shortest path from $(-3, 0, 1)$ to $(1, 0, -1)$ is

$$shortest\_path = (2, 1, -1) - (-3, 0, 1)$$
$$= (5, 1, -2)$$
$$= (4, 0, -3)$$

All shortest paths have $4\hat{u}$ steps and $-3\hat{v}$ steps.

A Very Simple Game

HexGame is a very simple game. It starts by asking for the location of two players: the Chaser and the Target. At each round, HexGame computes the shortest path between Chaser and Target, and moves Chaser one step toward Target. The "game" ends when Chaser catches Target. It goes quickly, and the Chaser always wins. Needless to say, HexGame is not destined to be the next game craze with sales in the millions. But it does show a few basics. A more interesting version requires the Target to move too.

Implementation Comments

Natural hexgrid coordinates are easy to use because they describe the shortest path between points. However, it takes three integers to store them, and one is redundant. In the implementation module, the "unnatural" coordinate with $w = 0$ is used so only u and v are stored. Method get() is the only routine that must calculate the MID of the stored u and v values and the implied $w = 0$ value. Methods getXY() and setXY() benefit from the unnatural $w = 0$ coordinate; they are simple linear transformations between (u, v) and (x, y). The hexgrid region classes also benefit from unnatural coordinates; they call methods $x()$ and $y()$ to access coordinates u and v. HexPoint should make these methods protected and declare the Region and Xform classes as friends. But there are too many Region and Xform subclasses.

Shortest Path Proof

This section proves natural coordinates give the shortest path between two cells. If you are willing to take my word for it, you can skip this proof.

THEOREM: The shortest path between the two points (u_1, v_1, w_1) and (u_2, v_2, w_2) is

$$shortest\_path = (\Delta u - \text{MID})\hat{u} + (\Delta v - \text{MID})\hat{v} + (\Delta w - \text{MID})\hat{w}$$

where $\Delta u = u_2 - u_1$, $\Delta v = v_2 - v_1$, $\Delta w = w_2 - w_1$, and $\text{MID} = \text{MID}(\Delta u, \Delta v, \Delta w)$. The length of the shortest path is

$$dist = \text{MAX}(\Delta u, \Delta v, \Delta w) - \text{MIN}(\Delta u, \Delta v, \Delta w)$$

PROOF: Subtract (u_1, v_1, w_1) from all coordinates. This makes point 1 the new origin, and moves point 2 to $(\Delta u, \Delta v, \Delta w) = (u_2 - u_1, v_2 - v_1, w_2 - w_1)$. Every $(\Delta u, \Delta v, \Delta w)$ describes a path from point 1 to point 2. The length of this path is the sum of the absolute value of the three coordinate differences. Because of the redundancy in the three coordinates, $(\Delta u + k)\hat{u} + (\Delta v + k)\hat{v} + (\Delta w + k)\hat{w}$ is also a path from point 1 to point 2 for all values of k. The length of the path is

$$dist = |\Delta u + k| + |\Delta v + k| + |\Delta w + k|$$
$$= |\text{MAX} + k| + |\text{MID} + k| + |\text{MIN} + k|$$

What value of k minimizes *dist*? The proof consists of five separate cases:

$0 < \text{MIN}$	All three coordinates are positive. Decreasing k by 1 decreases the path length by 3. Increasing k by 1 increases the path length by 3.
$\text{MIN} \le 0 < \text{MID}$	MID and MAX are positive, MIN is zero or negative. Decreasing k by 1 decreases the path length by 1. Increasing k by 1 increases the path length by 1 or 3.
$\text{MID} = 0$	MIN is negative or zero; MAX is positive or zero. Decreasing k by 1, the MIN and MID terms increase by 1 each, which outweighs any decrease in the MAX term, so the total path length increases. Increasing k by 1, the MID and MAX terms increase by 1 each, which outweighs any decrease in the MIN term, so the total path length increases again.
$\text{MID} < 0 \le \text{MAX}$	MIN and MID are negative. MAX is zero or positive. Increasing k by 1 decreases the path length by 1. Decreasing k by 1 increases the path length by 1 or 3.
$\text{MAX} < 0$	All three coordinates are negative. Increasing k by 1 decreases the path length by 3. Decreasing k by 1 increases the path length by 3.

Applying these five cases repeatedly to any coordinate moves MID to zero. The third case shows that $\text{MID} = 0$ is a stable minimum of the path length. Thus, setting $k = -\text{MID}$ produces the coordinate that describes the minimum path. The length of this path is

$$dist = |\text{MAX} - \text{MID}| + |\text{MID} - \text{MID}| + |\text{MIN} - \text{MID}|$$

Using the fact that $\text{MIN} \le \text{MID} \le \text{MAX}$, this can be simplified to $dist = \text{MAX} - \text{MIN}$. ∎

Source Code

File HexPoint.hpp

```
#ifndef _HEXPOINT_HPP
#define _HEXPOINT_HPP
//**********************************************************************
// TITLE: HexPoint -- Operations on hexagonal grid coordinates
```

```
//
// AUTHOR: Scott N Gerard, Rochester, MN
// LANGUAGE: C++
//
// FUNCTION:
//    This class provides the basic operations for a hexagonal grid
//    (three axes that are 120 degrees apart).  "HexPoints" describe the
//    points formed by the intersection of the axes.  This class can be
//    used to describe a plane full of hexagons (as are used in many
//    modern games).
//
//    Each HexPoint is conceptually composed     +v \        / -w
//    of the three integer values (u,v,w).          \      /
//    Each coordinate represents the number          \    /
//    of units along each of three axes: the   -u     \ /        +u
//    u-axis, v-axis, and w-axis.  The axes     ---------*----------
//    are shown at right.                             / \
//                                                   /   \
//    One of the 3 coordinates is redundant,        /     \
//    but maintaining all three preserves the   +w /       \ -v
//    natural symmetry of the grid.  This
//    redundancy can be expressed as
//
//         (u, v, w) = (u+k, v+k, w+k)  for all k
//
//    The value k can be chosen as desired      MAX(u,v,w) >= 0
//    to get an infinite set of coordinates     MID(u,v,w)  = 0
//    which all represent the same point.       MIN(u,v,w) <= 0
//    When k is chosen so to make the
//    relations at right hold, it is called the "natural" form of a
//    coordinate.  The natural form gives the shortest path between a
//    HexPoint and the origin.  get always returns the natural form.
//
//    HexPoints only store one of the redundant forms of (u+k,v+k,w+k).
//    However, we do NOT store the natural form because it is more
//    difficult to decipher (see get).  For the purposes of storage, k
//    is chosen to make w=0.  Thus there is no need to explicitly
//    store w.
//
//    This class is a leaf class -- it has no virtual functions.
//    Therefore instances to not contain a vtbl pointer that would
//    dramatically increase its size.
//
// CHANGE LOG:
//    11Apr88 - Initial coding.  SN Gerard
//    08Feb92 - Convert to C++.  SN Gerard
//    29Jun93 - Add hash().  SN Gerard
//***********************************************************************
#include <iostream.h>
#include "Bool.hpp"
#include "Point2.hpp"
```

(continued)

File HexPoint.hpp *(continued)*

```cpp
class HexPoint {

   typedef HexPoint ThisClass;

public:
   //**********************************************************************
   // Constructor
   //**********************************************************************
   HexPoint(int u=0, int v=0, int w=0): uu(u-w), vv(v-w) {};

   //**********************************************************************
   // set HexPoint to new coordinates
   //**********************************************************************
   HexPoint& set( int u, int v, int w) {
      uu = u-w;
      vv = v-w;
      return *this;
   };

   //**********************************************************************
   //* return natural coordinates.
   //**********************************************************************
   const HexPoint& get (int& u, int& v, int& w) const;

   //**********************************************************************
   // These routines convert between HexPoint coordinates and
   // rectangular coordinates (x,y).  They are useful for graphing.
   //
   //    u = x                                +u axis = +x axis
   //    v = -1/2 * x + SQRT(3) * y / 2       +v is in second quadrant
   //    w = -1/2 * x - SQRT(3) * y / 2       +w is in third quadrant
   //
   // Note: For proper scaling, mulitply the (x,y) values returned by
   // getxy by ( 1/2, sqrt(3)/2 ).  Divide by these values before
   // calling setxy.
   //
   // setXY() returns the HexPoint closest to (x,y) position.  exact is
   // TRUE iff (x,y) converted exactly; otherwise exact is FALSE.
   //**********************************************************************
   Point2 getXY () const;

   HexPoint& setXYEx (const Point2& p, BOOL& exact);
   HexPoint& setXY   (const Point2& p) {
      BOOL    exact;
      setXYEx(p,exact);
      return *this;
   };

   //**********************************************************************
   // are the two HexPoints equal ?
   //**********************************************************************
```

```
friend BOOL operator == (const HexPoint& a, const HexPoint& b)
   { return BOOL( a.uu == b.uu && a.vv == b.vv); };

friend BOOL operator != (const HexPoint& a, const HexPoint& b)
   { return BOOL( !(a==b) ); };

//****************************************************************
// Add and subtract two HexPoints
//   (ua,va,wa) + (ub,vb,wb) = (ua+ub, va+vb, wa+wb)
// This is useful with "a" and "b" are thought of as vectors.
//****************************************************************
friend HexPoint operator + (const HexPoint& a, const HexPoint& b)
   { return HexPoint( a.uu+b.uu, a.vv+b.vv, 0); };

friend HexPoint operator - (const HexPoint& a, const HexPoint& b)
   { return HexPoint( a.uu-b.uu, a.vv-b.vv, 0); };

HexPoint& operator += (const HexPoint& p) {
   uu += p.uu;
   vv += p.vv;
   return *this;
};

HexPoint& operator -= (const HexPoint& p) {
   uu -= p.uu;
   vv -= p.vv;
   return *this;
};

HexPoint& operator - () {                    // unary minus
   uu = -uu;
   vv = -vv;
   return *this;
};

//****************************************************************
// Compute the minimum distance between two points
//****************************************************************
int dist (const HexPoint& b);

//****************************************************************
// hash
//****************************************************************
long int hash () const;

//****************************************************************
// routines for minimums and maximums
//****************************************************************
HexPoint& minValue();
HexPoint& maxValue();
```

(continued)

File HexPoint.hpp *(continued)*

```cpp
    HexPoint& min (const HexPoint& p);
    HexPoint& max (const HexPoint& p);

    //********************************************************************
    // IO operations using external format "(u,v,w)"
    //********************************************************************
    friend istream& operator >> (istream&, HexPoint&);
    friend ostream& operator << (ostream&, const HexPoint&);

// protected: for Region and Xform derived classes.
    //********************************************************************
    // set and change coordinates the u and v coordinates directly.
    // The Region and Xform classes use x() and y() for their
    // transformations.  HexPoint does not know all the classes that
    // will need to use it.  Particularly the Board classes that have a
    // user-defined cell class.
    //********************************************************************
    int x () const    { return uu; };
    int y () const    { return vv; };

    HexPoint& x(const int X)  { uu = X;  return *this; }
    HexPoint& y(const int Y)  { vv = Y;  return *this; }

private:
    //********************************************************************
    // Coordinates.  Note that w is always assumed to be zero and thus
    // does not need to be stored explicitly
    //********************************************************************
    int uu, vv;

};

#endif
```

File HexPoint.cpp

```cpp
//********************************************************************
// TITLE: HexCoord -- Operations on hexagonal grid coordinates
//
// AUTHOR: Scott N Gerard, Rochester, MN
// LANGUAGE: C++
//
// FUNCTION:
//    This class provides the basic operations for a hexagonal grid.
//
```

```
// MACRO VARIABLES:
//    If the macro variable VERT_U is defined, u will be aligned
//    vertically (along the +y axis).  If VERT_U is not defined (the
//    normal case), u will be aligned horizontally (along the +x axis).
//
// CHANGE LOG:
//    11Apr88 - Initial coding.  SN Gerard
//    08Feb92 - Convert to C++.  SN Gerard
//    29Jun93 - Add hash().  SN Gerard
//***********************************************************************
#include <limits.h>
#include <math.h>
#include "IntMath.hpp"
#include "HexPoint.hpp"
#include "SimpHasher.hpp"


//***********************************************************************
// Convert a HexCoord back into its three values (u,v,w)
//***********************************************************************
const HexPoint& HexPoint::get (int& u, int& v, int& w) const {

    // Determine MID(uu,vv,ww).  Then subtract it from stored values.
    if (( uu >= 0 && vv <= 0 ) || ( uu <= 0 && vv >= 0)) {
        u = uu;                           // ww=0 is MID
        v = vv;
        w = 0;

    } else if (abs(uu) >= abs(vv)) {      // vv is MID
        u = uu - vv;                      // = uu - vv
        v = 0;                            // = vv - vv
        w = -vv;                          // = ww - vv = 0 - vv

    } else {                              // uu is MID
        u = 0;                            // = uu - uu
        v = vv - uu;
        w = -uu;                          // = ww - uu = 0 - uu
    };
    return *this;
};


//***********************************************************************
// Compute the minimum distance between two points
//***********************************************************************
int HexPoint::dist (const HexPoint& hc) {
    int u, v, w;
    HexPoint diff;

    diff = *this - hc;                    // vector from hc to this
    diff.get(u, v, w);                    // get natural coords of vector
    return abs(u) + abs(v) + abs(w);      // distance of shortest path
};
```

(continued)

File HexPoint.cpp *(continued)*

```cpp
//**********************************************************************
// hash
//**********************************************************************
long int HexPoint::hash () const {
    SimpHasher<int> h;
    h << uu << vv;
    return h.result();
};


//**********************************************************************
// routines for minimums and maximums
//**********************************************************************
HexPoint& HexPoint::minValue() {
    uu = INT_MIN;
    vv = INT_MIN;
    return *this;
};

HexPoint& HexPoint::maxValue() {
    uu = INT_MAX;
    vv = INT_MAX;
    return *this;
};

HexPoint& HexPoint::min (const HexPoint& p) {
    uu = ::min(uu, 0+p.uu);              // NOTE: 0+p.uu is not const
    vv = ::min(vv, 0+p.vv);
    return *this;
};

HexPoint& HexPoint::max (const HexPoint& p) {
    uu = ::max(uu, 0+p.uu);
    vv = ::max(vv, 0+p.vv);
    return *this;
};

//**********************************************************************
// IO operations using external format "(u,v,w)"
//**********************************************************************
ostream& operator << (ostream& os, const HexPoint& hc) {
    int u, v, w;

    hc.get(u,v,w);
    os << "(" << u << "," << v << "," << w << ")";
    return os;
};

istream& operator >> (istream& is, HexPoint& hc) {
    int u, v, w;
    char leftp, com1, com2, rightp;
```

```
    is >> leftp >> u >> com1 >> v >> com2 >> w >> rightp;

    if (is && (leftp=='(' && com1==',' && com2==',' && rightp==')'))
        hc.set(u,v,w);
    else
        is.clear( ios::badbit | is.rdstate() );
    return is;
};


//*********************************************************************
// These two routines convert between HexPoint coordinates and
// rectangular coordinates (x,y).
//
//                      active version          commented out
//      +u axis             +x axis                +y axis
//      +v axis         in 2nd quadrant        in 3rd quadrant
//      +w axis         in 3rd quadrant        in 4th quadrant
//
// These routines are useful for graphing and mouse handling.
//*********************************************************************

// Convert a HexPoint into an (x,y) pair
Point2 HexPoint::getXY () const {
    #ifndef VERT_U                                  // use horizontal u
        return Point2( 2 * uu - vv,  vv);           // +u = +x
    #else                                           // use vertical u
        return Point2( -vv, 2 * uu - vv);           // +u = +y
    #endif
};

// Given an (x,y) position, find the closest, legal HexPoint
HexPoint& HexPoint::setXYEx (const Point2& p, BOOL& exact) {
    #ifndef VERT_U                                  // use horizontal u
        uu = (p.x() + p.y()) / 2;
        vv =  p.y();
        exact = BOOL( (p.x() + p.y()) % 2 == 0 ); // any rounding on uu?
    #else                                           // use vertical u
        uu = (p.y() - p.x()) / 2;
        vv = -p.x();
        exact = BOOL( (p.x() - p.y()) % 2 == 0 ); // any rounding on uu?
    #endif
    return *this;
};
```

File Reg2Hexagon.hpp

```
#ifndef _REG2HEXAGON_HPP
#define _REG2HEXAGON_HPP
//*********************************************************************
// TITLE: Reg2Hexagon  -- 2D hexagonal region
//
```

(continued)

File Reg2Hexagon.hpp *(continued)*

```
// AUTHOR: Scott N Gerard, Rochester, MN
// LANGUAGE: C++
//
// FUNCTION:
//    Maps a hexagonal region.  For example, defining a hexagon with
//    edge=3 gives this mapping on a HexGrid.
//
//                        33    34    35    36
//                    28    29    30    31    32
//                22    23    24    25    26    27
//            15    16    17    18    19    20    21
//                 9    10    11    12    13    14
//                 4     5     6     7     8
//                      0     1     2     3
//
// CHANGE LOG:
//    11Apr88 - Initial coding.  SN Gerard
//    23Jun90 - Divide up hex mapping routines.  SN Gerard
//    26May93 - Convert to C++.  SN Gerard
//*******************************************************************
#include <stdlib.h>
#include "IntMath.hpp"
#include "Reg2Trap.hpp"

template <class P>
class Reg2Hexagon: public Region<P> {

    typedef Region<P> BaseClass;
    typedef Reg2Hexagon<P> ThisClass;

public:
    //***************************************************************
    // constructor
    // A hexagon is two trapezoids divided horizontally thru the center.
    //***************************************************************
    Reg2Hexagon (int edge, BOOL chkBounds=TRUE);

    //***************************************************************
    // make a copy
    //***************************************************************
    ThisClass* copy() const { return (ThisClass*) _copy(); };

    //***************************************************************
    // change checkBounds
    //***************************************************************
    virtual void setCheckBounds(BOOL checkBounds) const;

    //***************************************************************
    // where is Point?
    // Don't let Reg2YSplit do checking.  It won't handle boundaries
    // correctly.
    //***************************************************************
```

```
    virtual BOUNDS boundsEx (const P p, BOOL& exact) const {
       exact = TRUE;

       // check p against these boundaries (e is the edge)
       // (-e,-e) -> ( 0,-e)    ==>    0 <= e      + v
       // ( 0,-e) -> ( e, 0)    ==>    0 <= e - u + v
       // ( e, 0) -> ( e, e)    ==>    0 <= e - u
       // ( e, e) -> ( 0, e)    ==>    0 <= e      - v
       // ( 0, e) -> (-e, 0)    ==>    0 <= e + u - v
       // (-e, 0) -> (-e,-e)    ==>    0 <= e + u
       return int2Bounds(
          min(
             min( edge - abs(p.x()), edge - abs(p.y()) ),
             edge - abs(p.y()-p.x())
          )
       );
    };

    //*******************************************************************
    // return enclosing box
    //*******************************************************************
    virtual void enclosure (P& low, P& high) const;

    //*******************************************************************
    // rank
    //*******************************************************************
    virtual long rankEx (const P p, BOOL& exact) const {
       if (p.y() < 0)
          return bot.rankEx(p-p1, exact);
       else {
          P skewp = p - p2;
          skewp.x( skewp.x() - skewp.y() );
          return top.rankEx( skewp, exact) + botSize;
       };
    };

    //*******************************************************************
    // unrank
    //*******************************************************************
    virtual P unrank (long rank) const {
       if (rank < botSize)
          return bot.unrank(rank) + p1;
       else {
          P skewp = top.unrank(rank-botSize);
          skewp.x( skewp.x() + skewp.y() );
          return skewp + p2;
       };
    };

protected:
    int edge;                        // remember the edge

    P  p1, p2;                       // origin offsets
```

(continued)

File Reg2Hexagon.hpp *(continued)*

```
    Reg2Trap<P> bot;               // bottom trapezoid
    Reg2Trap<P> top;               // top trapezoid

    int botSize;                   // size of bottom trapezoid

    virtual RootClass* _copy() const { return new ThisClass(*this); };
};

#endif
```

File Reg2Hexagon.cpp

```
//**********************************************************************
// TITLE: Reg2Hexagon  -- 2D hexagonal region
//
// AUTHOR: Scott N Gerard, Rochester, MN
// LANGUAGE: C++
//
// FUNCTION:
//    Maps a hexagonal region.
//
// CHANGE LOG:
//    11Apr88 - Initial coding.  SN Gerard
//    23Jun90 - Divide up hex mapping routines.  SN Gerard
//    26May93 - Convert to C++.  SN Gerard
//**********************************************************************
#include "Reg2Hexagon.hpp"

//**********************************************************************
// constructor
// A hexagon is two trapezoids divided horizontally thru the center.
//**********************************************************************
template <class P>
Reg2Hexagon<P>::Reg2Hexagon (int Edge, BOOL chkBounds)
    :Region<P>(chkBounds),
    edge(Edge),
    bot( edge, edge-1, +1, chkBounds),     p1(-edge, -edge),
    top( 2*edge, edge, -1, chkBounds),  p2(-edge,    0),
    botSize( bot.size() )
    { elems = bot.size() + top.size(); };

//**********************************************************************
// change checkBounds
//**********************************************************************
template <class P>
void Reg2Hexagon<P>::setCheckBounds(BOOL checkBounds) const {
    BaseClass::setCheckBounds(checkBounds);
    bot.setCheckBounds(checkBounds);
    top.setCheckBounds(checkBounds);
};
```

```
//********************************************************************
// return enclosing box
//********************************************************************
template <class P>
void Reg2Hexagon<P>::enclosure (P& low, P& high) const {
   low = P(-edge,-edge);
   high = P(edge, edge);
};
```

File HexGame.cpp

```
//*********************************************************************
// TITLE: HexGame -- A simple chase on a hexgrid
//
// AUTHOR: Scott N Gerard, Rochester, MN
// LANGUAGE: C++
//
// FUNCTION:
//    This is a very simple game with two markers on a hexgrid.  One
//    marker is a stationary target.  The other marker, the chaser,
//    steps closer to the target on each move.  The distance and
//    shortest path from chaser to target is displayed every move.
//
// CHANGE LOG:
//    10Feb92 - Initial Coding.  SN Gerard
//*********************************************************************
#include <iostream.h>
#include "HexPoint.hpp"

void main() {
   HexPoint chaser, target, shortestPath;
   int u,v,w;                               // coordinates of shortestPath
   int d;                                   // distance between chaser & target

   const HexPoint U (1,0,0), V (0,1,0), W (0,0,1);

   cout << "Coordinates of Target:";
   cin  >> target;
   cout << "Coordinates of Chaser:";
   cin  >> chaser;

   cout << "\nTarget: " << target << endl;
   while (1) {
      shortestPath = target - chaser;    // path from chaser to target
      d = chaser.dist(target);           // distance of shortest path
      cout << "Chaser: " << chaser
           << " shortest path=" << shortestPath
           << " distance=" << d << endl;

      // have we reached target ? (distance is zero?)
      if (d == 0) {
```

(continued)

File HexGame.cpp   *(continued)*

```cpp
            cout << "Chaser captured Target" << endl;
            break;
      };

      // move chaser one unit towards the target
      // get natural coordinates of shortest path.
      shortestPath.get(u,v,w);
      if        (u > 0) chaser += U;
      else if (u < 0) chaser -= U;
      else if (v > 0) chaser += V;
      else if (v < 0) chaser -= V;
      else if (w > 0) chaser += W;
      else if (w < 0) chaser -= W;
   };
};
```

PART FOUR

Calculation Modules

9

Calculator

This chapter begins a section on data types. To make experimentation easy and to help me test my ideas during development as I was writing the first data type, I also started writing a small calculator. The strategy was so successful that when I started writing the other data types I copied the code and made the changes necessary for that data type. This process continued with other data types. Then, of course, I wanted to enhance one of the calculators. But instead of many not-quite-identical copies of the calculator code, I had several different versions with no easy way to propagate new features to all calculators. It was now obvious that the bulk of the calculators could share common code. This chapter is the result of that effort.

I believe you will find these calculator pieces as useful as I have. Regardless of whether you are relatively new to C++ and are writing your first Complex class, or are working on more advanced data type classes, it is a fairly simple task to construct a calculator for it. Adhoc testing becomes very easy.

These calculator classes are used by all the calculators in this book: REALCALC (in this chapter), FUNCALC and AUTOCALC in Chapter 10, PERMCALC in Chapter 12, and PARTCALC in Chapter 14. This chapter describes the common details about the implementation and provides information so you can extend or write a new calculator for your data types.

This chapter covers REALCALC: a calculator for double floating point values. I purposely chose a simple data type (doubles) for the first calculator so the data type details would not obscure the calculator.

Note: the calculators do not prevent every possible mistake. They prevent some obvious errors, but you can crash it in many of the same ways you can crash the underlying class with your own C++ program. This is in keeping with the goal of the calculators being a test bed.

Starting REALCALC

Go to any DOS command line and fire up REALCALC.

```
C>REALCALC
```

After a one-line help message, the REALCALC prompt is displayed.

```
REALCALC>
```

Two commands you should remember are help and quit. help displays a list of the valid commands, and quit returns to DOS. All the calculators are case-sensitive, so HELP and Help are invalid commands.

Literals

Each calculator works with a different data type and therefore has different rules for literal values. For REALCALC, a literal is a double floating point value. Literals are read using iostream and so follow its syntax rules for doubles. To display the value of a literal precede it with an equal sign. Extra spaces in the input line are ignored by the calculator's parser.

```
REALCALC> = 9.15
9.15
```

Variables

The calculator maintains a list of named, double floating point variables. To assign a value to a variable, type

```
REALCALC>s=9.15
s=9.15
```

REALCALC assigns the value 9.15 to variable *s* and echoes the result.

Commands

The calculator also supports commands. To execute a command, type in the command name (in the proper case) and any parameters. For example, to look at the list of all named variables and their values, enter the list command.

```
REALCALC>list
  1: s=9.15
```

It is easy to add new commands to a calculator for either testing a particular feature, or accessing subroutines that use the data type (see "Writing Your Own Calculator" later in this chapter).

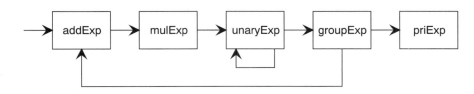

FIGURE 9.1
REALCALC **expression objects.**

Expressions

Rather than simply printing and assigning literal values to variables, an expression may follow the equal sign.

```
REALCALC>z=2*(s+1)
z=20.3
```

The operators vary from calculator to calculator depending on the data type. For example, PERMCALC does not support an addition operator because addition of permutations makes no sense.

In most programming languages, multiplication has higher **precedence** than addition, so in expressions without parentheses, multiplication is done before addition. Therefore, 3 + 4 * 5 is evaluated as 3 + (4 * 5) rather than (3 + 4) * 5. Multiplication and division have the same precedence. Neither one takes precedence over the other; they are evaluated left-to-right.

The calculator classes let you define the operators that are meaningful to your data type, and let you set their relative precedence levels. To get a list of the valid operators and their precedence levels for a calculator, enter the command helpExp. The operators with the smallest indentation have a lower precedence level than operators indented further. Operators with the same indentation have the same precedence.

Figure 9.1 shows the expression objects for REALCALC. Each object parses part of an expression. Object addExp reads expressions with addition and subtraction operators; mulExp reads expressions with multiplication and division operators, and so forth.

Addition and subtraction (addExp) have the lowest precedence, followed by multiplication and division (mulExp). The unary operators unary plus, unary minus, and logical not (unaryExp) are next in precedence. The arrow from unaryExp to itself shows that a unary operator can be followed by an expression that also allows unary operators. That is, a groupExp can be preceded by multiple unary operators. Parentheses, square brackets, and curly braces (groupExp) contain a full expression, as shown by the arrow from groupExp to addExp. The highest precedence object is priExp (primary expression), which parses literals, variables, and symbol names.

Besides the operators, each calculator may define symbols that can be used in expressions (but not on the left-hand side). helpSym lists the valid symbols.

REALCALC defines symbols pi and e, which return the value of those famous constants. It also defines symbols for log(x) and exp(x). The argument for these symbols can be another full expression.

```
REALCALC>q=exp( 1 + log(s+pi) )
q=33.412013
```

Comments

Any characters between // and the end of line are a comment and are ignored. An entire line may be a comment, or a line may contain an expression or command that ends with a comment.

```
REALCALC>// This is a full line comment
REALCALC>area=pi*radius*radius  // compute the area of a circle
```

Line Continuation

A single command or expression can split across multiple input lines. Any line that ends with a "\" and a carriage return is continued on the next line. Multiple lines can be concatenated by placing a "\" at the end of every line except the last.

```
REALCALC>x = 2 * \
REALCALC> 3
x=6
```

Line continuations are processed before looking for comments, so this is a single, multiline comment:

```
REALCALC>// This is one  \
REALCALC>really, really, \
REALCALC>long comment
```

Interrupting Execution

To stop a long-running calculation, press control-break.

Common Commands

The common calculator code defines a number of commands that are independent of the data type. Every calculator has these commands.

General commands:

new Reinitialize the calculator. This resets the internal state of the calculator, and deletes all variables.

quit   Exit the calculator and return to DOS.

dos   Execute a DOS command. The rest of the characters following this command are passed to the DOS command shell. For example, to get a list of all files in the current directory, enter

```
REALCALC>dos dir *.*
```

The help commands return information that was compiled into the calculator. They are independent of the current state of the calculator.

help   List all commands alphabetically. Each line shows the command name, a summary of the parameters it requires (if any), a colon, and a brief description.

helpSym   List all symbols alphabetically. Each line shows the symbol name, a summary of the parameters it requires (if any), a colon, and a brief description.

helpExp   List all operators. Operators are grouped into precedence levels, and indented. Higher precedence operators are indented further than lower precedence operators.

There are two ways to list the currently defined variables:

list   List all variables and their current value. Entries are listed in the order they were defined.

listValue   List all variables by value. Variables with the same value are listed together. The values are listed in "hash" order, which looks essentially random. This information is a direct byproduct of the structures needed for the name command and the various table commands in later calculators.

Commands to work with individual variables:

delete   Delete a variable from the variable list.

name   Evaluate an expression and print the name of a variable with that value (if any).

hash   Evaluate an expression and return its hash value. Every data type must provide a hash method (for class AttrList to work) so this command is always possible. However, you might want to remove this command from a production-level calculator. See "Hashing" in Chapter 5 for more information on hashing.

All calculators have three internal flags, and a corresponding command to set or query its value. A "Y" argument turns the flag on; an "N" argument turns the flag off; no argument prints the flag's current value.

change   Whenever any existing variable's value changes, this flag is set on. The includeChg command uses this flag.

echo   Controls whether input lines are echoed to the output. Normally, echo is off when reading from the terminal, and on when reading from a file.

unknown   If an unknown variable name is encountered when parsing an expression, should a variable be created with a default value (Y), or should an error be reported (N)?

The include commands read and evaluate each line in a DOS file. The argument to these commands is a DOS filename. Include files may include other files. There is no maximum depth for include files. The only constraint is the amount of memory.

include   Read and evaluate every line in the file. Stop at end-of-file.

includeChg   Include the file repeatedly until the change flag stays off. The change flag is turned off at the beginning of every pass. It iterates a file of expressions until their values stabilize.

REALCALC **Specific Commands**

REALCALC defines one extra command. Later calculators define different commands.

precision   Change the precision for printing doubles to *n* digits.

Implementation Comments

This section describes the classes that make up the calculator. They are interesting in their own right. But if you are primarily interested in extending an existing calculator, or writing your own calculator, skip to "Writing Your Own Calculator" on page 157 and refer back to this section as needed.

Some of the calculator classes require typedef CalcType to be set to the data type for the calculator. CalcType is set to Real in the main source file (RealCalc.cpp for REALCALC).

Real Class

C++ doubles provide almost all the operations REALCALC requires. Unfortunately, doubles have neither a hash() method nor a valid() method. hash() is required by classes AttrList and SetOfList to construct hash tables. Since hash() is a member function, and C++ forbids adding a member function to a fundamental data type, we must define a new class.

Class Real is quite simple. It has a constructor that accepts a double, and it can be cast to a double. These methods allow us to assign Reals to doubles in both directions. It is important to note that the constructor also acts as a default constructor. The calculator classes assume CalcType has a default constructor.

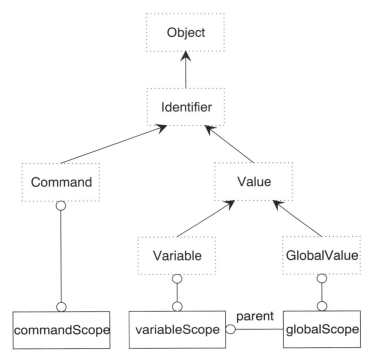

FIGURE 9.2
Identifier classes.

Real also has the hash() method we need. valid() is called by the calculator to insure the value is in a valid state. For Real, valid() simply returns TRUE. For more complex types, the checks are more substantial.

File RealCalc.cpp defines two routines used during expression evaluation. isLiteral() returns TRUE if the character it is passed begins a Real literal; double integers can begin with either a digit, a decimal point, a plus, or a minus. getLiteral() reads a literal from the input stream and returns its value.

Identifier

Identifier Class

Identifier is the abstract class for all identifiers in the calculators. Figure 9.2 shows the Identifier class hierarchy. Its constructor accepts the name of the identifier (the name the user will type on input), a brief description used for help text, and a description of the parameters (parameter help text). Method isChangeable() distinguishes between identifiers that can change values (variables) and those that can't.

Identifier is derived from class Object in Borland's class library. It contains a number of methods to fit into their structure.

Command Class

Commands are Identifiers, so they have a name, help text, and parameter help text. They also contain a pointer to a function that implements the command. Method execute() invokes that function. The function may read arguments from the passed istream and may write results on the passed ostream. Command objects are simply intermediaries that tie a name (and help text) to a function.

Simply declaring a new command object makes it active. Nothing else is necessary. Command's constructor adds its name to the commandScope. A commandScope is a sorted list of commands. The commands can be declared in any order, but the help list will always be sorted alphabetically. The common calculator commands are declared in Calc.cpp. But each calculator can declare additional commands in other files, like RealCalc.cpp.

Value Class

A Value is also an Identifier with a name and help text. But instead of an execute() method, it introduces a value() method to return a value of type CalcType. value() is a pure virtual function so Value is an abstract class. Value has an integer userValue. This value is available for use by user commands and symbols. Some calculators don't use it at all.

Variable Class

An object of this class is a named variable with a value. Identifier's name is used for the variable's name, but the help and parameter descriptions are not used. This is the only class derived from Identifier that returns TRUE for isChangeable(), and it adds a setValue() method to do the job.

Variables add themselves to the variableScope. Once added, a client can find a varaible in variableScope given either the variable's name or its value.

GlobalValue Class

GlobalValues are used for all nonvariable symbols; those listed by command helpSym. This class is derived from Value. Like Variables, GlobalValues can return a value of type CalcType. But since they are not changeable, they do not have a setValue() method.

The value() method may read parameters from the input stream, but it doesn't have to. For example, the symbol pi in REALCALC does not need any parameters. But log() and exp() need to read a left parenthesis, a CalcType expression, and a right parenthesis. Any errors in this syntax are reported to the user. Like Commands, GlobalValues have a function pointer and are intermediaries between the symbol's name and the function pointer. When a GlobalValue is defined, its adds itself to the globalScope. helpSym lists all names in globalScope, sorted alphabetically.

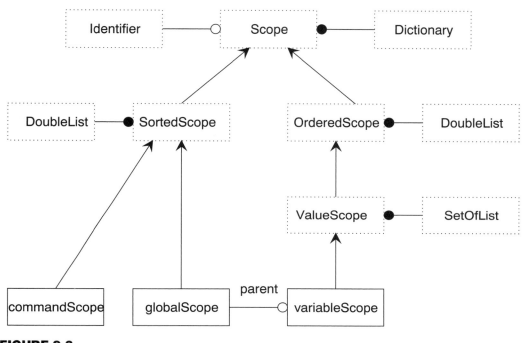

FIGURE 9.3
Scope class hierarchy.

Scopes

A scope is a collection of Identifier objects (see Figure 9.3). Every scope provides methods to add(), change(), and detach() variables. Each of these methods calls an internal version that performs any processing specific to its derived class, and then calls the same procedure in its base class. Every scope object collects various kinds of information about the Identifiers it contains.

Scope Class
Scope is the common base class for all the scope classes. It has a dictionary so it can look up an Identifier by name.

Every scope can have a parent scope. Block structured languages can be implemented with a nested scope containing a pointer to its parent. Method lookupThisScope() searches just the current scope; method lookup() continues searching all parent scopes if a local match is not found. In the current calculators, globalScope is the parent of variableScope. commandScope has no parent.

Scope is derived from Borland's TShouldDelete class, which controls whether a container "owns"—and therefore should delete—the elements it contains.

SortedScope Class

This scope has a sorted list of all the elements it contains. A SortedScope has both a dictionary (from class Scope) for lookup by name, and a sorted list of identifiers (from class SortedScope) for printing out all Identifiers alphabetically by name. Both the globalScope of Identifier names, and the commandScope of command names are SortedScopes. Class SortedScopeIterator is used for walking alphabetically through the Identifiers.

OrderedScope Class

An OrderedScope also maintains a list of all the elements it contains. But instead of maintaining the list sorted alphabetically by name, it maintains its list in creation order. Like SortedScope, an OrderedScope contains both a dictionary (from class Scope) and a list (from OrderedScope). The `list` command walks down the ordered list to show all the variables. It also has a corresponding iterator class: OrderedScopeIterator.

ValueScope Class

Besides looking up Variables by name and creation order, a ValueScope can look up Variables by value. variableScope is an instance of ValueScope. Looking up Variables by value is necessary for later calculators to print out different kinds of tables. ValueScope has a SetOfList which implements this support.

SetOfList Class

Some calculator commands (e.g., `name` and `close` in `AUTOCALC`) look up variables given a value. For instance, is there a variable with value 9.15? SetOfList provides this capability.

SetOfList is a set of lists (AttrList). Each list contains Variables (Figure 9.4). All variables with the same value (attribute) are in the same list. Variables with different values are in different lists (Figure 9.5). Given a value, SetOfList finds the one list with that value. If there is no list, then no variable has that value.

SetOfList is derived from Borland's Set class. The elements in the set are always instances of class AttrList. An AttrList (attribute list) is a list of other classes (Variables in this case) that have the same value of some attribute (the Variable's value). Method getAttr() returns the common value of all the Variables in an AttrList. Method getAny() selects and returns one of the Variables.

When a Variable is added to a SetOfList, it uses the Variable's value to find the AttrList with the same value. The Variable is added to that AttrList. When a Variable's value changes, the change() method removes the Variable from the AttrList for its old value and adds it to the AttrList for its new value.

The `name` command allows by-value lookups from the calculator command line. It searches the SetOfList contained in variableScope to find the matching AttrList. It then prints out the name of one of the Variables in that AttrList.

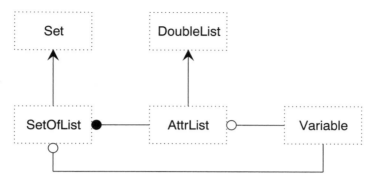

FIGURE 9.4
SetOfList class hierarchy.

Expressions

Exp Class

Exp is the abstract class for all expression classes. The expression class hierarchy is shown in Figure 9.6 and the grammar supported by these classes is shown in Figure 9.7.

A full expression tree is a collection of expression objects. Expression objects contain characters for operators (like "+" and "*") and pointers to subexpression objects. The most important expression method is eval(). eval() reads and parses characters

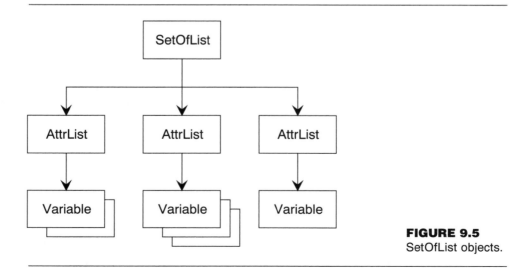

FIGURE 9.5
SetOfList objects.

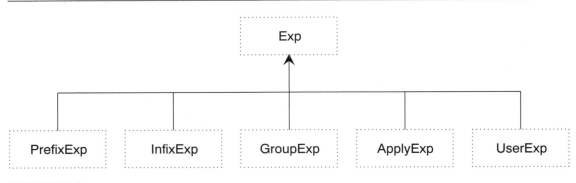

FIGURE 9.6
Expression class hierarchy.

from the passed istream, and parsing errors are written to the passed ostream. The eval() method of most expression classes parses just a few characters and calls eval() on a subexpression. The specific characters and the subexpression pointers are different for every expression tree. The best solution would be to pass these characters and pointers as parameters on the constructor. However, this is not possible since the objects form a circular graph (see Figure 9.1). There are cases where a pointer to an object is required before it can be constructed. Therefore, each concrete expression class has various add() methods to add this information to the object. The add() methods also accept help text for each operator.

The constant MAX_OPS declares the maximum number of operators for one expression object. Its current value of 5 should be large enough for most situations.

Command `helpExp` calls the other important method for expressions: printOn(). It walks an expression tree and prints out help text. printOn() prints the character(s) for each operator, indented, followed by its help text. If the operator has stepInto = TRUE, printOn() is called for the operator's subexpression with a larger indentation. Since most expression trees are circular graphs, stepInto *must* be FALSE somewhere to prevent infinite recursion. Most operators in an expression point to the same subexpression. Setting stepInto = TRUE on just the last operator produces a concise and readable listing.

PrefixExp Class

PrefixExp parses prefix operators. It allows up to MAX_OPS prefix operators and subexpressions, plus an "else" subexpression that is used when no prefix operator matches the next input character. The subexpression for a prefix operator usually points back to itself so multiple prefix operators like "+!exp" can be handled. After the "+" operator is recognized, PrefixExp recursively calls itself as the subexpression. The second copy of PrefixExp recognizes the "!" operator, and again calls itself. The third copy of PrefixExp presumably does not find any prefix operators, and calls the else

Exp = PrefixExp | InfixExp | GroupExp | ApplyExp | UserExp;

PrefixExp = (op_char Exp
* | ...*
* | op_char Exp*
* | Exp);*

InfixExp = Exp (op_char Exp
* | ...*
* | op_char Exp) *;*

GroupExp =   op_char Exp op_char
* | ...*
* | op_char Exp op_char*
* | Exp;*

ApplyExp = Exp (op_char Exp op_char
* | ...*
* | op_char Exp op_char);*

UserExp =   beginFn ExpFn
* | ...*
* | beginFn ExpFn;*

FIGURE 9.7
Grammar for
expression classes.

subexpression that matches "exp." As the calls return, the "!" and "+" operators are evaluated.

The else subexpression points to the next higher precedence level. Prefix operators can also signal a subexpression of a different type. For example, a "%" prefix operator might evaluate an integer subexpression, and "\" might evaluate a character expression.

I find it most natural to set stepInto = TRUE on just the else subexpression.

InfixExp Class
This class parses binary, infix operators. It actually parses a list of binary operators since most expression grammars allow lists of such operators. A purer approach would not support the looping feature. If you prefer that approach, it is an easy class to write. It will most likely run somewhat slower since it will have to make more recursive calls to itself.

InfixExp has a first expression that is shared by all operators, and up to MAX_OPS operator characters and subexpression pointers.

In most InfixExp objects, all subexpressions point to the next higher precedence level. StepInto = TRUE is set on for just the last operator.

GroupExp Class

This class is for parsing bracketed expressions that have an opening character, a subexpression, and a closing character. The three common forms are "(exp)", "[exp]" and "{exp}". If the closing character is not found, GroupExp calls parseError().

Usually, GroupExp is the one that creates the circular graph since it points back to the top node in the expression tree. Therefore setting stepInto = TRUE for any of these operators would cause an infinite amount of bad news.

ApplyExp Class

This unusual class is for handing the function apply operator "function(x)" and the subscript operator "array[i]". It has a first expression that is shared by all its operators, and up to MAX_OPS operators that are an opening character, a subexpression, and a closing character. ApplyExp signals a parsing error if it cannot match the closing character. At first, this might seem to be a duplication of GroupExp, but it is not. A GroupExp cannot follow an identifier without an intervening operator.

ApplyExp can only handle functions and arrays with a single subexpression. Multiple parameters/indices can be handled by pointing to an InfixExp whose operator is ", ".

Again, set stepInto = TRUE only for the last operator.

UserExp Class

All the other expression classes match a few characters, and then call a subexpression to finish their job. UserExp objects break the cycle by escaping to user-written C++ functions. These functions can perform any parsing activities that do not fit into the rest of the model.

Each UserExp "operator" is a pair of C++ functions. If the first function returns TRUE when passed the next input character from the istream, then the second function will be called to return a value. The logic is just an if-else-if chain. The first operator whose first function returns TRUE is called to parse the next characters. There is no "else" operator, but it can be easily simulated by a final operator whose first function always returns TRUE. If no first function returns TRUE, parseError() is called.

The calculators have one UserExp object with two operators. The first operator reads a literal. In REALCALC, its first function returns TRUE if the current character is a digit, a decimal point, a plus, or a minus. Its second function calls iostream to read a double integer value.

The second operator retrieves the value of a variable or symbol. Its first function checks for characters that can begin an identifier name. Its second function calls getVarInScope() (in Calc.cpp) to read an identifier name (variable or symbol) and looks up its value.

Evaluation Routines

Routine evalPrint() parses a single character string. It decides which strings are commands and which are expressions. It also handles expressions that assign a value to a variable.

Routine evalPrintLoop() reads each line from an istream and passes the line to evalPrint. This routine continues reading lines until end of file or the internal variable quit becomes TRUE. The `quit` command sets on the quit flag.

Routine parseError() marks the current position in the input stream and prints an error message. Routines match() and matchEof() are widely used routines, that either match something in the input stream or call parseError().

Writing Your Own Calculator

Writing a calculator for your data type, or extending an existing calculator, is fairly straightforward.

1. First declare the data type for the calculator, and typedef CalcType to it. All the calculator routines work in terms of type CalcType.
2. Include the common calculator code by including file Calc.hpp (or Calc.cpp).
3. Write the code to handle CalcType expressions. Look at procedure RealExp-Tree in RealCalc.cpp for an example. You'll need routines to perform operations like add and multiply. You must declare C++ routines because the expression objects take a function pointer; not a member pointer.

   Then declare one expression object, at file scope, for each precedence level. And write a function (RealExpTree) to add each operator to one of those objects. This routine is called by main(). You can parse CalcType expressions using

   ```
   value = calcExp->eval(is,os);
   ```

4. Write the C++ functions to handle any additional commands you need. The function will be passed an istream and an ostream. Read any arguments you need from the istream. Print your result on the ostream and return. Routines parseError, match(), and matchEof() will help you do the parsing. Routine setQueryBool is a nice routine for handling flags like `changed`.

   As a matter of style, command functions should always call matchEof() to make sure there are no spurious parameters on the command line.

   Then construct a Command object passing it the function, the name of the command, and help and parameter text. Simply constructing the command object is all you need to do to get it properly integrated into the calculator. Command names must be unique.

5. Write the C++ functions to handle any symbols you need. This function will be passed an istream and an ostream. Read any arguments you need from the istream. Whereas commands parse an entire line, symbols are buried in the middle of expressions. Your function must not start eating the next piece of the expression. Normally, arguments should be surrounded with parentheses so there is no ambiguity in the end of the parameter list. Symbols only use the

ostream for error conditions. They return a result of type CalcType. The same parsing commands—except for matchEof()—are useful for parsing symbol arguments.

Construct a GlobalValue object passing it the function, the name of the symbol, and help and parameter text. Simply constructing the object is all you need to do. Symbol names must be unique.

Remember, symbols produce values but they are never assigned a value. They are not variables.

6. If you don't have any code to run when the calculator is reinitialized with new, skip this step. Otherwise, you'll need to adjust some pointers in main().

new actually calls through the function pointer init to perform initialization. Your function will need to save the old value of init, and call that old function at some point during your initialization function. Then change init to point to your initialization function. See the code sample below or look in FUNCALC.

7. Code your main() function like this:

```
void main() {
    initFunCalcPrev = init;            // save old init fn pointer
    init = initFunCalc;                // set new init fn pointer

    calcExp = FunExpTree();            // build expression tree
    init();                            // initialize calculator
    cout << "\"help\" or \"quit\"\n";
    evalPrintLoop(cin, "FUNCALC>", cout);  // start calculator
};
```

The first two lines are needed only if you require your own initialization routine (see step 6). The next line sets the pointer to the expression tree. Then the calculator is initialized. Finally, tell the user about the two most important commands, and call evalPrintLoop() to begin the interaction.

Possible Extensions

There are many ways to extend REALCALC by adding new commands and symbols. You might consider doing the following:

- Add trigonometric or hyperbolic-trig functions.
- Add commands for common DOS commands like dir and type.
- Add a beep(a,b) command to simplify testing. It would beep if expression a and b were not equal. Or perhaps set a foundError flag instead of, or in addition to, beeping. The value of the flag could be set and queried like the changed flag.
- Add a valid exp command. It would run the valid() method on the resulting CalcType. Note this would be useful only if you have turned off assertion checking. Personally, I leave assertion checking on as much as possible. The computer checks values more regularly than I remember to.

The calculator could be enabled for batch execution. If the calculator was invoked with command line arguments, then evaluate those arguments as a single command using evalPrint(). That command could evaluate one expression or it could be an include command to kick off an entire sequence of operations.

An obvious direction for extension is to give the calculator a graphical user interface. I choose not to pursue this because it would complicate things and it would tend to obscure the data types themselves.

It is tempting to combine multiple data types in a single calculator. However, this produces mixed-mode expressions. Either operators must be defined for each *pair* of classes, or a run-time type checking scheme must be implemented.

The expression classes currently support single character operators. You might consider adding a full tokenizer and change the expression classes to match tokens rather than characters. Because of this limitation I was forced to use "&" rather than "&&" for logical-and in FUNCALC and AUTOCALC.

Add new expression classes:

* Add an InfixExp class that does not loop.
* Add a PostfixExp class. The only postfix operators in C++ are "++" and "−−". But since the parser does not support double character operators, I left this class out.
* Add a TrinaryInfixExp class to handle expressions like "a ? b : c".

One particularly interesting direction would be to add a compile() method to the expression classes. Rather than returning a single value, it would return a syntax tree of the expression it found. This compiled expression could then be evaluated separately. Furthermore, constant folding could compress constant expressions during parsing but leave references to variables intact. A spreadsheet built using these expression classes would want to use this approach.

Add a startScope command to dynamically allocate a new ValueScope whose parent is the current ValueScope (the value of variableScope). Any new variables would be added to this nested scope, but the scope lookup() method would still search all nested scopes. Command endScope would delete the current scope and reset to the previous scope.

Change all symbols to use parentheses even if they have no arguments, for example, pi() rather than pi. This might be less confusing to users.

Add String expressions. These could be called by include/includeChg and dos.

Source Code

File CalcIdent.hpp

```
#ifndef _CALCIDENT_HPP
#define _CALCIDENT_HPP
```

(continued)

File CalcIdent.hpp *(continued)*

```
//*********************************************************************
// TITLE: CalcIdent -- calculator identifiers
//
// PROGRAMMER: Scott N Gerard
// LANGUAGE: C++
//
// FUNCTION:
//    Define calculator identifiers classes.
//
//    Identifier  - root of all identifiers
//    Command     - identifiers that have an execute method
//    Value       - identifiers that return a value of type T
//    GlobalValue - identifiers that add themselves to a scope.
//    Variable    - values that can change their value.
//
// CHANGE LOG:
//    11Oct92 - Initial coding.  SN Gerard
//    03Mar93 - Delete Literal class.  SN Gerard
//    17Apr93 - Convert Value, Variable and GlobalValue to template
//              classes.  SN Gerard
//    24Jun93 - Rename Symbol to Identifier.  SN Gerard
//*********************************************************************
#include <assert.h>
#include <strng.h>


//*********************************************************************
// Identifier is an abstract class.
//*********************************************************************
class Identifier: public Object {
protected:
    String*    nam;
    String*    hlp;
    String*    parmhlp;

public:
    Identifier(const String& name,
        const String& help = "",
        const String& parmhelp = "");
    virtual ~Identifier();

    // return information about the identifier
    virtual const String name() const {
        assert(valid());
        return *nam;
    };

    virtual const int nameWidth()  {
        assert(valid());
        return strlen(*nam);
    };
```

```
    virtual const String help() const {
        assert(valid());
        return *hlp;
    };

    virtual const String parmhelp() const {
        assert(valid());
        return *parmhlp;
    };

    virtual BOOL isChangeable() const {
        assert(valid());
        return FALSE;
    };

    // comparison operators for sorting by name
    friend BOOL operator < (Identifier& a, Identifier& b) {
        assert(a.valid() && b.valid());
        return BOOL(*a.nam < *b.nam);
    };
    friend BOOL operator == (Identifier& a, Identifier& b) {
        assert(a.valid() && b.valid());
        return BOOL(*a.nam == *b.nam);
    };

    // standard object methods
    hashValueType hashValue() const {
        assert(valid());
        return nam->hashValue();
    };

    int isEqual(const Object& testObject) const {
        assert(valid());
        return nam == ((const Identifier& )testObject).nam;
    };
    classType isA() const { return 1234; };
    int isSortable() const {return 1; };
    char* nameOf() const { return "Identifier"; };
    void printOn( ostream& os ) const {
        assert(valid());
        os << "Identifier " << *nam;
    };
    virtual BOOL valid() const
        { return BOOL( nam != 0 ); }; };
};

//*****************************************************************
// commands contain a pointer to a function.
//*****************************************************************
class Command: public Identifier {

    typedef void (*FUNCTION)(istream& is, ostream& os);
    FUNCTION f;
```

(continued)

File CalcIdent.hpp *(continued)*

```cpp
public:
   Command(const FUNCTION fun,
      const char* name,
      const char* help  = 0,
      const char* parms = 0);

   ~Command();

   // execute the comand
   virtual void execute(istream& is, ostream& os) {
      assert( valid() );
      f(is,os);                            // call the function
   }

   void printOn( ostream& os ) const {
      assert(valid());
      os << "Command " << name();
   };
};

//*******************************************************************
// base class for identifiers with a value of type T
//*******************************************************************
template <class T>
class Value: public Identifier {
public:
   Value(
      const String& name,
      const String& help = "",
      const String& parmhelp = "")
   : Identifier(name, help, parmhelp) {};

   // return the value of the identifier.  The identifier can read more
   // characters from istream.
   virtual const T value (istream& is, ostream& os) = 0;

   int userValue;                         // available for user
};

//*******************************************************************
// Variables have changable values.
//*******************************************************************
template <class T>
class Variable: public Value<T> {
   typedef Value<T> BaseClass;

   T       val;                       // the value of the variable

public:
   Variable(const String& nam);
   Variable(const String& nam, const T& value);
```

```
   ~Variable() {};

   const T value (istream& is, ostream& os) { return val; };
   const T* value() const        { return &val; };
   void setValue (const T value) { val = value; };

   BOOL isChangeable() const { return TRUE; };

   void printOn( ostream& os ) const {
     assert(valid());
     os << "Variable " << *nam;
   };

   BOOL valid() const
       { return BOOL( BaseClass::valid() && val.valid() ); };
};

//*********************************************************************
// GlobalValues add themselves to the global scope.
//*********************************************************************
template <class T>
class GlobalValue: public Value<T> {
   typedef const T (*FUNCTION)(istream& is, ostream& os);
   FUNCTION f;

public:
   GlobalValue(
//       const FUNCTION fun,
       const T (*fun)(istream& is, ostream& os),
       const String& name,
       const String& help = "",
       const String& parmhelp = "");

   ~GlobalValue();

   virtual const T value (istream& is, ostream& os) {
       assert( valid() );
       return f(is,os);
   };
};

#endif
```

File CalcIdent.cpp

```
//*********************************************************************
// TITLE: CalcIdent -- calculator identifiers
//
// PROGRAMMER: Scott N Gerard
// LANGUAGE: C++
//
```

(continued)

File CalcIdent.cpp *(continued)*

```
// FUNCTION:
//    Define calculator identifiers classes.
//
//    Identifier
  - root of all identifiers
//    Command     - identifiers that have an execute method
//    Value       - identifiers that return a value of type T
//    GlobalValue - identifiers that add themselves to a scope.
//    Variable    - values that can change their value.
//
// CHANGE LOG:
//    ??????79 - Initial version in TINY BASIC.  SN Gerard
//    31DEC84 - Convert to Turbo Pascal from TINY BASIC version. SNG
//    09Dec90 - Convert to Modula-2.  SN Gerard
//    29Dec90 - Use hash table to speed look up of existing
//              permutations.  SN Gerard
//    27Jan91 - Change from $VERB to VERB.  This will invalidate many
//              old perm files.  SN Gerard
//    28Feb91 - Add routines to support names rather than numbers. SNG
//    15Apr91 - Improve performance of CLOSE.  SN Gerard
//    09Jul91 - Add conjugate table.  SN Gerard
//    11Oct92 - Convert to C++.  SN Gerard
//    03Mar93 - delete Literal class.  SN Gerard
//    17Apr93 - Convert Value, Variable and GlobalValue to template
//              classes.  SN Gerard
//********************************************************************


//********************************************************************
// Identifiers
//********************************************************************
Identifier::Identifier(
   const String& name,
   const String& help,
   const String& parmhelp)
   : nam(new String(name)),
     hlp(new String(help)),
     parmhlp(new String(parmhelp))
   {};

Identifier::~Identifier() {
   assert(valid());
   delete nam;
   delete hlp;
   delete parmhlp;
};


//********************************************************************
// Commands
//********************************************************************
```

```
Command::Command(
     const FUNCTION fun,
     const char* name,
     const char* help,
     const char* parmhelp)
   : Identifier(name, help, parmhelp), f(fun)
{
   commandScope.add(*this);             // add command to commandScope
};

Command::~Command() {
   commandScope.detach(*this);
   f = 0;
};

//******************************************************************
// Variables are a subclass of Values that have changable values.
// Variables are instances of this class.
//******************************************************************
template <class T>
Variable<T>::Variable(const String& nam): Value<T>(nam) {};

template <class T>
Variable<T>::Variable(const String& nam, const T& value)
   : Value<T>(nam), val(value) {};

//******************************************************************
// GlobalValues are a subclass of Values that have changable values.
// Calculator identifiers are instances of this class.
//******************************************************************
template <class T>
GlobalValue<T>::GlobalValue(
//       FUNCTION fun,
     const T (*fun)(istream& is, ostream& os),
     const String& name,
     const String& help,
     const String& parmhelp)
   : Value<T>(name, help, parmhelp), f(fun)
   { globalScope.add(*this); };

template <class T>
GlobalValue<T>::~GlobalValue() {
   assert( valid() );
   globalScope.detach(*this);
   f = 0;                               // destroy function pointer
};
```

File CalcScope.hpp

```
#ifndef _CALCSCOPE_HPP
#define _CALCSCOPE_HPP
```

(continued)

File CalcScope.hpp   *(continued)*

```
//********************************************************************
// TITLE: CalcScope -- calculator name scopes
//
// PROGRAMMER: Scott N Gerard
// LANGUAGE: C++
//
// FUNCTION:
//    Define calculator scope:
//
//    Scope          - root of all scopes.  Provides lookup by name
//    SortedScope    - maintain sorted list of names.
//    OrderedScope   - maintain names in create order
//    ValueScope     - provide lookup by value.  Need for closure and
//                     addtable kinds of commands.
//
//    Classes Identifier and Variable must already be defined.
//
// CHANGE LOG:
//    01Nov92 - Initial coding.  SN Gerard
//    17Apr83 - Convert to template classes.  SN Gerard
//********************************************************************
#include <shddel.h>
#include <dict.h>
#include <assoc.h>
#include <dlistimp.h>
#include <dbllist.h>

#include "CalcIdent.hpp"
#include "SetList.hpp"


//********************************************************************
// Scope: A basic scope of variable and/or identifier names.
//********************************************************************
template <class T>
class Scope: public TShouldDelete {
   Scope*     parent;

protected:
   Dictionary names;

   // internal routines that actually perform the work.  The public
   // versions check whether or not the operator is legal.
   virtual void _add     (Identifier& sym);
   virtual void _change  (Variable<T>& var, const T& newValue);
   virtual void _detach  (Identifier& sym);

public:
   Scope(Scope* parentScope = NULL): parent(parentScope) {};
   virtual ~Scope()              { names.flush(); };
```

```
    virtual void add      (Identifier& sym);
    virtual void change   (Variable<T>& var, const T& newValue);
    virtual void detach   (Identifier& sym);

    virtual Identifier* lookupThisScope (const String& name);
    virtual Identifier* lookup          (const String& name);

    virtual void assign  (const String& name, const T& value);

    int numIdents() const       { return names.getItemsInContainer(); };
    int nameWidth();

    // Scope::ownsElements calls operate directly on names.ownsElements
    int ownsElements()          { return names.ownsElements(); };
    void ownsElements(int del)  { names.ownsElements(del); };

    virtual void flush(DeleteType dt = DefDelete);
    void printOn( ostream& os ) const;
};

//********************************************************************
// SortedScope: A scope of variables sorted by variable name.
//********************************************************************
template <class T>
class SortedScope: public Scope<T> {
    typedef Scope<T> BaseClass;
    friend class SortedScopeIterator<T>;

protected:
    BI_ISDoubleListImp<Identifier> sortedSyms; // list of identifiers

    virtual void _add      (Identifier& sym);
    virtual void _detach   (Identifier& sym);

public:
    SortedScope(Scope<T>* parentScope = NULL): Scope<T>(parentScope) {};
    void flush(DeleteType dt = DefDelete); // delete all identifiers in scope
};

//********************************************************************
// An iterator for a SortedScope
//********************************************************************
template <class T>
class SortedScopeIterator: public BI_IDoubleListIteratorImp<Identifier> {
public:
    SortedScopeIterator(const SortedScope<T>& scope)
      :BI_IDoubleListIteratorImp<Identifier>(scope.sortedSyms) {};
};

//********************************************************************
// OrderedScope: A scope that maintains the order elements were added
//********************************************************************
```

(continued)

File CalcScope.hpp *(continued)*

```cpp
template <class T>
class OrderedScope: public Scope<T> {
   typedef Scope<T> BaseClass;
   friend class OrderedScopeIterator<T>;

protected:
   // NOTE:  The current implementation of BI_IDoubleListImp (Borland
   // C++ Ver3.0) "owns" its contents and will destruct them when
   // removed from the list.  BI_DoubleListImp does not "own" is
   // contents.
   BI_DoubleListImp<Variable<T>*> vars;

   virtual void _add      (Identifier& sym);
   virtual void _detach  (Identifier& sym);

public:
   OrderedScope(Scope<T>* parentScope = NULL): Scope<T>(parentScope) {};
   virtual void flush(DeleteType dt = DefDelete);
};

//*********************************************************************
// An iterator for a OrderedScope
//*********************************************************************
template <class T>
class OrderedScopeIterator: public BI_DoubleListIteratorImp<Variable<T>*> {
public:
   OrderedScopeIterator(const OrderedScope<T>& scope)
      : BI_DoubleListIteratorImp<Variable<T>*>(scope.vars) {};
};

//*********************************************************************
// A scope with lookup by value
//*********************************************************************
template <class T>
class ValueScope: public OrderedScope<T> {
   typedef OrderedScope<T> BaseClass;

protected:
   virtual void _add      (Identifier& sym);
   virtual void _change  (Variable<T>& var, const T& newValue);
   virtual void _detach  (Identifier& sym);

public:
   // values is public because many different commands need access to it
   SetOfList<Variable<T>,T> values;  // value to variable mapping

   ValueScope(Scope<T>* parentScope = NULL)
      : OrderedScope<T>(parentScope)
   {
      values.ownsElements(0);
   };
```

```
      // return the identifier with specified value or NOOBJECT
      const Identifier* getAny (const T& value);
      unsigned valueCount  (const T& value) const;

      virtual void flush(DeleteType dt = DefDelete);
      void printOn( ostream& os ) const;
};

#endif
```

File CalcScope.cpp

```
//**********************************************************************
// TITLE: CalcScope -- calculator name scopes
//
// PROGRAMMER: Scott N Gerard
// LANGUAGE: C++
//
// FUNCTION:
//    Define calculator scope:
//
//    Scope        - root of all scopes.  Provides lookup by name
//    SortedScope  - maintain sorted list of names.
//    OrderedScope - maintain names in create order
//    ValueScope   - provide lookup by value.  Need for closure and
//                   addtable kinds of commands.
//
// CHANGE LOG:
//    01Nov92 - Initial coding.  SN Gerard
//    17Apr93 - Convert to template classes.  SN Gerard
//**********************************************************************
#include "SetList.cpp"

//**********************************************************************
// Scope
//**********************************************************************
template <class T>
void Scope<T>::_add(Identifier& sym) {
   Association* assocp =
      new Association(*new String(sym.name()), sym);
   names.add(*assocp);
};

template <class T>
void Scope<T>::_change (Variable<T>& var, const T& newValue) {
   var.setValue(newValue);
};

template <class T>
void Scope<T>::_detach(Identifier& sym) {
   Association* assoc = &names.lookup(sym.name());
```

(continued)

File CalcScope.cpp   *(continued)*

```
      names.detach(*assoc);
};

template <class T>
void Scope<T>::add(Identifier& sym) {
   _add(sym);
};

template <class T>
void Scope<T>::change (Variable<T>& var, const T& newValue) {
   // change the current value of the variable.
   if (newValue != *var.value() ) {
      valueChanged = TRUE;
      _change(var, newValue);
   };
};

template <class T>
void Scope<T>::detach(Identifier& sym) {
   if (sym.isChangeable())
      _detach(sym);
};

template <class T>
Identifier* Scope<T>::lookupThisScope(const String& name) {
   Association* assoc = &names.lookup(name);     // is it in our dict?
   if (*assoc != NOOBJECT)
      return (Identifier*) &assoc->value();
   else
      return (Identifier*) &NOOBJECT;
};

template <class T>
Identifier* Scope<T>::lookup(const String& name) {
   Identifier* symp = lookupThisScope(name);
   if (*symp != NOOBJECT)
      return symp;
   else if (parent != NULL)
      return parent->lookup(name);
   else
      return (Identifier*) &NOOBJECT;
};

template <class T>
void Scope<T>::assign (const String& name, const T& value) {
   Identifier* symp = lookupThisScope(name);
   if ( *symp == NOOBJECT)                 // create a new Variable
      add( *new Variable<T>(name, value) );

   else if ( symp->isChangeable() )      // change existing variable
      change( *(Variable<T>*) symp, value);
```

```
      else
         cout << "Assignement not allowed to " << symp->nameOf() << endl;
};

template <class T>
int Scope<T>::nameWidth () {
   int width = 0;
   for (ContainerIterator* i = &names.initIterator(); *i; ++*i ) {
      Association* assocp = (Association*) &i->current();
      Identifier* symp = (Identifier*) &assocp->value();
      int symWidth = symp->nameWidth();
      if ( width < symWidth )
         width = symWidth;
   };
   return width;
};

template <class T>
void Scope<T>::flush( TShouldDelete::DeleteType dt) {
   names.flush(dt);
};

template <class T>
void Scope<T>::printOn( ostream& os ) const {
   os << "Scope {\n";
   names.printOn(os);
   os << "\n}";
};

//*********************************************************************
// SortedScope:  This scope does not own its contents, they are owned
// in the base class.
//*********************************************************************
template <class T>
void SortedScope<T>::_add(Identifier& sym) {
   sortedSyms.add(&sym);
   BaseClass::_add(sym);
};

template <class T>
void SortedScope<T>::_detach(Identifier& sym) {
   sortedSyms.detach(&sym);
   BaseClass::_detach(sym);
};

template <class T>
void SortedScope<T>::flush( TShouldDelete::DeleteType dt) {
   sortedSyms.flush(dt);
   BaseClass::flush(dt);
};
```

(continued)

File CalcScope.cpp *(continued)*

```cpp
//*********************************************************************
// OrderedScope
//*********************************************************************
template <class T>
void OrderedScope<T>::_add(Identifier& sym) {
   Variable<T>* varp = (Variable<T>*) &sym;
   vars.addAtTail(varp);
   BaseClass::_add(sym);
};

template <class T>
void OrderedScope<T>::_detach(Identifier& sym) {
   Variable<T>* varp = (Variable<T>*) &sym;
   vars.detach(varp);
   BaseClass::_detach(sym);
};

template <class T>
void OrderedScope<T>::flush( TShouldDelete::DeleteType dt ) {
   vars.flush(dt);
   BaseClass::flush(dt);
};


//*********************************************************************
// ValueScope
//*********************************************************************
template <class T>
void ValueScope<T>::_add(Identifier& sym) {
   Variable<T>* varp = (Variable<T>*) &sym;
   values.insert(*varp);
   BaseClass::_add(sym);
};

template <class T>
void ValueScope<T>::_change (Variable<T>& var, const T& newValue) {
   values.remove(var);
   BaseClass::_change( var, newValue);
   values.insert(var);
};

template <class T>
void ValueScope<T>::_detach(Identifier& sym) {
   Variable<T>* varp = (Variable<T>*) &sym;
   values.remove(*varp);
   BaseClass::_detach(sym);
};

template <class T>
const Identifier* ValueScope<T>::getAny (const T& value) {
```

```cpp
    Variable<T>* searchFor = new Variable<T>("temp", value);
    const Identifier* found = values.getAny(*searchFor);
    delete searchFor;
    return found;
};

template <class T>
unsigned ValueScope<T>::valueCount (const T& value) const {
    Variable<T>* searchFor = new Variable<T>("temp", value);
    unsigned count = values.valueCount(*searchFor);
    delete searchFor;
    return count;
};

template <class T>
void ValueScope<T>::flush( TShouldDelete::DeleteType dt ) {
    vars.flush(dt);
    values.flush(dt);
    BaseClass::flush(dt);
};

template <class T>
void ValueScope<T>::printOn( ostream& os ) const {
    os << "ValueScope {\n";
    values.printOn(os);
    os << "}\n}";
};
```

File RealCalc.cpp

```cpp
//********************************************************************
// TITLE: RealCalc -- calculator for reals
//
// PROGRAMMER: Scott N Gerard
// LANGUAGE: C++
//
// FUNCTION:
//     Calculator for reals (doubles).
//
// CHANGE LOG:
//     11Oct92 - Initial coding.  SN Gerard
//     02Mar93 - Add control-break handling. SN Gerard
//********************************************************************
#include <iostream.h>
#include <iomanip.h>
#include <ctype.h>
#include <limits.h>
#include <math.h>
#include <new.h>
#include "Bool.hpp"
```

(continued)

File RealCalc.cpp *(continued)*

```cpp
// This class is needed so we can add methods hash & valid to doubles.
class Real {
public:
   Real(double real=0.0): r(real) {};
   operator double() const { return r; };

   unsigned hash () const { return unsigned(r) % UINT_MAX; };
   BOOL valid() const { return TRUE; };

   double r;
};


typedef Real CalcType;


#include "Calc.hpp"


Exp<CalcType>* calcExp;


// Define the scopes
SortedScope<CalcType> globalScope;                     // Values
SortedScope<CalcType> commandScope;                    // Commands
ValueScope<CalcType>  variableScope(&globalScope);     // Variables


#include "Calc.cpp"

//*********************************************************************
// User expressions
//*********************************************************************
CalcType getLiteral (istream& is, ostream& os) {
   double val;
   is >> val;
   if ( !is )
      os << "Invalid Literal\n";
   return val;
};


int isLiteral (const char ch) {
   return ( '0' <= ch && ch <= '9' || ch == '.'
         || ch == '+' || ch == '-');
};


CalcType getVariable (istream& is, ostream& os)
   { return getVarInScope(is, os, variableScope); }


//*********************************************************************
// Build Expression tree for Reals
//*********************************************************************
InfixExp <CalcType>  addExp;
InfixExp <CalcType>  mulExp;
```

```
PrefixExp<CalcType>  unaryExp;
GroupExp <CalcType>  groupExp;
UserExp  <CalcType>  priExp;

CalcType add    (CalcType a, CalcType b) { return a.r + b.r; };
CalcType sub    (CalcType a, CalcType b) { return a.r - b.r; };
CalcType mul    (CalcType a, CalcType b) { return a.r * b.r; };
CalcType div    (CalcType a, CalcType b) { return a.r / b.r; };

CalcType uplus  (CalcType a) { return +a.r; };
CalcType uminus (CalcType a) { return -a.r; };
CalcType not    (CalcType a) { return !a.r; };

Exp<CalcType>* RealExpTree () {

   addExp.first(mulExp);
   addExp.add( '+', mulExp, add, "addition" );
   addExp.add( '-', mulExp, sub, "subtraction", TRUE );

   mulExp.first(unaryExp);
   mulExp.add( '*', unaryExp, mul, "multiplication" );
   mulExp.add( '/', unaryExp, div, "division", TRUE );

   unaryExp.add( '+', unaryExp, uplus,  "unary plus" );
   unaryExp.add( '-', unaryExp, uminus, "unary minus" );
   unaryExp.add( '!', unaryExp, not,    "logical-not" );
   unaryExp.add( groupExp, TRUE);

   groupExp.add( '(', addExp, ')', "Parentheses" );
   groupExp.add( '[', addExp, ']', "Brackets" );
   groupExp.add( '{', addExp, '}', "Braces" );
   groupExp.add( priExp, TRUE);

   priExp.add( isLiteral, getLiteral,  "double literals: -9.15" );
   priExp.add( isIdent,   getVariable, "variables and symbols" );

   return &addExp;
};

//*****************************************************************
// set precision
//*****************************************************************
void setPrecision (istream& is, ostream& os) {
   int digits;
   is >> digits;
   if ( !matchEof(is,os) ) return;

   os << setprecision(digits);
};
Command setPrecisionCmd( setPrecision, "precision",
   "set floating point precision", "int" );
```

(continued)

File RealCalc.cpp   *(continued)*

```cpp
//*********************************************************************
// Return Pi.  From CRC Standard Mathematical Tables. 17th ed. 1969
//*********************************************************************
const CalcType pi (istream& is, ostream& os) {
    return 3.141592653589793;
};
GlobalValue<CalcType> piVal(pi, "pi", "return the value of pi", "" );

//*********************************************************************
// Return e.  From CRC Standard Mathematical Tables. 17th ed. 1969
//*********************************************************************
const CalcType e (istream& is, ostream& os) {
    return 2.718281828459045;
};
GlobalValue<CalcType> eVal(e, "e", "return the value of e", "" );

//*********************************************************************
// Natural log
//*********************************************************************
const CalcType logReal (istream& is, ostream& os) {
    CalcType value;

    if ( !match(is,os,'(') ) return value;
    value = calcExp->eval(is, os);
    if ( !match(is,os,')') ) return value;

    return log(value);
};
GlobalValue<CalcType> logVal( logReal, "log",
    "natural logarithm", "(exp)");

//*********************************************************************
// Exponential
//*********************************************************************
const CalcType expReal (istream& is, ostream& os) {
    CalcType value;

    if ( !match(is,os,'(') ) return value;
    value = calcExp->eval(is, os);
    if ( !match(is,os,')') ) return value;

    return exp(value);
};
GlobalValue<CalcType> expVal( expReal, "exp",
    "exponential", "(exp)");

void main() {
    calcExp = RealExpTree();
    init();
    cout << "\"help\" or \"quit\"\n";
    evalPrintLoop(cin, "REALCALC>", cout);
};
```

10

Functions

Functions are the workhorse of mathematics—they are used everywhere. They naturally show up in programs, and it is worthwhile designing a C++ class to work with them.

C++ uses the term "function" for a block of code. To avoid confusion in this chapter, I will use the term "routine" for a block of C++ code.

A completely general description of mathematical functions would be able to handle real-valued functions like $f(x) = x^2$ and $g(x) = \sin(x) + \cos(x)$. Such a C++ class would have to deal with functions symbolically. PC packages like Maple, Mathematica, and Derive can be used for this level of flexibility. But many applications do not need that much generality.

In this chapter, I present a C++ class for functions with a **finite, discrete domain.** They are finite because their domain is a finite set. They are discrete because the domain set can be represented as integers. Functions with a real domain are neither finite (there are an infinite set of reals in any range) nor discrete (between any two reals is another real). But simplifying to functions with a finite, discrete domain yields a class that is quite useful. They describe character translation tables, finite state machines, and semigroups, and are the foundation for Chapter 12, on permutations.

Some class libraries contain a class usually called a "Map." While similar in some ways, the function classes support different operations than a classic Map, including componentwise operations like $f(x) * g(x)$, and function composition $g(f(x))$.

Background

As a simple refresher, a function is a mapping between two sets called the **domain** set and the **range** set. Every element in the domain is assigned a *single* element in the range. The domain and range of a function f are defined with the notation

$$f\text{:}domain \mapsto range$$

When the domain and range sets are understood, a similar notation is used to show how each element in the domain is mapped to an element in the range. For example, the square function could be written

$$square\text{: } x \mapsto x^2$$

Since we are concerned only with finite, discrete functions, we can list the value of the function by listing the range element for each domain element.

Take the example of the function "square" whose domain is the set of integers between 0 and 5, and whose range is the set of integers between 0 and 25. In this case, the domain and range sets have the same type (integer), but are not the same since they have different elements. Element x in the domain is assigned the value x^2 in the range. Square is written

$$square = \begin{bmatrix} domain\text{: } 0 & 1 & 2 & 3 & 4 & 5 \\ range\text{: } 0 & 1 & 4 & 9 & 16 & 25 \end{bmatrix}$$

This "two-row" notation is read from top to bottom. The elements in the top row are almost always sorted. The function takes the element at the top of each column and moves, or maps, it to the element at the bottom of the same column. Because the first column has a 0 on top and a 0 on the bottom, square maps 0 to 0. In C++ this is written square(0) = 0. Reading the other columns, square(1) = 1, square(2) = 4, ..., square(5) = 25.

Two-row notation is a little verbose, but it simplifies some discussions. But since the domain elements in the top row are sorted, they don't add any information. Dropping the top row, square can be written more efficiently in "one-row" or simply "row" notation.

$$square = \begin{bmatrix} 0 & 1 & 4 & 9 & 16 & 25 \end{bmatrix}$$

The limitation to finite functions is now quite clear; we cannot list every value of a function with an infinite domain.

The domain and range do not have to be mathematical values like integers. The function age:people $\mapsto$ integer maps each person to their current age. The function parmCount:routine $\mapsto$ integer is a function from C++ routines to the number of their parameters.

If we went no further, our function class would not be substantially different than a classic Map class, which is present in many class libraries. But many functions can be added, subtracted, multiplied, and so on. Specifically, we can create a new function $h(x) = f(x) + g(x)$. Clearly, $f(x)$ and $g(x)$ must have exactly the same domain. Addition of functions requires addition of range elements. If the ranges of f and g are integers, then function addition is based on integer addition at each domain element.

$$square2 = square + square$$

$$square2 = \begin{bmatrix} 0 & 2 & 8 & 18 & 32 & 50 \end{bmatrix}$$

Similarly, subtraction, multiplication, and division of integer functions are defined by subtracting, multiplying, or dividing range elements. These are **componentwise** operations. However, functions whose range is "vehicle" (presumably) cannot be added.

Both $f(x)$ and $g(x)$ must define a range element for *every* domain element. The domain of a classic Map can change so dynamically that it is unlikely that two maps have the same domain.

Functions can also be **composed**. That is, we can define a new function $p(x) = g(f(x))$. $p(x)$ maps x first through $f(x)$ and takes that result and maps it through $g(x)$. A classic Map does not support either componentwise operations or function composition.

Class Overview

DSet Class

The domain of every function, and the range of all FunDRngImp functions and its derivatives, must be a finite, discrete set of values. The template class DSet embodies this concept. A DSet knows how to convert an object of class T (the template parameter) back and forth to unsigned integers. The DSet class hierarchy supports discrete sets of integers, enumerations, and floating point numbers that follow linear, logarithmic, exponential, and power curves (see Figure 10.1).

Fun Class

Functions use a handle/body framework (see "Handles and Bodies" in Chapter 5). The Fun classes are handles to the FunImp classes where the real work goes on. Figure 10.2 shows the function class hierarchy. FunImp is an abstract class, so you can't create objects of this type.

FunImp sets up the common methods for all function implementations. Conceptually, a FunImp is an array of range values. There is one range value for every element of the function's domain. The function's domain DSet handles any conversion from external domain values the user works with (say floating point values) to unsigned integers used to index the internal array added by derived classes.

Fun and FunImp make no assumptions about the range type. It can be integer, floating point or Employee.

FunGRng Class

FunGRng is a concrete class that, like Fun, makes almost no assumptions about its range type. FunGRng stands for "functions with general range." I like to pronounce it

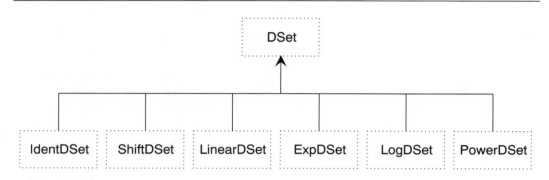

FIGURE 10.1
Domain set class hierarchy.

"fungy-range." FunGRngs work well when the range cannot be mapped to unsigned integers, or when you know very little about the range type. You can also use it when you don't need member functions rank(), unrank() or random(). FUNCALC is a calculator for FunGRng objects.

FunDRng Class

Concrete class FunDRng is for functions with a finite, discrete *range*. Therefore, its range type must be convertible to unsigned integers using a DSet. I like to pronounce this class "fundy-range" or even "fun-deranged."

FunDRngs are best suited for functions that map to enumerations, or when the function will be involved in many composition operations. You can use a floating point type as the range type, but the values will be rounded (by the range DSet) to a finite set of values. FunDRng introduces the member functions rank(), unrank() and random().

AutoFun Class

AutoFun is a function that maps a set to itself. That is, its domain set is exactly the same as its range set. Given this restriction, function composition can be—and is—made a member function of AutoFun.

While there seems to be no commonly accepted name for this kind of function many functions have exactly this property. The term "auto" is supposed to suggest the fact that it maps a set to itself. As we will see in the sample application section below, AutoFuns describe translation tables, finite state machines, and semigroups. AUTOCALC is a calculator for AutoFuns.

Perm Class

Permutations are specialized AutoFuns; they are functions from a set to itself. Whereas AutoFuns can be any function of a set to itself, permutations are one-to-one

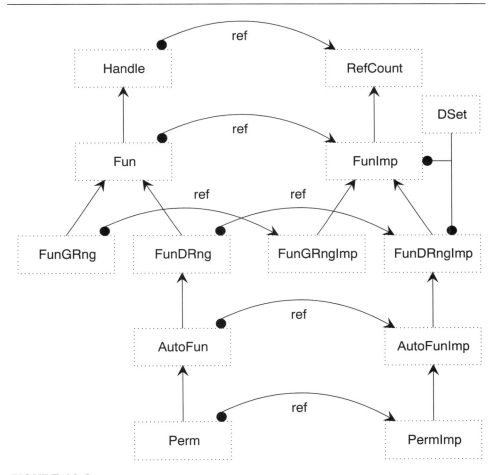

FIGURE 10.2
Function classes.

and onto functions. Therefore, we can define the "inverse" of a permutation function (under function composition). Chapter 12 is devoted to looking at this special class of functions. PERMCALC is a calculator for permutations.

Element Class

Many of the calculators on the diskette manipulate data types that have subpieces (elements): AUTOCALC from this chapter; PERMCALC from Chapter 12; and PARTCALC from Chapter 14. They use the common class Element as the data type for their subpieces. AUTOCALC and PERMCALC use Element as the domain and range type.

An object of type Element is basically an integer between 0 and *n*. But it can be read and written in three different formats. It can be a decimal integer, the letters A, B, ... Z, AA, AB, ... ZZ, AAA, ..., or a list of user-defined names. The format is controlled by the calculator element commands.

Function Calculator

FUNCALC, a calculator for FunGRng function, is based on the calculator classes in Chapter 9. It allows you to interactively play with the FunGRng class without having to write any programs. For complicated problems you can either extend FUNCALC or you can write a new program using the C++ FunGRng class (see "Writing You Own Calculator" in Chapter 9 for more information). FUNCALC has a lot of infrastructure, so a separate program will be much smaller.

Start the function calculator by entering FUNCALC at any DOS command line.

```
C>FUNCALC
```

Let's build a FunGRng "square" that maps the integers 0..5 to 0..25. First we need to define the domain DSet. By default FUNCALC sets the domain to the 25 integers $0 \le x \le 25$. You change this with the domain command.

```
FUNCALC>domain I 5
```

The "I" means the domain will be an IdentDSet, and 5 is the largest element in the domain (0..5). Now, whenever any new functions are constructed, they will have this default domain. Note that setting the domain size to 32,000 will terminate FUNCALC when it tries to allocate its first function due to a lack of memory.

Declare the square function, and assign it a value.

```
FUNCALC>square = [0 1 4 9 16 25]
square=[0 1 4 9 16 25]
```

Functions can be combined in expressions. For example, given function square, we can compute

```
FUNCALC>square2 = square + square
square2=[0 2 8 18 32 50]
FUNCALC>fourth = square * square
fourth=[0 1 16 81 256 625]
```

Functions can be added, subtracted, multiplied and divided. They can also be logically and-ed (&), or-ed (|) and negated (!) where 0 is FALSE and anything else is TRUE.

FUNCALC adds more commands to those in REALCALC (see "Common Commands" in Chapter 9):

isConstant   Evaluates an expression and prints 1 if it is a constant function. Otherwise, it prints 0.

get   Maps a domain element through the function, and prints the result.

```
FUNCALC>get(square,2)
4
```

compare   Command that evaluates two function expressions and compares them. It prints either "Equal" or "Not Equal."

FUNCALC adds two new symbols that can be used in expressions:

constant   Returns a constant function.

```
FUNCALC>=constant(4)
[4 4 4 4 4]
```

set   Symbol that returns a modified function where one domain element has been changed.

```
FUNCALC>=set(square,4,99)
[0 1 4 9 99 25]
```

C++ Source Code

Functions in C++ source code mirror FUNCALC commands. They are template classes. The first template parameter is the type of the domain elements; the second is the type of the range elements. The domain type can be any type, but it must be a convertible to an unsigned integer using a DSet. The range type can be anything: integers, floats, employees, whatever.

Both domain and range types must support iostream input and output with operators << and >>. In addition, the range type must have a default constructor, support assignment and support operator != (not equal).

Let's code the square example above in C++. The FunGRng.hpp and FunGRng.cpp files on the diskette contain the definition and implementation for FunGRng functions. Their inheritance relationships are shown in Figure 10.2.

```
#include <iostream.h>
#include "FunGRng.cpp"

void main() {
   IdentDSet<double>    domain(5);

   FunGRng<double,double> square(domain, "[0 1 4 9 16 25]" );
   cout << square << '\n';
};
```

First we need a DSet for the domain. A simple IdentDSet of doubles works nicely for this example. It creates a DSet whose values are $0.0, 1.0, 2.0, \ldots 5.0$.

The square function is a FunGRng. The template parameters are the domain and range types, which are both double. The initial value of square is specified on the constructor. Function literals are null-terminated character strings, so they must be enclosed in double quotes. iostream operators $<<$ and $>>$ read and write functions using the same syntax used for literals.

Function constructors always require the domain DSet (and range DSet for FunDRngs). Different constructors initialize the function

- to a constant value from a string literal.
- from a user-defined C++ routine.
- from an existing function object.

The calculator classes require a default constructor, so the function handle classes provide one that initializes the handle pointer to null. The first use of a handle class that contains a null pointer will initialize the handle class with a user-defined, default function. The variable Fun::defaultFun points to the default function handle, and you can change it at any point within your program. It *must* be set before the first reference to a null handle class.

```
Fun<int,int>      f1, f2;        // = null pointer
IdentDSet<int>    domain(5);     // domain = 0..5
FunGRng<int,int> g(domain);

f1.get(3);                       // illegal
f1 = g;                          // assign a value to f1
f1.get(3);                       // OK now

f2.get(3);                       // illegal
Fun::defaultFun = g;             // initialize default function
f2.get(3);                       // OK now
```

In the first and third calls to get(), f1 and f2 are null and defaultFun has not been set. Operations on f1 are legal after it has been initialized with g. Operations on any null handle class are legal after defaultFun has been set.

Function expressions are straightforward. However, since FunGRng does not assume its range type supports arithmetic operations, we have a small amount of extra work.

```
double addDouble (const double a, const double b) { return a + b; };
double mulDouble (const double a, const double b) { return a * b; };

FunGRng<double,double>  square2(domain), fourth(domain);

square2 = component( square, addDouble, square);
fourth  = component( square, mulDouble, square);
```

First we declare C++ routines to add and multiply two range elements. Then component() is called to combine square with itself in two different ways.

As a last example, let's build a function called Sin whose domain is the 9 angles (in radians) that are multiples of 45 degrees, between 0 and 180 degrees. LinearDSet is perfect for the domain DSet.

```
#include <math.h>
#include <iostream.h>
#include <iomanip.h>
#include "FunGRng.cpp"

double pi=3.1416;
LinearDSet<double>   domain(0,pi,9);

void main() {
   FunGRng<double,double>  Sin(domain,sin);
   cout << setprecision(2);
   cout << Sin << '\n';
};
```

The constructor for Sin specifies the standard math function sin, which is called for each of the 9 angles in the domain, and those values are used to initialize Sin. The output is

```
[0 0.38 0.71 0.92 1 0.92 0.71 0.38 -7.35e-06]
```

A **constant function** has the same range value over its entire domain. Class Fun has both a constructor for constant functions, as well as a member function constant(). Class member isConstant() returns TRUE if the function is constant.

```
FunGRng<double,double>   zero(domain);   // use default range ctor
FunGRng<double,double>   two(domain,2); // as a constructor
two.constant(2);                        // or as a member function
```

FUNCALC's constant() symbol returns a constant function.

```
FUNCALC>two = constant(2)
two=[2 2 2 2 2]
FUNCALC>isConstant two
TRUE
```

Member function, and FUNCALC command, compare() compares two functions. It returns TRUE if corresponding domain elements have the same range value. If two functions are different at even one domain point, the functions are not equal. It is easy to consider other ways to compare two functions that would return more information. For example, you might consider returning a TotalCompare (total comparison) or PartCompare (partial comparison) type. But these usually assume various operators (like <) are defined on the range type. Fun operators == and != are inline calls to compare().

There are a number of methods that work with individual elements. Method get() takes a domain element and returns the range value to which it is mapped. Method

geti() is similar, but it takes an unsigned integer. geti() is used internally since it eliminates conversions through the domain DSet. Operator() is equivalent to get() and has a
more familiar look. set() changes the range value for a specific domain element, and
can be used to touch up a nearly correct function, or to build a function from scratch.
seti(), like geti(), takes an unsigned integer rather than a value of the domain type.

```
FunGRng<double,double>  f(domain);

f.set(5,12);                      // map 5 to 12
cout << 5 << " is mapped to " << f(5)      << "\n";
cout << 5 << " is mapped to " << f.get(5) << "\n";
```

In FUNCALC, command get and symbol set get and change functions.

Method domainSet() returns the DSet used to convert domain values. Note that a
function makes a copy of the DSet passed on the constructor. Therefore, you must delete the DSet you pass on the constructor.

DSet Class

Every application does not call for functions with the evenly spaced domain elements
produced by LinearDSet. The DSet class hierarchy provides a number of different ways
to convert domain values to the unsigned integers required by FunImp's implementation.

The DSet classes are template classes that convert between the template parameter class and unsigned integers. DSets allow the user to work with the domain type
while FunImp's internals work with unsigned integers.

Each DSet makes increasing demands on its template class. IdentDSet requires only
assignment to and from unsigned integers. ShiftDSet requires addition and subtraction
on the template type. LinearDSet requires multiplication and division. ExpDSet,
LogDSet, and PowerDSet require functions exp(), log(), and pow()—like those defined in math.h—to be defined on the template type. Data types that do not provide,
and do not require, all operations can live nicely with the simple DSet classes.

While IdentDSets can be defined for integers, floating point, enumerations, and
many user-defined classes, ExpDSet, LogDSet, and PowerDSet are essentially limited
to floating point types. Since exp(), log(), and pow() in math.h work specifically on
doubles, you will need to define additional versions before you can use these DSets for
long double types.

In the following sections, t is a variable of type T (the template parameter) and u
is an unsigned integer; a and b are constants computed by the constructors.

IdentDSet Class

This class converts domain values by simple assignment. So a floating point 1.0 is
mapped to unsigned 1, and vice versa. In addition, floating point numbers truncate on
assignment to integral types so floating point 1.9 also maps to unsigned 1.

$$t = u$$

The IdentDSet constructor specifies the largest element in the set. Zero is always the smallest element in the set.

The default domain DSet for `FUNCALC` is set with the `domain` command followed by "I" or "i" for an IdentDSet followed by the highest value in the DSet.

`FUNCALC>domain I` <u>`last`</u>

ShiftDSet Class

A ShiftDSet contains every integral element between the first and last values specified on the constructor. This set is nice for functions whose domain is the years 1950 though 2000. Internally, it simply adds and subtracts the first element during conversions, so it is quite fast.

$$t = u + \mathit{first}$$

A ShiftDSet is declared in `FUNCALC` as

`FUNCALC>domain S` <u>`first`</u> <u>`last`</u>

LinearDSet Class

This set is similar to ShiftDSet but also allows domain values to be something other than one unit apart. The LinearDSet constructor takes the first and last elements in the set, and a count of the number of elements in the set (including first and last). It uses a linear transformation for conversions, and that requires the domain type to support multiplication and division.

$$t = au + b$$

The constructor computes the proper values of a and b. First can be larger than last. In `FUNCALC`, a LinearDSet is declared as

`FUNCALC>domain L` <u>`first`</u> <u>`last`</u> <u>`count`</u>

ExpDSet Class

This class uses an exponential equation to convert elements. Like LinearDSet, its constructor specifies the first and last elements in the set, and the number of elements in the set. However, the points are not equally spaced. The first and last values must have the same sign.

$$t = be^{au}$$

It is declared as

```
FUNCALC>domain E first last count
```

LogDSet Class

This class uses a logarithmic equation to convert elements. Its constructor specifies the first and last elements in the set, and the number of elements in the set.

$$t = a\log(++u) + b$$

u is incremented in this equation to avoid log(0), which is negative infinity. LogDSets are declared as

```
FUNCALC>domain G first last count
```

PowerDSet Class

PowerDSet converts elements using a power curve equation. Its constructor also specifies the first and last elements, and the number of elements in the set. The first and last values must have the same sign.

$$t = b(++u)^a$$

u must be incremented here too so that constants a and b can be found to match $u = 0$ with the first value in the domain.

```
FUNCALC>domain P first last count
```

Component Operations

After mapping a domain value to a range value, the most common operations on functions are componentwise addition, subtraction, multiplication, and division. That is, function h is the sum of functions f and g when

$$h(x) = f(x) + g(x) \quad \text{for all } x$$

Function addition is not part of Fun's class interface because addition may not be defined for the range type. Instead, the component() method allows functions to be combined with a user-defined routine. Function addition is then

```
FunGRng<Dom, Rng>  f(domain), g(domain), h(domain);

Rng addRng(const Rng a, const Rng b) { return a + b; };

h = component(f, addRng, g);
```

Function subtraction and so forth are handled in a similar way. The mathematical properties of component() are dependent on the user routine. $f + g$ is commutative and associative if and only if the user routine has those properties.

There are both friend and member function versions of component() that operate on a single function with a unary operator.

```
Rng notRng (const Rng a) { return !a; };

h = component(f, notRng);
```

FUNCALC, since its range type is known to be double, does support function addition (+), subtraction (−), multiplication (∗), and division (/). It also supports the logical operations and (&), or (|), and not (!). The "and" and "or" operators are single characters (& and |) rather than double characters (&& and ||) due to limitations in the parsing code. A full tokenizing parser would be needed to fix this shortcoming. Command helpExp shows the full list of operators, and their precedences (see "Possible Extensions" in Chapter 9).

FunDRng Class

FunDRngs are functions with a finite, discrete domain and range. That is, their range values must be convertible to unsigned integers. So it is not surprising FunDRng constructors also need a range DSet. Every element in the range does not have to be used. The only requirement is every range element that is used must be part of the range DSet.

FunDRng adds three member functions. rank() converts a function to a unique long integer, and unrank() reverses the conversion. Member random() returns a random function. All three of these functions depend on knowing the number of elements in the range set. The rank value is between 0 and (domain size) ∗ (range size) − 1. If you try to compute rank() of a function with a large domain or a large range, integer overflow will occur. random(), however, can handle FunDRngs with large domains and ranges because it is not subject to integer overflow.

There is no calculator for FunDRngs because it is possible to use many different range DSets. While it might be possible to write a calculator that has a scope for DSet values, this is left as an exercise for the reader (one approach would add an Ordered-Scope of DSet values and then build FunDRngs using user-defined domain and range DSets). Another problem with writing a FunDRng calculator is FunDRngs become most powerful when different types are used for different FunDRngs.

Function Composition

Function composition merges two functions quite differently than the componentwise operation. A new function $h(x)$ is the composition of functions $f(x)$ and $g(x)$ when

$$h(x) = g(f(x)) \quad \text{for all} \, x$$

The range of *f* must be a subset of the domain of *g*. The domain of *h* is the domain of *f*, and the range of *h* is the range of *g*. *h* maps any element *x* first through *f* and then maps the result through *g*.

Following many mathematical texts, this is often written as $h = f{\circ}g$. Notice that *f* and *g* are reversed in this notation. This notation makes sense if you write *f(x)* as *(x)f* with the function name on the right. Then $f{\circ}g = h$ is just $((x)f)g = (x)h$.

Function composition is associative. That is, for any three functions *f*, *g* and *h*:

$$(f{\circ}g){\circ}h = f{\circ}(g{\circ}h)$$

It is not, in general, commutative, nor is there an inverse to composition.

In the C++ classes, function composition is a routine with three Fun parameters: *f*, *g* and *h*. Each of these three functions is a template class with a domain and range class.

```
template <class R, class S, class T>
void compose (
   const Fun<R,S>& f,
   const Fun<S,T>& g,
         Fun<R,T>& h);
```

R is the domain of *f* and *h*, S is the range of *f* and the domain of *g*, and T is the range of *g* and *h*. *f* will be evaluated only at points in the domain of *h*, and *g* will be evaluated only at points in the range of *f*.

Because of C++'s rules for template resolution (Stroustrup, 1991, §r. 14.4), template functions match function calls only where the template parameters *exactly* match the function arguments. So a template function that takes three Funs will not match calls that specify derived classes, say three FunDRngs. There are two ways to get around this problem. The first is to cast all derived classes to the base class like this:

```
FunDRng<R,S> f(rDSet, sDSet);
FunDRng<S,T> g(sDSet, tDSet);
FunDRng<R,T> h(rDSet, tDSet);

compose( (Fun<R,S>&) f, (Fun<R,S>&) g, (Fun<R,S>&) h );
```

The second way is to define more compose() routines that take derived types and expand to an inline call to the compose of Funs. Since you will most likely be composing functions of the same derived class, there are versions of compose tailored to Fun-GRng and FunDRng. AutoFun and its derived class Perm do not need a special version of compose() because they have compose() as a member function. Since AutoFuns map a set to itself, the first AutoFun forces R = S, and the second forces S = T. So there is only one template type and it matches the template type of AutoFun.

AUTOCALC **and AutoFun**

AUTOCALC is a calculator for AutoFuns. Our discussion will be in terms of AUTOCALC, but the primitive operations apply to the AutoFun C++ class in the obvious way.

AUTOCALC manipulates AutoFuns with a domain and range of type Element (see "Element Class" on page 193). It shares much of the code with the other calculators, but it also adds features specific to AutoFuns. The most important extension is the addition of operator "^" for function composition.

```
AUTOCALC>domain I 4
AUTOCALC>f=[0 4 3 2 1]
AUTOCALC>g=[4 3 1 1 2]
AUTOCALC>=f ^ g
[4 2 1 1 3]
```

The **identity** AutoFun maps every element to itself.

$$identity = \begin{bmatrix} 0 & 1 & 2 & 3 & 4 & 5 \\ 0 & 1 & 2 & 3 & 4 & 5 \end{bmatrix}$$

This simple AutoFun plays the same role as 1 does for real number multiplication. When you want to multiply a list of numbers together, initialize the product to 1; when you want to compose a list of AutoFuns together, initialize the product to identity.

Many of the AUTOCALC specific commands are related to function composition.

ident
This symbol returns the identity function for composition. Any function f, when composed with the identity function, is unchanged. That is, f ^ ident $= f$. The identity maps every element of the domain to itself.

```
AUTOCALC>=ident
[0 1 2 3 4 5]
```

isIdent
This command evaluates a function expression and determines whether or not it is the identity function.

power
Symbol power takes a function expression and an integer exponent as arguments. It returns the expression composed with itself exponent times. A function to the 0-th power returns the identity. Thus power$(f, 0)$ = ident, power$(f, 1)$ = f, power$(f, 2)$ = f ^ f, power$(f, 3)$ = f ^ f ^ f, ...

Since AutoFuns do not have inverses in general, it is an error to specify a negative exponent. PERMCALC removes this restriction.

Class AutoFun has two power member functions. Member power() is a mutator; it changes the value of *this. Member powerPure() is a pure function. It does not change *this. Rather, it creates a new function whose value is *this raised to the exponent power. The difference between these functions is similar to the difference between "+" and "+=." The friend function power() calls powerPure().

powers
This command takes an integer argument and prints a table of each variable raised to every power between 1 and the number specified on the command. It is similar to the name command in that it computes a function and looks for a variable with that value.

```
AUTOCALC>domain I 5
AUTOCALC>f=[1 2 0 1 2 0]
AUTOCALC>g=power(f,2)
AUTOCALC>h=power(f,3)

AUTOCALC>powers 10
1 2 3 4 5 6 7 8 9 10
f g h f g h f g h f
g f h g f h g f h g
h h h h h h h h h h
```

comptable　This table says power$(g, 8) = f$, and that all powers of h equal h. This command prints a function composition table of every variable composed with every other variable. With the 3 variables f, g, and h defined above

```
AUTOCALC>comptable
^ f g h
f g h f
g h f g
h f g h
```

close　That is, since row f, column g contains h, $f \circ g = h$ or $((x)f)g = (x)h$. The function composition and powers tables will contain "?" entries when no variable is currently defined with that value. The `close` command composes every variable with every other variable and if no variable has that value, a new variable is added. Newly added variables are also composed with all other variables. When `close` completes, `comptable`, which now includes all newly added variables, will not have any "?" entries.

Close is useful for semigroups (see "Semigroups" in Chapter 11).

The rank(), unrank(), and random() member functions in class FunDRng are available:

rank　This command evaluates a function expression and prints its rank value. The rank is an unsigned long integer that uniquely identifies the function. No other function with the current domain size will have the same rank value. rank() may produce integer overflow if the domain size is too large. The total number of possible functions from a domain of size s to itself is s^s. On a machine where an unsigned long is 32 bits, the largest domain size is 9.

unrank　This symbol converts an integer into a function. The result depends on the number of elements in the domain.

random　This symbol returns a random function of the current domain. It is not limited by the size of the domain as rank() and unrank() are. It can return a random function of any size domain.

randomDist This command generates n random functions and computes their chi-squared statistic. The chi-squared value gives a measure of whether or not random() is biased.

```
AUTOCALC>domain I 3
AUTOCALC>randomDist 5000
   Number of values=5000    recommended minimum=2560
..............................................
   Degrees of Freedom=255   Chi-squared range (90%) =224 .. 288
   Chi-square=240.115036
```

If random() is not biased, approximately 90 percent of the time the chi-squared value will be between 224 and 288 (Sedgewick, 1984:41). Since the chi-square for this sample of 5000 AutoFuns is about 240, random() appears to be unbiased. On my computer, random() usually does fall within the specified bounds. If it doesn't on your computer, check your rand() routine in math.h.

randomDist allocates a counter for each possible function. A check prevents requests that require more than 64K of memory. The largest domain size is 5.

If the "l" (lowercase L) option is used, every possible function is listed along with the number of times it was generated. If added to the example above, all 256 AutoFuns of four elements would be printed along with their frequency.

Element Class

The Element class is used as a flexible domain and/or range type. AUTOCALC, PERMCALC, and PARTCALC use Element. Element instances are constructed from unsigned integers, and that unsigned value can be extracted later. The major reason for this class is their iostream operators. Elements can be read and written in three different formats:

- as unsigned integers,
- as strings of letters: A, B, . . ., Z, AA, AB, . . ., AZ, BA, . . ., ZZ, AAA, . . ., and
- as user-defined names (character strings).

Calculators that deal with elements have the following additional commands:

elemFormat Change the I/O format for elements. "I" specifies integer format, "A" specifies alpha or letter format, and "N" specifies name format.

elemName This command adds new user-defined element names. The first name is a synonym for 0, the next name is a synonym for 1, etc. New names are added to the end of the list. elemName accepts a blank separated list of names.

```
AUTOCALC>elemName Apple Banana Cantaloupe Date
```

listElem   List all user-defined element names and the unsigned integers to which they correspond.

newElem   Delete all existing element names.

The `elemFormat` command sets the format for elements.

```
AUTOCALC>domain I 5
AUTOCALC>elemFormat a
AUTOCALC>autoA=[A C C B D]
[A C C B D]
```

`elemFormat` can also switch `AUTOCALC` to names defined by the `elemName` command.

```
AUTOCALC>elemName alice bob cindy dave elizabeth frank
AUTOCALC>elemFormat n
AUTOCALC>=autoA
[alice cindy cindy bob dave]
```

Option I switches back to integers.

```
AUTOCALC>elemFormat i
AUTOCALC>=autoA
[0 2 2 1 3]
```

Note: *first* and *last* values on the domain command must be specified in the proper element format. Use "`domain I F`" after "`elemFormat a`."

Implementation Comments

This section discusses some of the internals of the function classes. If you just want to use these classes, you can ignore this section and skip to Chapter 11.

Memory Layout

As shown in Figure 10.2, functions are implemented as two parallel class hierarchies. The handle class hierarchy is derived from class Handle; the body class hierarchy is derived from class RefCount (also see "Handles and Bodies" in Chapter 5).

The memory layout of the handle hierarchy is trivial. Every element in the handle hierarchy contains exactly one pointer to an instance in the body hierarchy (plus a pointer to its virtual method table).

The real implementation and data for functions are in the body hierarchy. Function implementations have a reference count that is used by the handle classes. Implementations also contain a pointer to a domain DSet, which they own and will destroy. FunDRng and its derivatives also contain a pointer to a range DSet. AutoFuns actually have two copies of the DSet: one for their domain and one for their range. Deriving AutoFunImp directly from FunImp would eliminate this data duplication at the cost of some code duplication.

Every implementation has a pointer to an array of range elements that is dynamically allocated from the heap. In FunGRngImp, it is an array of the range template type. In FunDRngImp, it is an array of unsigned integers. The range DSet is used to convert these integers to actual range element values as needed.

Domain and Range Types

The class used for a domain type must support

- construction from an unsigned integer
- casting to an unsigned integer
- iostream operators $<<$ and $>>$

The class used for a range type must support

- a default constructor
- assignment and a copy constructor
- casting to an unsigned integer
- iostream operators $<<$ and $>>$
- comparison operator != (dependence on this could easily be changed to just operator ==)

Since AutoFunImps and PermImps have a single type for both their domain and range, that type must support all of these operations.

Binary Operators

Member functions compare() and component() are binary operators. They have two parameters of type FunImp (one is `*this`). The virtual function call effectively tells us the actual type of one of the parameters (`*this`). But all we know about the other parameter is that it is derived from FunImp.

C++ does not have a nice, straightforward means of implementing binary operators like this. The scheme proposed by Meyers (1992) is the cleanest one I have seen for safe, run-time type testing.

The base class declares a set of virtual functions castToX() that cast the object to a derived type X. By default, all of these functions return a null pointer. Only in derived class X is method castToX() overridden to return the `this` pointer. Method X::castToX() will only be executed if `this` really points to an instance of class X (or one of its derived classes). Therefore, returning `this` as a pointer of type X is always safe. castToX() returns a valid pointer if the object is indeed of derived type X. Otherwise, it returns a null pointer.

```
class FunImp ... {
   ...
   virtual FunGRngImp<Dom,Rng>* castToFunGRngImp() const { return 0; };
   virtual FunDRngImp<Dom,Rng>* castToFunDRngImp() const { return 0; };
};

class FunGRngImp ... {
   ...
   virtual FunGRngImp<Dom,Rng>* castToFunGRngImp() const { return this; };
};

class FunDRngImp ... {
   ...
   virtual FunDRngImp<Dom,Rng>* castToFunDRngImp() const { return this; };
};
```

Unfortunately, I am unable to compile this code with the current version of the compiler. It seems to be a compiler bug involving forward references to template classes. Rather than requiring a particular level of the compiler, I changed the cast-ToX() method to an isX() method that returns a boolean. The isX() methods in the base class (FunImp) return FALSE. In derived class X, isX() is overridden and returns TRUE.

Possible Extensions

If a function's range type is not totally ordered, compare() could return a partially ordered value instead of a boolean (see "Partial Compare" in Chapter 4). Specifically, compare(f, g) could return

PartEQ   if $f(x) = g(x)$ for all x
PartLT   if $f(x) \leq g(x)$ for all x
PartGT   if $f(x) \geq g(x)$ for all x
PartUN   if $f(x) > g(x)$ for some x and $f(y) < g(y)$ for some y

Functions have many properties not supported by the current implementation.

isMonotonic   A function is **monotonic** if it either increases or decreases over its entire range. This member function would return one of "strictly decreasing," "decreasing or equal," "constant," "increasing or equal," or "strictly increasing." It generalizes and replaces isConstant(). isMonotonic() only makes sense if both the domain and range types are totally ordered.

isOnto   A function is **onto** if it maps some domain element to every possible range element. This only makes sense for FunDRngs and its derivatives, which have a finite, discrete range.

isOneToOne A function is **one-to-one** if every domain element maps to a single range element (this is always true for functions), and every range element maps to a single domain element. This is exactly the definition of a permutation function. But this query function might be useful for FunDRngs and AutoFuns.

It might be useful to add a method to DSet that returns a default value. This would be used by FunDRng to set the default range value for constant functions. DSets might also return a random element in their set. These two methods would not be used by FunGRng since it doesn't have a range DSet.

The function composition routine in AutoFunImp could be speeded up by using the translation (xlate) instruction available in many machine instruction sets.

The implementation of powerPure() assumes that the exponent is a small number (say less than 10 or 20). If larger exponents are computed frequently, the following loop can be substituted for the final for loop. It is faster when power is a large number.

```
AutoFun<int>  p, result;  // p is input.
result.ident();
for (;;) {
   if (exponent & 1)        // is exponent odd?
      result.compose(p);    // result = result * p
   exponent /= 2;
   if (exponent == 0)
      break;
   p.compose(p);            // square p
};
```

Domain values are implicit in function literals. Two extensions could be made in readFrom() to make domain values explicit and perhaps more obvious. The first extension would support an "@ dom" syntax. It identifies the next domain value to be set. If constant functions are used a lot, a second extension would support a " = range" syntax, to set the default range value. Any domain value not assigned a specific value would get the default range value. Currently the default Rng constructor is used as the default range value. Combining these two ideas would support the following function literals for a function whose domain is the integers 1..6 and whose range is integers.

```
[ 1 2 3 4 5 6 ] = [1 2 3 4 5 6]
[=4] = [4 4 4 4 4 4]
[=4 2 3] = [2 3 4 4 4 4]
[@1 4 @2 5 @3 10 @4 1 @5 7] = [4 5 10 1 7 0]
[=99 @1 3 4 @5 9 10 @4 14 15] = [3 4 99 14 15 10]
```

In the last example, domain element 5 is set to 9 and is then overwritten by 15.

Another way to handle constant functions would be to support assignment of a range value to a function with an operator= routine. This construct can also be added to the calculators by adding another operator to the priExp expression object.

It is possible to create function classes that have two (or more) distinct domain types to represent functions with two independent variables. Internally, it would allocate a two-dimensional array of range values. Many of the member routines carry over naturally. However, it isn't clear what happens to function composition. The first function returns a single range value, and that would not be enough to determine both domain values required by the second function.

It would be very nice to combine all the different calculator programs into a single program. However, rank() is not supported by FunGRng. So some kind of runtime type checking would be needed to reject such requests. This also has all the problems of mixed-mode expressions (see "Possible Extensions" in Chapter 9).

Source Code

File Function.hpp

```
#ifndef _FUNCTION_HPP
#define _FUNCTION_HPP
//**********************************************************************
// TITLE: Function --  functions with a finite, discrete domain.
//
// AUTHOR: Scott N Gerard, Rochester, MN
// LANGUAGE: C++
//
// FUNCTION:
//    A function maps every value in the domain to a value in the range.
//
// CHANGE LOG:
//    11Jan91 - Initial coding.  Modified version of Perm.  SN Gerard
//    03Jan93 - Convert to C++.  SN Gerard
//    16Jan93 - Rework from Xlate to Fun.  SN Gerard
//**********************************************************************
#include <iostream.h>
#include <limits.h>

#include "Bool.hpp"
#include "DSet.hpp"
#include "Handle.hpp"

//**********************************************************************
//
//                    FunImp (Abstract Base Class)
//
// Function base class.
//**********************************************************************
typedef unsigned DomI;               // internal Domain type

template <class Dom, class Rng>
class FunImp: public RefCount {

    typedef RefCount BaseClass;
    typedef FunImp<Dom,Rng> ThisClass;
```

```
protected:
    //******************************************************************
    // Constructor
    //******************************************************************
    FunImp(const DSet<Dom>& domainSet)
        :siz(domainSet.count()), domSet(domainSet.copy()) {};

public:
    typedef Rng (*UNARY_FN) (Rng a);
    typedef Rng (*BINARY_FN)(Rng a, Rng b);

    //******************************************************************
    // Destructor
    //******************************************************************
    virtual FunImp();

    //******************************************************************
    // Assignment operators
    //******************************************************************
    FunImp& operator = (const char*);             // set from string
    FunImp& operator = (Rng(*fn)(Dom d));         // set from routine

    //******************************************************************
    // copy creates a copy but doesn't downcast the ref to the base class.
    //******************************************************************
    FunImp* copy () const  { return (ThisClass*) _copy(); };
    virtual void init() = 0;

    //******************************************************************
    // Return the size and domain DSet.
    //******************************************************************
    DomI domainSize () const { return siz; };
    DSet<Dom>& domainSet () const { return *domSet; };

    //******************************************************************
    // Set a function to a constant value
    //******************************************************************
    virtual FunImp& constant(const Rng k) = 0;
    virtual BOOL  isConstant() const = 0;

    //******************************************************************
    // Get and set the d-th element.
    //******************************************************************
    virtual Rng     get (const Dom d) const;
    virtual FunImp& set (const Dom d, const Rng r);

    virtual const Rng operator () (const Dom d) const
        { return get(d); };

    //******************************************************************
    // Get and set the d-th element.  These are different than get()
    // and set() in that they use the internal domain index rather than a
    // Dom value.
    //******************************************************************
```

(continued)

File Function.hpp   *(continued)*

```
    virtual const Rng geti (const DomI di) const = 0;
    virtual FunImp&    seti (const DomI di, const Rng r) = 0;

    //**********************************************************************
    // Compare two functions.
    //**********************************************************************
    virtual BOOL compare (const FunImp& b) const;

    //**********************************************************************
    // Component-wise operations
    //**********************************************************************
    virtual FunImp& component (BINARY_FN binFn, const FunImp& b);
    virtual FunImp& component (BINARY_FN binFn, Rng k) = 0;
    virtual FunImp& component (UNARY_FN unaryFn) = 0;

    //**********************************************************************
    // Compute a hash value for a function.
    //**********************************************************************
    virtual unsigned hash () const = 0;

    //**********************************************************************
    // IO operations using an external format that lists the range value
    // for each domain element enclosed in square brackets.  For example,
    // "[0 1 2 3]" is the identity function.  Unspecified values are set
    // by Rng's default constructor.
    //**********************************************************************
    virtual ostream& printOn  (ostream& os) const;
    virtual istream& readFrom (istream& is);

    //**********************************************************************
    // Convert a string to a function.  Return TRUE if conversion was ok.
    //**********************************************************************
    virtual BOOL readString (const char *s);

    //**********************************************************************
    // Consistency checkers.
    //**********************************************************************
    virtual BOOL valid () const;                // is Fun valid?
    virtual BOOL validDom (const Dom d) const;  // is d in domain ?
    virtual BOOL validRng (const Rng r) const;  // is r in range ?

    //**********************************************************************
    // Run-time type queries.  Only need first level derived classes.
    //**********************************************************************
    virtual BOOL isFunGRngImp() const { return FALSE; };
    virtual BOOL isFunDRngImp() const { return FALSE; };

protected:
    //**********************************************************************
    // Domain information
    //**********************************************************************
```

```
    DomI siz;                          // size of domain and the number
                                       // of allocated elements.
    DSet<Dom>* domSet;                 // for converting Dom values

    virtual FunImp* _copy () const = 0;
};

//*********************************************************************
//
//                          Fun
//
//*********************************************************************
template <class Dom, class Rng>
class Fun: public Handle< FunImp<Dom,Rng> > {

    typedef Handle< FunImp<Dom,Rng> > BaseClass;
    typedef Fun<Dom,Rng> ThisClass;
    typedef FunImp<Dom,Rng> RefClass;

protected:
    Fun(RefClass& t);
    Fun(RefClass* t);

    const RefClass& readRef () const
        { return (RefClass&) _readRef(); };
    RefClass& writeRef () const
        { return (RefClass&) _writeRef(); };

public:
    //*****************************************************************
    // Funs built with the default constructor will be set to this value
    // when they are first referenced.  If defaultFun is not set when the
    // value of the function is required, the program halts.
    //*****************************************************************
    static Fun* defaultFun;

    //*****************************************************************
    // Constructors
    //*****************************************************************
    Fun() {};
    Fun(const Fun& copy);

    //*****************************************************************
    // Delegate operations to FunImp
    //*****************************************************************
    ThisClass& operator = (const ThisClass& copy);
    ThisClass& operator = (const char *string);
    ThisClass& operator = (Rng(*fn)(Dom d));

    virtual void init() { writeRef().init(); };

    DomI domainSize () const { return readRef().domainSize(); };
    DSet<Dom>& domainSet () const { return readRef().domainSet(); };
```

(continued)

File Function.hpp *(continued)*

```cpp
ThisClass& constant(const Rng k);
BOOL isConstant() const;

//*******************************************************************
// Get and set the d-th element.
//*******************************************************************
Rng get (const Dom d) const { return readRef().get(d); };
ThisClass& set (const Dom d, const Rng r);
const Rng operator () (const Dom d) const
   { return readRef().operator()(d); };


//*******************************************************************
// Get and set the i-th element.  These are different than get()
// and set in that they use the internal domain index rather than a
// Dom value.
//*******************************************************************
const Rng geti (const DomI di) const
   { return readRef().geti(di); };
ThisClass& seti (const DomI di, const Rng r);


//*******************************************************************
// Compare two functions.
//*******************************************************************
BOOL compare (const ThisClass& b) const
   { return readRef().compare(b.readRef()); };
friend  BOOL compare (const ThisClass& a, const ThisClass& b)
   { return a.readRef().compare(b.readRef()); };

friend BOOL operator == (const ThisClass& a, const ThisClass& b)
   { return a.readRef().compare(b.readRef()); };
friend BOOL operator != (const ThisClass& a, const ThisClass& b)
   { return BOOL( ! a.readRef().compare(b.readRef()) ); };


//*******************************************************************
// Component-wise operations
//*******************************************************************
ThisClass& component (RefClass::BINARY_FN binFn, const ThisClass& b);

friend ThisClass component (
   const ThisClass& a,
   RefClass::BINARY_FN binFn,
   const ThisClass& b);

ThisClass componentPure (
   RefClass::BINARY_FN binFn,
   const ThisClass& b) const
{
   ThisClass result = *this;
   result.component(binFn, b);
   return result;
};
```

```
ThisClass& component (RefClass::BINARY_FN binFn, Rng k);

friend ThisClass component (
   const ThisClass& a,
   RefClass::BINARY_FN binFn,
   Rng k);

ThisClass componentPure (RefClass::BINARY_FN binFn, Rng k) const {
   ThisClass result = *this;
   result.component(binFn, k);
   return result;
};

ThisClass& component (RefClass::UNARY_FN unaryFn);

friend ThisClass component (
   const ThisClass& a,
   RefClass::UNARY_FN unaryFn);

ThisClass componentPure (RefClass::UNARY_FN unaryFn) const {
   ThisClass result = *this;
   result.component(unaryFn);
   return result;
};

//******************************************************************
// Compute a hash value for a function.
//******************************************************************
unsigned hash () const;

//******************************************************************
// IO operations
//******************************************************************
ostream& printOn  (ostream& os) const;
istream& readFrom (istream& is);

friend ostream& operator << (ostream& os, const ThisClass& x);
friend istream& operator >> (istream& is,       ThisClass& x);

//******************************************************************
// Convert a string to a function.  Return TRUE if conversion was ok.
//******************************************************************
BOOL readString (const char *s);

//******************************************************************
// Consistency checkers.
//******************************************************************
virtual BOOL valid() const;
virtual BOOL validDom (const Dom d) const;
virtual BOOL validRng (const Rng r) const;

//******************************************************************
// Handle<T> primitives
//******************************************************************
```

(continued)

File Function.hpp *(continued)*

```
    virtual FunImp<Dom,Rng>* allocRef () const;
    virtual FunImp<Dom,Rng>* copyRef () const { return p->copy(); };
};

//*********************************************************************
//
//                      Function composition
//
// Function composition.  Return h(x) = g(f(x)), that is
// apply f first and then g to that result.
//*********************************************************************
template <class R, class S, class T>
void compose (
    const Fun<R,S>& f,
    const Fun<S,T>& g,
          Fun<R,T>& h);

#endif
```

File FunGRng.hpp

```
#ifndef _FUNGRNG_HPP
#define _FUNGRNG_HPP
//*********************************************************************
// TITLE: FunGRng --  functions with a finite, discrete domain.
//
// AUTHOR: Scott N Gerard, Rochester, MN
// LANGUAGE: C++
//
// FUNCTION:
//    A function maps every value in the domain to a value in the range.
//
// CHANGE LOG:
//    11Jan91 - Initial coding.  Modified version of Perm.  SN Gerard
//    03Jan93 - Convert to C++.  SN Gerard
//    16Jan93 - Rework from Xlate to Fun.  SN Gerard
//*********************************************************************
#include "UnInit.hpp"
#include "Function.hpp"


//*********************************************************************
//
//                           FunGRngImp
//
// Function with a general range.
//*********************************************************************
template <class Dom, class Rng>
class FunGRngImp: public FunImp<Dom,Rng> {

    typedef FunImp<Dom,Rng>  BaseClass;
    typedef FunGRngImp ThisClass;
```

```
protected:
    // Construct and leave uninitialized
    FunGRngImp(const DSet<Dom>& domainSet, UnInit u);

public:
    //*******************************************************************
    // Constructors and destructor
    //*******************************************************************
    FunGRngImp(const DSet<Dom>& domainSet);
    FunGRngImp(const DSet<Dom>& domainSet, const Rng k);
    FunGRngImp(const DSet<Dom>& domainSet, const char* string);
    FunGRngImp(const DSet<Dom>& domainSet, Rng(*fn)(Dom d));
    FunGRngImp(const FunGRngImp& g);

    virtual ~FunGRngImp();

    //*******************************************************************
    // Assignment operators
    //*******************************************************************
    FunGRngImp& operator = (const FunGRngImp& b);   // set from FunGRngImp

    BaseClass& operator = (const char * s)
        { return this->BaseClass::operator=(s); };

    BaseClass& operator = (Rng (*fn)(Dom d))
        { return this->BaseClass::operator=(fn); };

    //*******************************************************************
    // copy creates a copy but doesn't downcast the ref to the base class.
    //*******************************************************************
    ThisClass* copy () const { return (ThisClass*) _copy(); };
    virtual void init();

    //*******************************************************************
    // Set a function to a constant value
    //*******************************************************************
    virtual FunImp<Dom,Rng>& constant(const Rng k);
    virtual BOOL  isConstant() const;

    //*******************************************************************
    // Get and set the i-th element.
    //*******************************************************************
    virtual const Rng geti (const DomI di) const;
    virtual FunImp<Dom,Rng>& seti (const DomI di, const Rng r);

    //*******************************************************************
    // Compare two functions.
    //*******************************************************************
    virtual BOOL compare (const FunImp<Dom,Rng>& g) const;

    //*******************************************************************
    // Component-wise operations
    //*******************************************************************
```

(continued)

File FunGRng.hpp *(continued)*

```cpp
FunImp<Dom,Rng>& component (
    Rng (*binfn)(Rng a, Rng b),
    const FunImp<Dom,Rng>& g);

FunImp<Dom,Rng>& component (BINARY_FN binFn, Rng k);
FunImp<Dom,Rng>& component (UNARY_FN unaryFn);

//*********************************************************************
// Compute a hash value for a function.
//*********************************************************************
virtual unsigned hash () const;

//*********************************************************************
// Consistency checkers.
//*********************************************************************
virtual BOOL valid () const;

virtual BOOL isFunGRngImp() const { return TRUE; };

protected:
//*********************************************************************
// Store a pointer to the array of elements and the number of
// elements in the array.
//*********************************************************************
Rng* elem;                              // array of siz Rng elements

void alloc ();                          // allocate storage

virtual FunImp<Dom,Rng>* _copy () const
    { return new FunGRngImp<Dom,Rng>(*this); };
};

//*********************************************************************
//
//                          FunGRng
//
//*********************************************************************
template <class Dom, class Rng>
class FunGRng: public Fun<Dom,Rng> {

    typedef Fun<Dom,Rng> BaseClass;
    typedef FunGRng<Dom,Rng> ThisClass;
    typedef FunGRngImp<Dom,Rng> RefClass;

protected:
    FunGRng(RefClass& t);
    FunGRng(RefClass* t);

    //*****************************************************************
    // Extract reference
    //*****************************************************************
```

```
    const RefClass& readRef () const
        { return (RefClass&) _readRef(); };
    RefClass& writeRef () const
        { return (RefClass&) _writeRef(); };

public:
    //********************************************************************
    // Constructors and destructor
    //********************************************************************
    FunGRng() {};

    FunGRng(const DSet<Dom>& domainSet);
    FunGRng(const DSet<Dom>& domainSet, const Rng k);
    FunGRng(const DSet<Dom>& domainSet, const char *string);
    FunGRng(const DSet<Dom>& domainSet, Rng(*fn)(Dom d));
    FunGRng(const FunGRng& copy);

    //********************************************************************
    // Delegate operations to FunGRngImp
    //********************************************************************
    ThisClass& operator = (const ThisClass& b);
    ThisClass& operator = (const char *string);
    ThisClass& operator = (Rng(*fn)(Dom d));

    //********************************************************************
    // Component-wise operations
    //********************************************************************
    friend ThisClass component (
        const ThisClass& a,
        RefClass::BINARY_FN binFn,
        const ThisClass& b);

    friend ThisClass component (
        const ThisClass& a,
        RefClass::BINARY_FN binFn,
        Rng k);

    friend ThisClass component (
        const ThisClass& a,
        RefClass::UNARY_FN unaryFn);
};

//************************************************************************
//
//                        Function composition
//
// Function composition.  Return h(x) = g(f(x)), that is
// apply f first and then g to that result.
//************************************************************************
template <class R, class S, class T>
void compose (
```

(continued)

File FunGRng.hpp *(continued)*

```
   const FunGRng<R,S>& f,
   const FunGRng<S,T>& g,
         FunGRng<R,T>& h)
   { compose( (Fun<R,S>&) f, (Fun<S,T>&) g, (Fun<R,T>&) h); };


#endif _FUNGRNG_HPP
```

File Element.hpp

```
#ifndef _ELEMENT_HPP
#define _ELEMENT_HPP
//*********************************************************************
// TITLE: Element -- common sub-piece
//
// PROGRAMMER: Scott N Gerard
// LANGUAGE: C++
//
// FUNCTION:
//    Element type for calculators.  This class supports conversions
//    between an internal value and:
//    -- integers (beginning with 0),
//    -- strings of letters (A, B, ..., Z, AA, AB, ..., ZZ, AAA, ...)
//    -- user specified identifiers.
//
// CHANGE LOG:
//    11Oct92 - Initial coding.  SN Gerard
//*********************************************************************

#include <strng.h>
#include <vectimp.h>


//*********************************************************************
// Elements
//*********************************************************************
class Element {
public:
   enum ElementFormat {IntegerFormat, AlphaFormat, NameFormat};

protected:
   static ElementFormat format;
   int val;
public:
   Element(int value = 0): val(value) {};
   operator int () const { return val; };

   friend istream& operator >> (istream& is, Element& e);
   friend ostream& operator << (ostream& os, const Element& e);

   friend void setFormat (char* str);
};
```

```
//********************************************************************
// The array of element names
//********************************************************************
void addElemName(const String* name);   // add an element name
void flushElemNames();                   // delete all elem names

extern BI_CVectorImp<String> elemNames;

#endif
```

File Element.cpp

```
//********************************************************************
// TITLE: Element -- common sub-piece
//
// PROGRAMMER: Scott N Gerard
// LANGUAGE: C++
//
// FUNCTION:
//     Element type for calculators.  This class supports conversions
//     between an internal value and:
//     -- integers (beginning with 0),
//     -- strings of letters (A, B, ..., Z, AA, AB, ..., ZZ, AAA, ...)
//     -- user specified identifiers.
//
// CHANGE LOG:
//     11Oct92 - Initial coding.  SN Gerard
//********************************************************************
#include <ctype.h>
#include "Ident.hpp"
#include "Element.hpp"

Element::ElementFormat Element::format = IntegerFormat;
BI_CVectorImp<String> elemNames(5, 25);

void setFormat (char* str) {
   switch (str[0]) {
   case 'I': case 'i':
      Element::format = Element::IntegerFormat;
      break;
   case 'A': case 'a':
      Element::format = Element::AlphaFormat;
      break;
   case 'N': case 'n':
      Element::format = Element::NameFormat;
      break;
   default:
      cout << "Format must be I(nteger), A(lpha), or N(ame).\n";
   };
};
```

(continued)

File Element.cpp   *(continued)*

```cpp
//*********************************************************************
// Conversions between integers and an sequence of letters.
// A, B, ..., Z, AA, AB, ..., AZ, BA, ..., ZZ, AAA, ...
// The values are converted using A=0, ... Z=25.  The 26^ (i-1) strings of
// length i-1 precede strings of length i.  So 26 is added to strings
// of length 2; 26*26 is added to strings of length 3; etc.
//*********************************************************************
int readAlphaFormat (istream& is) {
   char ch;
   int x = 0;
   int x2 = 0;
   int power = 1;

   is >> ch;
   while ( is && isalpha(ch) ) {
      if ( 'A' <= ch && ch <= 'Z' )
         x = 26 * x + ch - 'A';
      else if ( 'a' <= ch && ch <= 'z' )
         x = 26 * x + ch - 'a';
      x2 += power;
      power *= 26;
      is.get(ch);
   };
   is.putback(ch);
   return x + x2 - 1;
};

void writeAlphaFormat (ostream& os, int x) {
   int power = 1;

   while ( 26*power <= x ) {
      power *= 26;
      x -= power;
   };

   while ( power != 0 ) {
      int digit = x / power;
      x %= power;
      power /= 26;
      os << char('A' + digit);
   };
};


//*********************************************************************
// Element name routines
//*********************************************************************
void addElemName(const String& name) {
   elemNames.add( *new String(name));
};
```

```
void flushElemNames() {
   elemNames.flush();
};

int readNameFormat(istream& is) {
   char token[MAX_SYMNAME_LEN];
   getIdent(is, token, sizeof(token));
   String name(token);
   for( int i = 0; i < elemNames.count(); ++i)
      if ( name == elemNames[i] )
         return i;

   // name string is not in names array.  add it and return new index
   elemNames.add(name);
   return elemNames.count() - 1;
};

void writeNameFormat(ostream& os, const int x) {
   if (x < elemNames.count())
      // x has a valid name.  Write it out the identifier
      os << elemNames[x];
   else
      // there is no name for x.  Write x as an integer
      os << x;
};

//*****************************************************************
// Add element names
//*****************************************************************
void elemName (istream& is, ostream& os) {
   char token[MAX_SYMNAME_LEN];
   while( is && !is.eof() ) {
      getIdent(is, token, sizeof(token));
      if ( strlen(token) > 0 ) {
         String name(token);

         for (int i=0; i < elemNames.count(); ++i)
            if ( name == elemNames[i] )
               return;                  // already have it.  Ignore it.

         elemNames.add(name);           // don't already have.
      };
   };
};
Command elemNameCmd(elemName, "elemName",
   "define element names", "name1 name2 ...");

//*****************************************************************
// List all element names
//*****************************************************************
```

(continued)

File Element.cpp   *(continued)*

```cpp
void listElem (istream& is, ostream& os) {
    os << "Elements:\n";
    for (int i = 0; i < elemNames.count(); ++i) {
        os << i << ": " << elemNames[i] << endl;
    };
};
Command listElemCmd(listElem, "listElem",
    "list all element names and their value");

//*********************************************************************
// Delete all element names
//*********************************************************************
void newElem (istream& is, ostream& os) {
    elemNames.flush();
};
Command newElemCmd( newElem, "newElem", "delete all element names");

//*********************************************************************
// set element format
//*********************************************************************
void elemFormat (istream& is, ostream& os) {
    char    token[MAX_SYMNAME_LEN];
    getIdent( is, token, sizeof(token) );
    setFormat(token);
};
Command elemFormatCmd( elemFormat, "elemFormat",
    "set element format", "a(lpha)i(nteger)n(ame)");

//*********************************************************************
// Input/output routines
//*********************************************************************
istream& operator >> (istream& is, Element& e) {
    switch (Element::format) {
    case Element::IntegerFormat: is >> e.val;                   break;
    case Element::AlphaFormat:   e.val = readAlphaFormat(is);   break;
    case Element::NameFormat:    e.val = readNameFormat(is);    break;
    };
    return is;
};

ostream& operator << (ostream& os, const Element& e) {
    switch (Element::format) {
    case Element::IntegerFormat: os << e.val;                   break;
    case Element::AlphaFormat:    writeAlphaFormat( os, e.val); break;
    case Element::NameFormat:     writeNameFormat( os, e.val); break;
    };
    return os;
};
```

11

Applications of Functions

Functions, functions everywhere.

Real Functions

Why use a FunGRng for Sin when sin() from math.h works just as well? If you have a graphics program that calls sin() a lot, it is more efficient to evaluate sin() once and look up the results each time they are needed. Assume you only need sin() and cos() evaluated to the nearest degree.

```cpp
#include <math.h>
#include "FunGRng.cpp"

const double pi=3.1416;
double   x=1, y=0;
double   x2, y2;

void main() {
    LinearDSet<double> angles(0,2*pi,361);  // 0..360 inclusive

    // Construct functions and initialize with sin and cos from math.h
    FunGRng<double,double>
                    Sin(angles,sin),
                    Cos(angles,cos);

    for (double ang = 0; ang <= 2*pi; ang += pi/180) {
        x2 = x * Cos(ang) - y * Sin(ang);
        y2 = x * Sin(ang) + y * Cos(ang);
```

```
        // plot point <x2,y2>
    };
};
```

In the loop, the values for sin and cos are looked up, not reevaluated.

Lookup Tables

Lookup tables occur quite often in computer programming. For example, a virtual memory translation maps logical addresses to physical addresses:

$$VirtualMemory: logicalAddress \mapsto physicalAddress$$

The mapping is done by dividing the logical address space into "frames" and the physical address space into "pages." Frames and pages are the same size—usually a power of 2, like 256 or 512 bytes. Then a function maps each logical frame to a physical page in main memory:

$$VirtualMemoryPage: logicalFrame \mapsto physicalPage$$

A function can also look up presidents of the United States:

```
enum Presidents {
    Washington, Adams, Jefferson, ... Reagan, Bush, Clinton};

LinearDSet<int> electionYears(1788, 1992, 52);  // every 4 years
FunDRng<int,Presidents> electionWinner(electionYears);

electionWinner.set(1788, Washington);
electionWinner.set(1792, Washington);
electionWinner.set(1796, Adams);
electionWinner.set(1800, Jefferson);
...
electionWinner.set(1980, Reagan);
electionWinner.set(1984, Reagan);
electionWinner.set(1988, Bush);
electionWinner.set(1992, Clinton);
```

Circuit Simulation

Functions can perform simple circuit simulation. Each function $f:time \mapsto boolean$ is the history of an electrical signal over time. The logical componentwise operations simulate logic gates.

```
FUNCALC>domain I 13
FUNCALC>in1=[0 0 0 1 1 1 1 0 0 0 1 1 0 0]
```

```
in1=[0 0 0 1 1 1 1 0 0 0 1 1]
FUNCALC>in2=[1 1 0 1 1 1 1 0 1 1 1 1 0]
in2=[1 1 0 1 1 1 1 0 0 1 1 1 1]

FUNCALC>and = in1 & in2
and=[0 0 0 1 1 1 1 0 0 0 1 1]
FUNCALC>equ = in1 & in2 | !in1 & !in2
equ=[0 0 1 1 1 1 1 1 1 0 1 1 0 1]
```

You might consider extending FUNCALC with NAND and NOR symbols.

Function Composition

Macro Functions

Many tools provide a macro facility. Basically, a macro is a name for a collection of primitive operations and/or other macros. Function composition can create "macro functions."

Suppose we have three functions: AB:A $\mapsto$ B, BC:B $\mapsto$ C and CD:C $\mapsto$ D. Function composition creates a macro function AD:A $\mapsto$ D = AB ^ BC ^ CD. AD has the same format as a primitive function, and can be further combined into larger macro functions. It is more efficient to map A to D using AD, than to map elements through each of the three primitive functions.

Why is it useful to even define the intermediate functions AB, BC, and CD when all we really want is AD? First, we may happen to already have those functions lying around. Second, we may want to reuse some of those functions in other macros. That is, they are common building blocks. And third, those functions represent pieces of information, and different people or different objects may be responsible for constructing and maintaining those individual pieces of information.

Consider a corporate example. The personnel department is responsible for keeping track of each employee's department (DEPT:employee $\mapsto$ dept). Now, suppose another group needs to hold a sitewide meeting, but there are too many employees to fit in the largest room available. They create another function that maps departments to meeting times (MEETING:dept $\mapsto$ time). A function that maps each employee to his scheduled meeting time is just the composition of the two functions: DEPT ^ MEETING.

The interface between functions DEPT and MEETING, and the interface between the personnel and meeting groups, is the common set dept. Both groups must agree what elements are in dept and what those elements mean. For example, is there a "dummy" department? When will personnel map an employee to the dummy department? After they leave the company? Are employees that have resigned in a different department than employees that have retired and still have the privilege of coming back to chat with (heckle?) their old comrades? What should the meeting group do with these special departments? Are they "don't care" departments, or must they be mapped to some reasonable time slot? Does the meeting set need a "no meeting" time slot?

Translation Tables

A very common use for Funs—and the original reason I wrote these classes—was to handle character translation tables. Each table is a function xlate:char ↦ char. Translation tables that map characters to their upper- or lowercase equivalents are common, as are tables that convert between ASCII and EBCDIC character sets. Like other functions, they can be combined into single macro functions by function composition. If AUpper is a function that maps ASCII characters to their uppercase equivalents, and A2E is a function that converts ASCII characters to EBCDIC characters, then AUpper ^ A2E converts an ASCII string to uppercase EBCDIC.

Color Palettes

Although the perception of a computer image involves many complex transformations, some transformations are functions that can be combined by composition. The process can be diagrammed as

where pixel is an (x, y) location, colorIndex is a one- or two-byte index into the color palette, RGB are red, green, and blue intensities, and IHS is the color represented as intensity, hue, and saturation. The whole process is represented by the function composition

```
image ^ colorPalette ^ humanEye
```

NASA uses color enhancements to highlight differences in an image. For example, you might increase the contrast in the image using a function doubleIntensity that doubles the intensity of each color (over a certain range). Colors that were one unit apart in intensity now become two units apart in intensity. The image designer does this by mapping existing RGB values to new RGB values (an AutoFun:RBG ↦ RGB). The new color palette is the function composition of old color palette times the changes: palette = palette ^ doubleIntensity.

Polynomials

The function class hierarchy can also perform addition and subtraction of polynomials of a single variable. A polynomial is a function POLY:power ↦ coefficient. That is, every power of x in the polynomial has a unique coefficient. Addition of two polynomials is just the componentwise addition of their coefficients. Member component() performs this operation nicely. Subtraction is handled the same way. By passing different routines to component(), polynomial operations might use modular-arithmetic. A number of applications use polynomials modulo 2.

Unfortunately, polynomial multiplication is not a componentwise operation. However, it would not be difficult to write that operation. Note that a polynomial is not a Fun because polynomials do not have a finite, discrete domain. Instead a polynomial *contains* a Fun.

Finite State Machines

Some electronic circuits are mathematical functions: their output completely depends on (is a function of) their current inputs. No other information is used to compute the output. NAND and NOR circuits are examples. Other circuits—and any C++ routine that uses static or global variables—remembers extra information called the current **state.** They use this information to affect their results.

Many of these circuits can be described by an abstract model called a **finite state machine** (FSM). A finite state machine is an abstract model of computation with five pieces:

I A set of **input symbols.** An input symbol is the only external input to an FSM.

O A set of **output symbols.** The FSM outputs an output symbol.

S A set of internal **states.** An FSM is always in exactly one state.

out A function:SxI $\mapsto$ O that computes the FSM's current output based on its current state and the current input.

next A function:SxI $\mapsto$ S that computes the next state of the FSM based on its current state and the current input.

A machine is initialized by setting its internal state to a certain value cleverly called the **start state.** When the first input $i1$ arrives at time $t1$, the machine's *out* function computes the "current" output $o1$, and its *next* function computes the next state. The next state is saved until both *out* and *next* are finished; the new state is active when the next input arrives. Subsequent input symbols cause the machine to move to new internal states, all the while outputting elements of the output set O.

This kind of machine is called a **Mealy machine.** Other variations also exist depending on how they handle output. In a **Moore machine** *out*:S $\mapsto$ O does not depend on the current input. In a **state machine** the internal state is the output. That is, O = S and *out* is the identity function. In an **autonomous machine**, there is no output at all. Even though these machines are slightly different, the input, states, and *next* function are the same, and that's the area where we will focus our efforts.

AutoFuns model finite state machines. The most important function is *next*. Rather than a single function of two arguments, we will create one AutoFun for each input value.

$$next_i(s) = next(s, i)$$

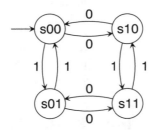

FIGURE 11.1
Finite state machine. Records
even/odd number of 0s and 1s in input.

$next_i(s)$ knows how to completely handle input i. It knows what happens to every possible internal state when input i is received. It is an S $\mapsto$ S mapping, and is declared in C++ as an AutoFun<State>. This function tracks all states simultaneously for one input.

Let's get to an example. Figure 11.1 shows a finite state machine. The set of states is S = {$s00, s01, s10, s11$}; and the input set is I = $[0, 1]$. The unlabeled arrow into $s00$ marks it as the start state. If a 0 is input while in $s00$, the next state is $s10$; inputting a 1 causes a transition to $s01$. This machine remembers whether it has seen an even or odd number of 0s and an even or odd number of 1s. The machine is represented by two AutoFuns: next0 and next1.

```
AUTOCALC>domain I 3
AUTOCALC>elemName s00 s10 s01 s11
AUTOCALC>elemFormat N
AUTOCALC>next0=[s10 s00 s11 s01]
AUTOCALC>next1=[s01 s11 s00 s10]
```

Command get computes the next state. If we are in the start state $s00$ and receive inputs 0, 1, and 0:

```
AUTOCALC>get(next0,s00)
s10
AUTOCALC>get(next1,s10)
s11
AUTOCALC>get(next0,s11)
s01
```

Evaluating state transitions step by step works, but it is tedious. Function composition provides a better way. If the machine starts in state s and receives inputs 0, 1, and 0, then it will end up in some state t:

$$t = next(next(next(s, 0), 1), 0)$$

$$t = next0(next1(next0(s)))$$

or using the $(x)f$ notation for functions,

$$t = (s)next0 \circ next1 \circ next0$$

That is, the function next0 ^ next1 ^ next0 maps any state *s* to the resulting state *t*. This is just a "macro function" built from next0 and next1.

```
AUTOCALC>next010=next0 ^ next1 ^ next0
next010=[s01 s11 s00 s10]
AUTOCALC>get(next010,s00)
s01
```

This is a powerful concept. The definition of a finite state machine means the entire input history is compressed (with a loss of information) into a single state *s*. These states remember all the important information about that input history (it is important because, by definition, all other information is discarded). Regardless of the current state, next010 knows which state the machine will end up in after receiving a 0, 1, and 0.

Composing longer streams of inputs is just as easy. The inputs 0, 1, 1, 0, 1 cause the state $\mapsto$ state function

```
AUTOCALC>next01101=next0 ^ next1 ^ next1 ^ next0 ^ next1
next01101=[s01 s11 s00 s10]
```

Some compositions tell a lot about this machine (in next01 and next10, the final *s00* state is suppressed by the output routine because it matches the default range value).

```
AUTOCALC>next00=next0^next0
next00=[s00 s10 s01 s11]

AUTOCALC>next01=next0^next1
next01=[s11 s01 s10]

AUTOCALC>next10=next1^next0
next10=[s11 s01 s10]

AUTOCALC>next11=next1^next1
next11=[s00 s10 s01 s11]
```

next01 is the same as next10. Therefore, switching adjacent 0s and 1s in the input stream does not affect the final state (it may, however, affect the output stream). That is, AutoFuns next0 and next1 commute; this property holds for this machine, but does not hold in general.

next00 and next11 are the identity function. After two adjacent 0s or two adjacent 1s, the state of the machine will be the same.

The function compositions so far have been of the form, "if the input stream contains a 0, then a 1, the state $\mapsto$ state mapping is ...." But the person or program supplying the input stream might check the current state of the machine before supplying the next input. This too is a function:

```
if ( currentState = s00 )
   input a 0;
```

becomes the identity function with domain value $s00$ changed to next0($s00$).

```
AUTOCALC>ifs00 = [s10 s10 s01 s11]
```

Semigroups

Finite state machines are closely related to the mathematical concept of a **semigroup.** A semigroup (S, ○) is a set of elements S and a binary operation ○ (often called "multiplication") that have the following properties:

- Multiplication of every pair of elements of the set is also an element of the set (the operation is "closed").
- The operation is associative.

If a semigroup contains an identity element, some authors call it a **monoid.** If a semigroup has an identity and inverse elements it is a group. We will look at groups in "Group Theory" in Chapter 13. In general, semigroups are not commutative.

Every FSM defines a semigroup. Each nexti transition function of an FSM is one element of a semigroup. The binary operation of the semigroup is function composition, which is associative.

For the example in Figure 11.1, next0 and next1 are two of the elements of the semigroup. But they are not the only elements. A semigroup must be closed, so the composition of every pair of elements must also be a member of the set. next0 ^ next0 is the identity function that is not an element of the set. next0 ^ next1 is also not in the set. At a minimum, both of these functions must be added to create a closed semigroup. Are there other elements in the semigroup? To get a complete (closed) set of semigroup elements that must be added, use AUTOCALC's close command. It composes every pair of variables and creates new variables (semigroup elements) for any unknown results.

```
AUTOCALC>new
AUTOCALC>domain I s11
AUTOCALC>next0=[s10 s00 s11 s01]
AUTOCALC>next1=[s01 s11 s00 s10]
AUTOCALC>close                    // compose all pairs of variables
Adding 3: next0_next0
Adding 4: next0_next1
Added 2 variables.
```

close creates two new variables: next0_next0 and next0_next1. close names new variables by concatenating the two variable names used in the composition, separated by an underscore. So next0_next0 = next0 ^ next0 and next0_next1 = next0 ^ next1. The four transition functions next0, next1, next0_next0, and next0_next1 are closed under function composition, and therefore form a semigroup.

Semigroups are often described by a multiplication table. It lists the product of every pair of elements. To see the multiplication table for this semigroup, use command `comptable` (composition table).

```
AUTOCALC>comptable
^            next0         next1         next0_next0 next0_next1
next0        next0_next0 next0_next1 next0         next1
next1        next0_next1 next0_next0 next1         next0
next0_next0 next0        next1         next0_next0 next0_next1
next0_next1 next1        next0         next0_next1 next0_next0
```

If the functions are not a closed set, some entries in the table will be "?".

Semigroup Representations

Every collection of AutoFuns defines a unique semigroup. In the example above, the semigroup has four elements (AutoFuns). However, other examples will have many more elements. The size of the semigroup can be very large. In general, a collection of AutoFuns with domain size d can have as many as d^d elements. It is not too difficult to construct semigroups that have this maximum number of elements. These functions generate a semigroup of every possible function of domain size 3.

```
AUTOCALC>domain I 2
AUTOCALC>a = [1 2 0]
AUTOCALC>b = [1 0 2]
AUTOCALC>c = [0 1 1]
AUTOCALC>close
```

Functions a and b generate the permutation group of three elements. Function c collapses two elements together. `close` generates the rest of the 27 functions.

However, the representation of a semigroup is not unique. The four-element semigroup in Figure 11.1 can also be represented as

```
AUTOCALC>next0=[s10 s00 s11 s01 t10 t00 t11 t01]
AUTOCALC>next1=[s01 s11 s00 s10 t01 t11 t00 t10]
```

All I've done is create a duplicate set of t states that map just like the s states. The point of this example isn't to find functions with ever larger domains. Rather, it is to demonstrate that the size of the domain is not closely tied to the number of elements in the semigroup.

Every set of AutoFuns defines a semigroup. But given a semigroup, how do you find a set of functions that represents it?

Given a semigroup's multiplication table (which completely defines the semigroup), the **right-regular representation** constructs a representation of the semigroup as AutoFuns. As an example, let's construct a representation for the semigroup whose elements are the eight subsets of $\{A, B, C\}$, and whose binary operation is set intersection. Variable Z represents the empty set $\{\}$, variable A represents the set $\{A\}$, and variable ABC represents the set $\{A, B, C\}$. Its multiplication table is

∩	Z	A	B	C	AB	AC	BC	ABC
Z	Z	Z	Z	Z	Z	Z	Z	Z
A	Z	A	Z	Z	A	A	Z	A
B	Z	Z	B	Z	B	Z	B	B
C	Z	Z	Z	C	Z	C	C	C
AB	Z	A	B	Z	AB	A	B	AB
AC	Z	A	Z	C	A	AC	C	AC
BC	Z	Z	B	C	B	C	BC	BC
ABC	Z	A	B	C	AB	AC	BC	ABC

We need eight AutoFuns, one for each element of the semigroup. The eight columns of the multiplication table build those functions. The eight elements of the semigroup serve double duty: they are the elements in the domain of the AutoFuns, and they are the elements of the semigroup. Semigroup element A is the function [Z A Z Z A A Z A]. It maps domain element Z ↦ Z, A ↦ A, B ↦ Z, C ↦ Z, ..., ABC ↦ A. The other columns of the table give the other semigroup elements. This table is commutative, so using the rows of this table also works. However, this does not work in general. Always use the columns.[1] Include INTERSEC.FUN, which contains

```
AUTOCALC>elemFormat n
AUTOCALC>elemName Z A B C AB AC BC ABC
AUTOCALC>domain I ABC

AUTOCALC>Z   = [Z   Z   Z   Z   Z    Z    Z    Z  ]
AUTOCALC>A   = [Z   A   Z   Z   A    A    Z    A  ]
AUTOCALC>B   = [Z   Z   B   Z   B    Z    B    B  ]
AUTOCALC>C   = [Z   Z   Z   C   Z    C    C    C  ]
AUTOCALC>AB  = [Z   A   B   Z   AB   A    B    AB ]
AUTOCALC>AC  = [Z   A   Z   C   A    AC   C    AC ]
AUTOCALC>BC  = [Z   Z   B   C   B    C    BC   BC ]
AUTOCALC>ABC = [Z   A   B   C   AB   AC   BC   ABC]
```

---

1. This assumes the notation $f \circ g = ((x)f)g$. If you change function composition to be $f \circ g = g(f(x))$, then you must use the rows rather than the columns.

```
AUTOCALC>comptable
^    Z    A    B    C    AB   AC   BC   ABC
Z    Z    Z    Z    Z    Z    Z    Z    Z
A    Z    A    Z    Z    A    A    Z    A
B    Z    Z    B    Z    B    Z    B    B
C    Z    Z    Z    C    Z    C    C    C
AB   Z    A    B    Z    AB   A    B    AB
AC   Z    A    Z    C    A    AC   C    AC
BC   Z    Z    B    C    B    C    BC   BC
ABC  Z    A    B    C    AB   AC   BC   ABC
```

The right-regular representation does not necessarily generate the smallest representation. A smaller representation of the set intersection semigroup is

```
AUTOCALC>elemFormat N
AUTOCALC>elemName   Z A B C
AUTOCALC>domain I C

AUTOCALC>Z    = [Z Z Z Z]
AUTOCALC>A    = [Z A Z Z]
AUTOCALC>B    = [Z Z B Z]
AUTOCALC>C    = [Z Z Z C]
AUTOCALC>AB   = [Z A B Z]
AUTOCALC>AC   = [Z A Z C]
AUTOCALC>BC   = [Z Z B C]
AUTOCALC>ABC  = [Z A B C]

AUTOCALC>comptable
```

These functions come from the first four rows of each of the eight columns in the multiplication table.

Why does the right-regular representation work? Because of Cayley's theorem. It is a very powerful result, and it applies to semigroups, groups and other mathematical structures. It states that every semigroup (group) is the same as a set of functions under function composition. Furthermore, the proof is constructive; it gives a procedure for building those functions. That construction produces the right-regular representation.

Cayley's theorem is usually written in terms of homomorphisms and isomorphisms. Since I have not covered those concepts in this book, this theorem is stated and proved in the limited context of auto functions and function composition.

CAYLEY'S THEOREM: The right-regular representation of a semigroup $(S, \circ)$ *with identity* constructs a collection of AutoFuns that represent the semigroup. Computing in the semigroup is the same as function composition of the AutoFuns.

PROOF: Let x and y represent AutoFun domain elements, and let f_x and f_y represent the corresponding AutoFun functions that are semigroup elements. We will also use the notation $(x)f$ rather than $f(x)$.

Mapping domain elements through a function gives the same answer as the semigroup operation:

$$(x)f_y = x \circ y$$

This is because, by definition, column y of the multiplication table maps domain element x to the semigroup product $x \circ y$. Composition of functions also gives the same answer as the semigroup operation:

$$(x)f_y \wedge f_z = ((x)f_y)f_z$$
$$= (x \circ y)f_z$$
$$= x \circ y \circ z$$
$$= (x)f_{y \circ z}$$

So,

$$f_y \wedge f_z = f_{y \circ z}$$

Therefore, composing two AutoFuns gives the AutoFun that corresponds to the semigroup product of the two elements. So computing with function composition gives the same results as computing with the semigroup operation. (There is a homomorphism between function composition of AutoFuns and the semigroup operation.) Since the semigroup is closed, every composition of functions produces an existing function (column in the multiplication table).

Since the identity i is an element of the semigroup, $(i)f_x = x$. Therefore every function is different at domain element i, and every function is unique. So there is a one-to-one correspondence between AutoFuns and semigroup elements. (The homomorphism is really an isomorphism.) ■

The right-regular representation can also construct a representation for a semigroup $(S, \circ)$ that does not have an identity. First, build a new semigroup $(S', \circ')$ whose set $S' = S + \{i\}$ and whose binary operation $\circ'$ is

$$x \circ' y = x \circ y$$
$$i \circ' x = x = x \circ' i$$
$$i \circ' i = i$$

where x and y are elements of S. $(S', \circ')$ is a semigroup with identity i.

Use the right-regular representation to build a set of AutoFuns for $(S', \circ')$. Now simply drop the AutoFun for the identity i to get a representation for the original semigroup $(S, \circ)$.

An example will make the process clearer. Let LZ be the semigroup ($\{A, B, C, D\}, \circ$) where the binary operation is $x \circ y = x$ for all elements x and y. LZ is a **left-zero** semigroup (because the left element acts like the zero of ordinary multiplication). LZ does not have an identity. Adding an identity I gives the multiplication table.

$\circ'$	**A**	**B**	**C**	**D**	**I**
A	A	A	A	A	A
B	B	B	B	B	B
C	C	C	C	C	C
D	D	D	D	D	D
I	A	B	C	D	I

Constructing AutoFuns for columns A, B, C and D (ignoring I) gives the representation

```
AUTOCALC>elemFormat N
AUTOCALC>elemName    A B C D I
AUTOCALC>domain I I

AUTOCALC>A = [A B C D A]
AUTOCALC>B = [A B C D B]
AUTOCALC>C = [A B C D C]
AUTOCALC>D = [A B C D D]
```

Notice how adding I and then dropping it do not quite cancel. The last row of the table and the last domain element of the function remain. Those remains make the functions unique.

12

Permutations

Background

Permutations are not as common as integers, real numbers, or even complex numbers. But they are very useful in some situations. They perfectly describe randomizing lists such as the list of answers to a multiple-choice question. They can randomize a deck of playing cards or simulate the act of shuffling. The matches in a round-robin tournament are generated by permutations. All Rubik's cube-type puzzles are based on permutations. For mathematical readers, I will show how permutations are natural representations of finite groups.

In this chapter I present a module for the "permutation" data-type. I have also included a simple permutation calculator so you can experiment with permutations. But first, what are permutations?

A **permutation** is a one-to-one and onto function of a set. Its domain and range are the same set. A permutation is a function that rearranges, or shuffles, the set. No elements are lost or created by the permutation. Every permutation data value represents one shuffling function.

We will begin rearranging the set of numbers [0..5]. Let permA be the permutation (in two-row notation):

$$permA = \begin{bmatrix} domain: 0 & 1 & 2 & 3 & 4 & 5 \\ range: 4 & 0 & 5 & 3 & 1 & 2 \end{bmatrix}$$

permA interchanges elements 2 and 5 by mapping 2 to 5 and mapping 5 to 2. Element 3 is not moved by permA. Since permutations are one-to-one and onto functions, each element appears exactly once in the top row and once in the bottom row. Routine valid() ensures a permutation is one-to-one and onto.

After rearranging elements using one permutation, we can rearrange the elements again using a second permutation. This is composition of functions. In Chapter 10, function composition was written as $f \circ g$. But in this chapter, since componentwise operations are not useful, I will use the term "multiplication" for function composition and write permA * permB to describe the final arrangement that results from rearranging the elements according to permA followed by rearranging the elements according to permB. The " ^ " operator in AUTOCALC is also redefined to be exponentiation (repeated multiplication) during input.

Let's compute permC = permA * permB where permB is

$$permB = \begin{bmatrix} 0 & 1 & 2 & 3 & 4 & 5 \\ 3 & 5 & 4 & 1 & 2 & 0 \end{bmatrix}$$

Compute the product by following the mapping of each element through the first (left, permA) permutation, and then through the second (right, permB) permutation. Since permA maps 0 to 4 and permB maps 4 to 2, permC maps 0 to 2. Multiplication (function composition), as always, is computed with permC[i] = permB[permA[i]]. The multiplication can also be illustrated graphically as

$$permC = \quad * \quad = \quad permA \begin{bmatrix} 0 & 1 & 2 & 3 & 4 & 5 \\ 4 & 0 & 5 & 3 & 1 & 2 \end{bmatrix} \quad \begin{bmatrix} 0 & 1 & 2 & 3 & 4 & 5 \\ 4 & 0 & 5 & 3 & 1 & 2 \end{bmatrix}$$
$$permB \begin{bmatrix} 0 & 1 & 2 & 3 & 4 & 5 \\ 3 & 5 & 4 & 1 & 2 & 0 \end{bmatrix} \quad * \quad = \quad * \begin{bmatrix} 4 & 0 & 5 & 3 & 1 & 2 \\ 2 & 3 & 0 & 1 & 5 & 4 \end{bmatrix}$$
$$= \begin{bmatrix} 0 & 1 & 2 & 3 & 4 & 5 \\ 2 & 3 & 0 & 1 & 5 & 4 \end{bmatrix}$$

The second and third expressions show permA written above permB. In the fourth expression, the columns of permB are sorted so that the top row of permB matches the bottom row of permA. The middle two rows are the same and are eliminated in the last expression to leave the top row of permA and the reordered bottom row of permB. This is the value of permC.

Unlike multiplication of integers and reals, permutation multiplication is not commutative: A * B $\neq$ B * A. permC = permA * permB is not the same as permD = permB*permA.

$$permD = \begin{bmatrix} 0 & 1 & 2 & 3 & 4 & 5 \\ 3 & 2 & 1 & 0 & 5 & 4 \end{bmatrix}$$

Some permutations do commute with each other, but not all of them do. Routine commute() returns TRUE if its two parameters commute with each other.

Permutations are also auto functions, so they share the same identity.

$$identity = \begin{bmatrix} 0 & 1 & 2 & 3 & 4 & 5 \\ 0 & 1 & 2 & 3 & 4 & 5 \end{bmatrix}$$

Because permutations are one-to-one and onto functions, every permutation has an "inverse." By definition, a permutation times its inverse is the identity. If a permutation maps 0 to 4, its inverse maps 4 right back to 0. The two-row notation for an inverse has the top and bottom rows interchanged. The inverse can be computed as permAi[permA[i]] = i. The inverse of permA is:

$$permAi = \begin{bmatrix} 0 & 1 & 2 & 3 & 4 & 5 \\ 1 & 4 & 5 & 3 & 0 & 2 \end{bmatrix}$$

A permutation always commutes with its inverse, so we get the identity regardless of whether we premultiply or postmultiply: permA $*$ permAi = identity = permAi $*$ permA. Since the inverse just flips rows, the inverse of permAi is permA again. Routine inverse() returns the inverse of a permutation.

Method power() multiplies a permutation times itself. Just as we use exponential notation for repeated multiplication of a real number, we can use exponential notation for repeated multiplication (function composition) of permutations. A^n means permutation A multiplied by itself n times: $A^1 = A$, $A^2 = A * A$, $A^3 = A * A * A$. Define A^0 as the identity, and A^{-1} as the inverse of A. The normal rules of exponents apply to permutations: $A^1 * A^{-1} = A^0 =$ identity, $A^n * A^m = A^{n+m}$, $A^{-n} = (A^{-1})^n = (A^n)^{-1}$, and $(A^n)^m = A^{nm}$. But since permutation multiplication is not commutative, $(A * B)^n \neq A^n * B^n$. For more information on permutations, see Knuth (1973c:11–18) or Fraleigh (1976:35–51).

Input and Output

Since permutations are functions, we can use row notations for permutation literals. Member row() writes permA as "[4   0   5   3   1   2]," and it writes the identity as "[0   1   2   3   4   5]" or "[]."

Permutations can also be written as "cycles." The cycle "(a1, a2, a3, . . . , an)" is the permutation that maps a1 to a2, maps a2 to a3, . . . and maps an to a1. In a cycle, each element is mapped to the element following it. The last element in the cycle is mapped to the first element.

To convert permA to cycle notation, write down "(0". permA maps 0 to 4 so write "4" following the 0. permA maps 4 to 1 so write "1" following the 4. permA maps 1 to 0. Since 0 is the first element in this cycle, finish this cycle by writing a ")". This completes the first cycle "(0   4   1)". Now pick the smallest unmapped element, 2. Following the same procedure, the next cycle is "(2   5)". The only element that has not yet been mapped is 3. Since it maps to itself, write the "singleton" cycle "(3)". This table shows some permutations written in both row notation and cycle notation.

Permutation	Row notation	Cycle notation	Comments
identity	[0 1 2 3 4 5] or []	(0)(1)(2)(3)(4)(5) or ()	identity
permA	[4 0 5 3 1 2]	(0 4 1)(2 5)(3)	permA
permAi	[1 4 5 3 0 2]	(0 1 4)(2 5)(3)	inverse of permA
permB	[3 5 4 1 2 0]	(0 3 1 5)(2 4)	permB
permC	[2 3 0 1 5 4]	(0 2)(1 3)(4 5)	permA * permB
permD	[3 2 1 0 5 4]	(0 3)(1 2)(4 5)	permB * permA

Member cycle() writes a permutation in cycle notation. It does not list singleton cycles (like (3) in permA). Any element not explicitly listed is assumed to map to itself. Since the identity permutation maps every element to itself, it is listed as "()" by cycle().

Member readFrom() reads a string and returns the permutation. It accepts a mixture of cycle notation, row notation, and exponential notation (using a "^" followed by an integer exponent). The exponents apply just to the preceding row or cycle. All rows and cycles are then multiplied together.

```
(1 2)                  ==> [0 2 1]
(1 2)(2 3)             ==> [0 3 1 2]
[4 0 5 3 1 2] (1 2)    ==> [4 0 5 3 2 1]
(0 1) [3 2 1 0] (3 4)  ==> [2 4 1 0 3]
(1 2 3 4 5)^2          ==> (1 3 5 2 4)
(1 2 3)(3 4 5)^-1      ==> (1 2 5 4 3)
```

A permutation literal can be a list of any number of cycles and rows. readFrom() stops reading when it encounters a character that cannot begin a row or cycle. This causes readFrom() to act naturally in most circumstances. However, when a program wants to read a permutation literal followed by another value that begins with either a "(" or a "[", readFrom() does not stop and tries to parse too many characters. So read-From() also allows a literal to be unambiguously ended by a "!" character. This is necessary only when a permutation literal is followed by a "(" or "[" character. Internally, class Perm uses the numbers 0 through $n - 1$ for the domain elements of the permutation. The permutation's DSet converts between internal integers and an external, user type T.

Permutation Calculator

Just like integer multiplication, permutation multiplication is not difficult, but it can be tedious. PERMCALC is a calculator for permutations. It is based on the calculator in Chapter 9 and provides those common commands.

Let's use PERMCALC to compute the products we computed earlier in this chapter. At the PERMCALC prompt enter

```
PERMCALC>permA=[4 0 5 3 1 2]      // row notation
permA=(0 4 1)(2 5)
PERMCALC>permB=(0 3 1 5)(2 4)      // cycle notation
permB=(0 3 1 5)(2 4)
```

Compute permC and permD:

```
PERMCALC>permC=permA*permB
permC=(0 2)(1 3)(4 5)
PERMCALC>permD=permB*permA
permD=(0 3)(1 2)(4 5)
```

The list command shows all the variables and their values.

```
PERMCALC>list
 1: permA=(0 4 1)(2 5)
 2: permB=(0 3 1 5)(2 4)
 3: permC=(0 2)(1 3)(4 5)
 4: permD=(0 3)(1 2)(4 5)
```

PERMCALC uses class Element ("Element Class" in Chapter 10) as its domain type. So all of the element commands are available to change the output format of elements. PERMCALC has commands and symbols similar to AUTOCALC. But it also adds and modifies some; use command help and helpSym for a complete listing.

permutations	Returns the number of permutations of *n* elements.
domain	Defines the domain DSet of all new permutations. It supports IdentD-Set, ShiftDSet and LinearDSet. See "DSet Class" in Chapter 10 for details.
format	Controls whether permutations are printed in cycle or row notation. format r prints permutations in row notation. format c switches back to cycle notation.
commute	Determines whether two permutations commute with each other.
shuffle	Returns a permutation for a perfect shuffling of a deck of cards:

```
PERMCALC>format r
PERMCALC>domain s 1 10
PERMCALC>=shuffle(10)
[2 4 6 8 10 1 3 5 7 9]
```

This means that card 1 moves to position 2, card 2 moves to position 4, card 3 moves to position 6, etc.

rotate	Returns a permutation that rotates the first n elements by one or more positions.
close	Ensures all products of existing pairs of permutations are variables. It also lists a set of generators for the group defined by the variables. However, this set of generators is neither unique nor minimal.
multable	Prints a table of every variable multiplied by (composed with) every other table. If the variables are closed, this is a group multiplication table.
conjtable	Similar to multable, but instead of listing the products row * col, lists the conjugates row^{-1} * col * row.
inversion	A *command* that prints the inversion array for a permutation expression (see "Inversions" on page 234).
inversion	A *symbol* that takes a list of unsigned integers that specify an inversion array, and returns the corresponding permutation.

```
PERMCALC>domain i 3
PERMCALC>=inversion(0,1,2,3)
[3 2 1 0]
```

Interpretations

Permutations can be interpreted as data values like numbers or they can be interpreted as operators. Assume we have a row of n boxes numbered 0 through $n - 1$ and n balls numbered 0 through $n - 1$. If each box holds exactly one ball, then we have a permutation between box number and ball number.

Permutations as Data Values

There are two ways to interpret a permutation as a data value. The first, and most common, interpretation is as a function that takes a box number (domain) and returns the ball number that is in that box (range). That is, "permA: box $\mapsto$ ball."

The second way to interpret data values is as a function that takes a ball number (domain) and returns the box number that holds that ball (range). If permA maps box i to ball j, the inverse of permA maps ball j to box i. So "permAi: ball $\mapsto$ box."

$$permA = \begin{bmatrix} box\text{: } 0 & 1 & 2 & 3 & 4 & 5 \\ ball\text{: } 4 & 0 & 5 & 3 & 1 & 2 \end{bmatrix}$$

$$permAi = \begin{bmatrix} ball\text{: } 0 & 1 & 2 & 3 & 4 & 5 \\ box\text{: } 1 & 4 & 5 & 3 & 0 & 2 \end{bmatrix}$$

The box $\mapsto$ ball interpretation is the inverse of the ball $\mapsto$ box interpretation, and vice versa.

Permutations as Operators

Permutations can also be used as operators. Let permS = (0   1). It swaps 0 and 1. But it swaps different things depending on how it is used. We can interchange the contents of box 0 and box 1 (regardless of the balls they contain), which is a box ↦ box interchange. Or we can interchange ball 0 and ball 1 (regardless of their containing boxes), which is a ball ↦ ball interchange.

Assume permA is a box ↦ ball data value. Multiplying permS on the "box-side" of permA interchanges the contents of boxes 0 and 1. That is premultiplication of permA by permS (permS * permA). This swaps the values on the top row of the two-row notation. Multiplying permS on the "ball-side" of permA interchanges the locations of balls 0 and 1. That is postmultiplication of permA by permS (permA * permS). This swaps the values on the bottom row of the two-row notation. In both cases, the result is a data value with the box ↦ ball interpretation, just like permA.

If permAi is a ball ↦ box interpretation, then to interchange boxes, postmultiply permAi by permS (permAi * permS) since the "box-side" of permAi is on the right. To interchange balls, premultiply permAi by permS (permS * permAi) since the "ball-side" of permAi is on the left. Again, the result is a ball ↦ box data value just like permAi.

$$
\text{box} \xrightarrow{\text{permS}} \text{box} \xrightarrow{\text{permA}} \text{ball} = \text{box} \xrightarrow{\text{permS*permA}} \text{ball}
$$

$$
\text{box} \xrightarrow{\text{permA}} \text{ball} \xrightarrow{\text{permS}} \text{ball} = \text{box} \xrightarrow{\text{permA*permS}} \text{ball}
$$

$$
\text{ball} \xrightarrow{\text{permS}} \text{ball} \xrightarrow{\text{permAi}} \text{box} = \text{ball} \xrightarrow{\text{permS*permAi}} \text{box}
$$

$$
\text{ball} \xrightarrow{\text{permAi}} \text{box} \xrightarrow{\text{permS}} \text{box} = \text{ball} \xrightarrow{\text{permAi*permS}} \text{box}
$$

Suppose we have a box ↦ box permutation. The "box-side" and "ball-side" mnemonics do not help any here. Suppose R = (A   B   C)(D   E   F) and T = (B   E). How do we decide between premultiplication T * R and postmultiplication R * T? Figure 12.1 shows R as two cycles. Premultiplying R by T = (B   E) interchanges the targets of B and E in R. That is, B now maps to E's old target (F) and E now maps to B's old target (C). The two cycles of R have been linked into one long cycle T * R = (A   B   F   D   E   C). Postmultiplying R by T, B's predecessor (A) now maps to E and E's predecessor (D) now maps to B. The two cycles of R have again been linked into one long cycle T * R = (A   E   F   D   B   C). Premultiplying by T switches the links out of B and E; postmultiplying by T switches the links into B and E.

You may want to multiply a data value by multiple permutation operations. For example, member shuffle() returns a permutation operation that is the same as shuffling a deck of cards. It is a box ↦ box operation. shuffle * cardDeck shuffles the deck of cards represented by the permutation cardDeck (box ↦ ball). shuffle *

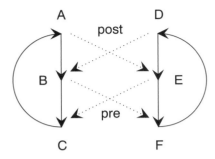

FIGURE 12.1
Premultiply versus postmultiply.
Premultiplication switches the out links;
postmultiplication switches the in links.

shuffle * cardDeck shuffles cardDeck twice. Permutation multiplication is associative: (A * B) * C = A * (B * C). Therefore, if you always shuffle the cards twice, you can compute shuffle2 = shuffle * shuffle once and then just compute shuffle2 * cardDeck each time. This is one of the big advantages of permutations. The detailed rearrangement is not hidden inside a procedure. It is visible as a data type. A whole sequence of mappings can be combined into a single mapping. When a rearrangement sequence is needed, one multiplication does everything. There is no need to continually call a whole list of subroutines.

Other Routines in Class Perm

Routine permutations() returns the number of permutations of n elements. Ball 0 can be placed in any one of the n boxes (n choices). Ball 1 can be placed in any box except the box containing ball 0 ($n - 1$ choices). Similarly, there are $n - 2$ choices for ball 2. In all, there are $n! = n * (n - 1) * (n - 2) * \ldots * 3 * 2 * 1$ different permutations of n elements. permutations() computes $n!$.

There are times when you may want to use a permutation to index into storage. rank() converts a permutation of n elements to a single, unique number in the range $[0..n! - 1]$. unrank() goes the other way: given a number in the range $[0..n! - 1]$, it generates the corresponding permutation. You can use unrank() to iterate through all permutations. See Ives (1976) for faster ways of iterating through all permutations.

Since rank() generates values in $[0..n! - 1]$, it cannot be used for large permutations (because $n!$ is too large). In those cases, use hash(). It returns an integer, but does not guarantee that different permutations return different hash values.

Member random() builds permutations by randomly selecting n random cycles, and then multiplying them together. One element of the cycle is always 0; the other is a random value in the range $0..n$.

$$Random = (n \quad 0..n)...(2 \quad 0..2)(1 \quad 0..1)(0 \quad 0..0)$$

For example, (2   0..2) means randomly select 0, 1, or 2 for the second value of the cycle. If n is chosen as the second value in (n 0..n), then this cycle is replaced by the identity.

Implementation Comments

Inversions

In a permutation p, if $i < j$ and $p[i] > p[j]$, then the ordered pair $(p[i], p[j])$ is one "inversion" in p (inversions are not the same as inverses). Every pair of numbers that are out of order is an inversion. Knuth (1973c:11–18) defines an "inversion table" of a permutation as an array b where $b[i]$ is the number of inversions of the form $(*, i)$. These inversion arrays have the form [0..n − 1, 0..n − 2, ..., 0..1, 0..0]. Class Perm defines the inversion table differently. The inversion array $b[i]$ is the number of inversions of the form $(i, *)$. This has very little practical difference, but changes the form of the inversion array to [0..0, 0..1, 0..2, ..., 0..n − 1]. With this new definition, inversion tables for permutations of $n − 1$ elements have the same form as inversion tables for permutations of n elements except for the last entry.

The rank() routine essentially converts a permutation to its inversion table and then computes a column-major offset as if the inversion table were an array. By using the modified definition of inversion table, rank() always returns values in the range [0..(n − 1)! − 1] if only the first $(n − 1)$ elements are moved by the permutation, and returns values in the range [0..n! − 1] if the nth element is also moved. This means that an application can allocate storage for the largest permutation it ever needs to handle. Permutations of fewer elements can be stored in these large arrays; the last elements map to themselves. The inversion table and rank() values are the same as if the highest elements were not included in the storage array at all. getInversion() and setInversion() are routines to convert between permutations and the inversion array $b[i]$.

Some applications need to know whether a permutation is "even" or "odd." This can be calculated by using getInversion and adding up all the values in the inversion array to get the total number of inversions. The sum is even or odd as the permutation is even or odd.

Possible Improvements

You might add an iterator to walk through a permutation in cycle order. It would be a general version of the solution described in "Moving Large Amounts of Data," in Chapter 13.

Iostream manipulators would be a good way to allow the user to dynamically control the output format for permutations.

```
cout << row << permA;
cout << cycle << permA;
```

The output format is better handled as an attribute of the output stream (ios::bitalloc) than as a static variable (cycleFormat) of class Perm. The row and cycle manipulators would set an attribute in the stream and Perm::printOn() would test it.

Source Code

File Perm.hpp

```cpp
#ifndef _PERM_HPP
#define _PERM_HPP
//**********************************************************************
// TITLE: Perm  --  permutation operations
//
// AUTHOR: Scott N Gerard, Rochester, MN
// LANGUAGE: C++
//
// FUNCTION:
//    A permutation is a rearrangement of the elements of a set.  In
//    this class, the internal set is the numbers 0 through n.  A
//    DSet converts internal integers to an external, user type.
//
// CHANGE LOG:
//    21May88 - Initial coding.  SN Gerard
//    19May90 - Add Sew coding.  SN Gerard
//    20Oct90 - Update description of Multiply. Also added Index and
//              Inversion routines.  SN Gerard
//    27Nov90 - Add IndexToPermImp routines.  SN Gerard
//    27Dec90 - Add Hash routine.  SN Gerard
//    09Feb91 - Rename Legal to Valid.  SN Gerard
//    27Nov92 - Convert to C++.  SN Gerard
//    05Feb93 - Derive from AutoFun.  SN Gerard
//**********************************************************************
#include <assert.h>
#include <limits.h>
#include <iostream.h>
#include "Bool.hpp"
#include "AutoFun.hpp"


//**********************************************************************
// Return the number of permutations of n things taken n at a time
//**********************************************************************
double permutations (unsigned n);

template <class Dom>
class PermImp: public AutoFunImp<Dom> {

    typedef AutoFunImp<Dom> BaseClass;
    typedef PermImp<Dom>    ThisClass;

protected:
    //**************************************************************
    // Construct and leave uninitialized
    //**************************************************************
    PermImp(const DSet<Dom>& convert, UnInit u);
```

(continued)

File Perm.hpp *(continued)*

```
public:
   //*********************************************************************
   // Constructors and destructor
   //*********************************************************************
   PermImp(const DSet<Dom>& convert);
   PermImp(const DSet<Dom>& convert, const char* string);
   PermImp(const DSet<Dom>& convert, Dom(*fn)(Dom d));
   PermImp(const PermImp& p);

   ~PermImp();

   //*********************************************************************
   // Assignment operators
   //*********************************************************************
   ThisClass& operator = (const ThisClass& b) {
      BaseClass::operator=(b);
      assert( valid() );
      return *this;
   };
   ThisClass& operator = (const char* string) {
      BaseClass::operator=(string);
      assert( valid() );
      return *this;
   };
   ThisClass& operator = (Dom (*fn)(Dom d)) {
      BaseClass::operator=(fn);
      assert( valid() );
      return *this;
   };

   //*********************************************************************
   // copy creates a copy but doesn't downcast the ref to the base class.
   //*********************************************************************
   ThisClass* copy () const { return (ThisClass*) _copy(); };
   virtual void init() { ident(); };
   //*********************************************************************
   // Set object to a "shuffle" permutation.  If "deck" is a deck of
   // cards, then "shuffle * deck" is the same as dividing the deck of
   // cards in half and interleaving them.  This is the normal deck
   // shuffling operation.  Create a shuffle of the first n cards.
   //*********************************************************************
   ThisClass& shuffle (unsigned n=UINT_MAX);

   //*********************************************************************
   // Set object to a permutation that rotates the first "n" elements
   // "shift" positions to the right.  shift can be positive (a shift to
   // the right), or negative (a shift to the left), and can be greater
   // than the size of the permutations.
   //*********************************************************************
   ThisClass& rotate (int shift=1, unsigned n=UINT_MAX);
```

```
//******************************************************************
// Return a random permutation of first n elements.
//******************************************************************
FunDRngImp<Dom,Dom>& random (unsigned n);


//******************************************************************
// Return pInv, the inverse of permutation p.  p * pInv = identity
//******************************************************************
ThisClass& operator ~ () const;
ThisClass& inverse ();


//******************************************************************
// Do two permutations commute with each other ?
//******************************************************************
friend BOOL commute (const ThisClass& a, const ThisClass& b);


//******************************************************************
// Pre- or post-multiply a permutation by the cycle (a,b).
// Note:  preCycle() is much faster than postCycle().
//******************************************************************
ThisClass& preCycle  (const Dom a, const Dom b);
ThisClass& postCycle (const Dom a, const Dom b);


//******************************************************************
// Multiplication (function composition)
//******************************************************************
      ThisClass& operator *= (const ThisClass& b);
friend ThisClass& operator *  (const ThisClass& a, const ThisClass& b);


//******************************************************************
// Since permutation multiplication is not communitive, there are two
// different ways to divide one permutation into another.  Unusual
// semantic:  there is no concept of "remainder" for permutations so %
// is used as one kind of division operator.
//
// if c = a / b (post-divide) then    c * b = a  and c =      a * ~b
// if c = a % b (pre-divide)  then b * c    = a  and c = ~b * a
//******************************************************************


//******************************************************************
// post-division
//******************************************************************
      ThisClass& operator /= (const ThisClass& b);
friend ThisClass& operator /  (const ThisClass& a, const ThisClass& b);


//******************************************************************
// pre-division
//******************************************************************
      ThisClass& operator %= (const ThisClass& b);
friend ThisClass& operator %  (const ThisClass& a, const ThisClass& b);
```

(continued)

File Perm.hpp   *(continued)*

```
//*********************************************************************
// power
//*********************************************************************
virtual BaseClass& power     (int exponent);        // mutator
virtual BaseClass& powerPure (int exponent) const; // pure function


//*********************************************************************
// Return the "rank" of a permutation P.  Each permutation has a
// unique rank in the range [0.. n!-1].
//*********************************************************************
virtual unsigned long rank() const;


//*********************************************************************
// Given a rank value in the range [0.. n!-1] (as returned by rank)
// return the corresponding permutation.
//*********************************************************************
virtual FunDRngImp<Dom,Dom>& unrank (unsigned long rank);


//*********************************************************************
// IO operations using external format of a list of cycles and/or rows.
// Cycle format is "(a b c)" which means a maps to b, b maps to c,
// and c maps to a.
// Row format is "[a b c]" which means the first element maps to a,
// the second element maps to b, and the third element maps to c.
//    - '()' and '[]' are the identity  permutation.
//    - on input, both cycles and rows may be intermixed.
//    - the list of cycles and rows are multiplied together.
// Any factor can be followed by '^' and an integer.  This raises
// the preceding factor to the specified power (which can be negative)
// A permutation ends when the next character is not a cycle or a
// row, or by an optional end of permutation character '!'.
//*********************************************************************
virtual ostream& printOn  (ostream& os) const;
virtual istream& readFrom (istream& is);

static void printAsCycles (BOOL b) { cycleFormat = b; };


//*********************************************************************
// Output permutation as a product of disjoint cycles.  Singleton
// cycles are not output.
//*********************************************************************
ostream& cycle (ostream& os) const;


//*********************************************************************
// Output permutation in row format by listing the contents of each
// position.
//*********************************************************************
```

```
   ostream& row (ostream& os) const;

   //*******************************************************************
   // Convert a permutation to an inversion (getInversion), and convert an
   // inversion to a permutation (setInversion).  Note: an inversion is
   // NOT the same as an inverse.
   //*******************************************************************
   void getInversion (unsigned* inversion) const;
   void setInversion (const unsigned* inversion);

   //*******************************************************************
   // Consistency checkers.
   //*******************************************************************
   BOOL valid () const;
   BOOL validInversion (const unsigned* inv) const;

protected:
   static BOOL cycleFormat;       // format for printOn()

   virtual FunImp<Dom,Dom>* _copy () const
      { return new ThisClass(*this); };
};


//*******************************************************************
//
//                              Perm
//
//*******************************************************************
template <class Dom>
class Perm: public AutoFun<Dom> {

   typedef AutoFun<Dom> BaseClass;
   typedef Perm<Dom> ThisClass;
   typedef PermImp<Dom> RefClass;

protected:
   Perm(RefClass& t);
   Perm(RefClass* t);

   //*******************************************************************
   // Extract referent
   //*******************************************************************
   const RefClass& readRef () const
      { return (RefClass&) BaseClass::readRef(); };
   RefClass& writeRef () const
      { return (RefClass&) BaseClass::writeRef(); };
```

(continued)

File Perm.hpp *(continued)*

```cpp
public:
    //*********************************************************************
    // Constructors and destructor
    //*********************************************************************
    Perm() {};
    Perm(const DSet<Dom>& domainSet);
    Perm(const DSet<Dom>& domainSet, const char* string);
    Perm(const DSet<Dom>& domainSet, Dom (*fn)(Dom d));
    Perm(const Perm& copy);


    //*********************************************************************
    // Delegate operations to PermImp
    //*********************************************************************
    ThisClass& operator = (const char *string);
    const ThisClass& operator = (Dom (*fn)(Dom d));
    const ThisClass& operator = (const ThisClass& b);


    //*********************************************************************
    // shuffle
    //*********************************************************************
    ThisClass shuffle (unsigned n=UINT_MAX);


    //*********************************************************************
    // rotate
    //*********************************************************************
    ThisClass rotate (int shift=1, unsigned n=UINT_MAX);


    //*********************************************************************
    // inverse
    //*********************************************************************
            ThisClass& inverse ();
    friend ThisClass operator  (const ThisClass& a);


    //*********************************************************************
    // commute
    //*********************************************************************
    friend BOOL commute (const ThisClass& a, const ThisClass& b);


    //*********************************************************************
    // multiply by a cycle
    //*********************************************************************
    ThisClass& preCycle  (const Dom a, const Dom b);
    ThisClass& postCycle (const Dom a, const Dom b);


    //*********************************************************************
    // multiplication
    //*********************************************************************
```

```
        ThisClass& operator *= (const ThisClass& b);
   friend ThisClass operator * (const ThisClass& a, const ThisClass& b);


   //*******************************************************************
   // post-division
   //*******************************************************************
        ThisClass& operator /= (const ThisClass& b);
   friend ThisClass operator / (const ThisClass& a, const ThisClass& b);


   //*******************************************************************
   // pre-division
   //*******************************************************************
        ThisClass& operator %= (const ThisClass& b);
   friend ThisClass operator % (const ThisClass& a, const ThisClass& b);


   //*******************************************************************
   // Output permutations
   //*******************************************************************
   ostream& cycle (ostream& os) const;
   ostream& row (ostream& os) const;

   static void printAsCycles (BOOL b)
      { RefClass::printAsCycles(b); };


   //*******************************************************************
   // Inversions
   //*******************************************************************
   void getInversion (unsigned* inversion) const;
   void setInversion (const unsigned* inversion);

   BOOL validInversion (const unsigned* inv) const
      { return readRef().validInversion(inv); };
};


#endif
```

13

Permutation Applications

Rearranging

It takes a little practice to spot applications where permutations can be put to good use. Here is a sample.

Randomizing Lists

When designing multiple-choice tests, teachers sometimes use subconscious patterns to place the correct answers. Some students learn to recognize such patterns. To totally scramble the choices and prevent any patterns, multiply the answer order by a random permutation.

I once wrote a flash-card program. I wanted to scramble the order in which the cards were displayed, so I used a program like random(). It gave me a completely random order, and yet each card appeared in the final list exactly once. I have seen other programs that generate a new random number each time another card is needed. It is very unlikely the user will see every card exactly once.

Card Games

Permutations naturally represent a deck of cards using a cardDeck: order ↦ card interpretation. To cut a deck of cards, use rotate(−cutPoint, 52). It generates a rotation of 52 cards by cutPoint positions. The first cutPoint cards are moved to the end of the deck, and all the other cards are moved up cutPoint positions. So cardDeck = rotate * cardDeck cuts the deck.

The shuffle() routine returns a permutation that shuffles a deck of cards. This is a "perfect" shuffle. The deck is divided exactly in half, and the cards are interleaved one by one to form the final deck. cardDeck = shuffle * cardDeck shuffles the deck. Beasley (1990:11–16) calls this an "in riffle" shuffle and discusses the randomness of it and various other shuffles. If you want to simulate a real-world shuffling more closely, you might rewrite shuffle() to randomly let two or three cards from one pile appear adjacent in the final deck.

You might want to add a deal() member function to Perm. It would group each player's cards together. If four players were dealt all 52 cards, it would place the cards for player 1 in the first 13 slots, the cards for player 2 in the next 13 slots, and so on.

```
deal = [ 1 14 27 40   2 15 28 41   3 16 29 42   ...   13 26 39 52 ]
```

Change Ringing

Change ringing is the practice of ringing *n* hand bells, or *n* large bells in a church tower, in all possible permutations. There are hundreds of different methods to generate "changes" or permutations. Each method generates changes in a different order. Some of the more well-known methods are Plain Bob, Kent Treble Bob, and Stedman Triples. Change ringing is practiced mostly in England.

As an example, we will generate the first few "changes" or permutations of Plain Bob using six bells, numbered 1 through 6. Bell 1 has the highest pitch, bell 2 has the second highest pitch, and so on. The highest-pitched bell is called the "treble" and the lowest-pitched bell is called the "tenor."

Plain Bob starts with the identity permutation [1   2   3   4   5   6] as its first "change." This means ring bell 1 first, then ring bell 2, bell 3, bell 4, bell 5, and finally bell 6. This is a permutation using the box ↦ ball interpretation, where the "boxes" are the order the bells are rung, and the "balls" are the different-pitched bells.

The second "change" or permutation of Plain Bob is [2   1   4   3   6   5]. It means ring bell 2 first, then bell 1, bell 4, and so forth. This permutation is the result of premultiplying the previous change by the box ↦ box permutation cross = (1   2)(3   4)(5   6).

The third change is [2   4   1   6   3   5]. It is the result of premultiplying the previous change by the box ↦ box permutation stretch = (2   3)(4   5). To get the next few changes, alternately premultiply by cross and stretch.

```
[1 2 3 4 5 6]
[2 1 4 3 6 5]   <= premultiplied by cross
[2 4 1 6 3 5]   <= premultiplied by stretch
[4 2 6 1 5 3]   <= premultiplied by cross
[4 6 2 5 1 3]   <= premultiplied by stretch
[6 4 5 2 3 1]   <= premultiplied by cross
[6 5 4 3 2 1]   <= premultiplied by stretch
[5 6 3 4 1 2]   <= premultiplied by cross
[5 3 6 1 4 2]   <= premultiplied by stretch
⋮
```

Additional permutations besides cross and stretch must be used at various points to get all 720 (6!) permutations.

I wrote a program primarily built on class Perm that read a pattern file describing a method and played each of the "changes" or permutations in turn. Each change is played through the speaker or sent to a musical keyboard using a MIDI (Music Instrument Digital Interface) interface. The bells are normally played at about 300 beats per minute with a one beat rest following each change.

For more information on change ringing, see Sadie (1990). Dorothy Sayers (1962) wrote a mystery novel in which the permutations of change bell ringing play an important role.

Moving Large Amounts of Data

Even when we are not explicitly multiplying permutations together, knowledge of permutations can improve an application's performance. The cycle notation of a permutation describes the fastest way to interchange large amounts of data, with little extra storage.

Suppose we need a routine to sort an array of records. Any of the common sort algorithms can be used to sort the data. Each record will be moved many times during the sort. If the records are large, these moves will dramatically slow the overall routine. Rather than moving the complete record each time, sort an array of record indices. When the sort is finished, permutations can quickly move each record directly to its proper place.

Let unsorted represent the original order of the records in the array. It is a box $\mapsto$ ball interpretation. Sorting gives sorted, another box $\mapsto$ ball permutation. unsorted and sorted are related by move, a box $\mapsto$ box permutation: sorted = move * unsorted. Note that we are not actually generating these permutations explicitly in storage. They just help organize our thinking about the problem.

Now, think of permutation move in cycle notation. Let $(a1, a2, \ldots, an)$ be one of its cycles. With one extra record of temporary storage, and one extra move, each record moves directly to its final position.

```
tempRecord = Record[an];
Record[an] = Record[an-1];
⋮
Record[a3] = Record[a2];
Record[a2] = Record[a1];
Record[a1] = tempRecord;
```

By interchanging records in cycle order, n records in c cycles can be rearranged using $n + c$ assignment statements. This can be improved slightly by not moving records in singleton cycles.

Round Robin Tournaments

Have you ever needed to generate a schedule for n teams to play each other in a round-robin tournament? Permutations provide the answer.

Assume there are an even number of teams. If there are an odd number of teams, add an extra dummy team. When a team plays the dummy team, they do not play that

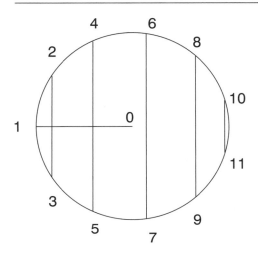

R = (0)(1 2 4 6 8 10 11 9 7 5 3)

Matches:

```
Start*R⁰  = [0   1   2   3   4   5   6   7   8   9  10  11]
Start*R¹  = [0   2   4   1   6   3   8   5  10   7  11   9]
Start*R²  = [0   4   6   2   8   1  10   3  11   5   9   7]
Start*R³  = [0   6   8   4  10   2  11   1   9   3   7   5]
Start*R⁴  = [0   8  10   6  11   4   9   2   7   1   5   3]
Start*R⁵  = [0  10  11   8   9   6   7   4   5   2   3   1]
Start*R⁶  = [0  11   9  10   7   8   5   6   3   4   1   2]
Start*R⁷  = [0   9   7  11   5  10   3   8   1   6   2   4]
Start*R⁸  = [0   7   5   9   3  11   1  10   2   8   4   6]
Start*R⁹  = [0   5   3   7   1   9   2  11   4  10   6   8]
Start*R¹⁰ = [0   3   1   5   2   7   4   9   6  11   8  10]
```

FIGURE 13.1
Round-robin tournament. Lines connect the two teams which play a match during a single round. Rotate the numbers around the perimeter to get the next round. (From Maurice Kraitchik, *Mathematical Recreations*; reprinted with permission.)

round: the team has a "bye." There will be $(n-1)$ rounds of $n/2$ matches each, and every team will play once each round. Kraitchik (1953:226–227) gives the solution, which is reproduced in Figure 13.1 for 12 teams.

The two teams at the end-points of each line play a match during one round. In the first round, team 0 plays team 1, team 2 plays team 3, and so on. The next round is generated by rotating all the line segments one position clockwise about the center. In the second round, team 0 plays team 2, team 4 plays team 1, team 6 plays team 3, and so on.

There are $n-1$ elements on the perimeter, so there will be $n-1$ different rounds as required. The team $\mapsto$ team permutation R = (0)(1 2 4 6 8 10 11 9 7 5 3) rotates the lines.

Let Start be a court $\mapsto$ team data value that assigns a court to a team. Normally, Start is the identity permutation or a random permutation. But Start can be used to "seed" teams into a particular order.

Start gives the court $\mapsto$ team mapping for the first round of matches. The second round is Start * R, which rotates the lines clockwise around the circle. In general, Start * R^{n-1} gives the matches for the nth round. Figure 13.1 shows the values of the permutations in row format. Start * R^2 shows the matches for the third round, where team 0 plays 4, 6 plays 2, and 8 plays 1, and so forth.

In the $n - 1$ rounds generated by R, every team plays every other team exactly once. Why is this so? Clearly, as the lines rotate around, team 0 (in the center) plays each of the other teams exactly once. Now look at the shortest line which initially connects teams 10 and 11. When a team is at the top end of the line (the 10 end), it plays the team which is one step clockwise around the perimeter. When a team is at the bottom end (the 11 end), it plays the team which is one step counter-clockwise around the perimeter. Since every team will be at both these positions once as the circle rotates, every team will play the two teams that are adjacent to it on the circle. The second shortest line is between teams 2 and 3. This line connects teams that are ±2 steps apart on the perimeter. The other lines connect teams which are ±3, ±4, and ±5 steps apart. As the lines rotate around, each team visits the end-point of every line once. So it plays the team five steps counter-clockwise from it, four steps counter-clockwise from it, ..., and five steps clockwise from it. Therefore, every team plays every other team in the list exactly once.

Kraitchik (1953:227–230) also shows how to place an odd number of elements around a circle, so that each element has distinct neighbors on both sides. While the details of the circle and the permutation R are somewhat different, permutations quickly give the results in a useful form.

Group Theory

Some applications are best described by groups. A **group** (G, $\circ$) is a set of elements G and an operation $\circ$ (often called "multiplication") that meet the following criteria:

- The multiplication of every pair of elements of the set is also an element of the set (the operation is "closed").
- The operation is associative.
- There is an identity element.
- Every element has an inverse.

The first two requirements are the definition of a semigroup (see "Semigroups" in Chapter 11) so every group is also a semigroup.

Group theory has been an important development in mathematics. It is an interesting field of study, but the only fact we will use here is that every group can be represented by a collection of permutations. There are many good books on introductory group theory. I have always liked Fraleigh (1976).

Symmetries of the Square

Among other things, groups describe the symmetries of plane shapes and solid bodies. Figure 13.2 describes the symmetries of the square using permutations. The corners of the square are labeled 0 through 3. Figure 13.2(a) shows the orientation of the square we will associate with the identity I = (). The square contains the character "F" to make it easier to see the effect of each permutation.

A 90° clockwise rotation of the square gives Figure 13.2(b). The square looks the same as in Figure 13.2(a). (After a rotation of 45° the square would not look the same.) Only the numbers labeling the corners and the "F" have moved. The permutation that describes this relabeling is R = (0 1 2 3). R moves the "0" corner of the identity position to the "1" corner of the identity position. Figure 13.2(b) shows the final location of each corner. R is one symmetry of the square. Another 90° rotation gives Figure 13.2(c). This symmetry is $R^2 = (0\ \ 2)(1\ \ 3)$. Two more rotations give R^3 (Figure 13.2(d)) and then I = () again.

The square can be picked up out of the plane, flipped over, and placed back down. Figure 13.2(e) shows this symmetry: F = (0 1)(2 3). Figures 13.2(f), (g), and (h) show the symmetries $F * R$, $F * R^2$, and $F * R^3$.

Figures 13.2(a)–(h) are the eight distinct symmetries of the square. There are no other symmetries. They are generated by multiplying permutations R and F together in every possible way. Since, $R^4 = F^2 = I$, and $R * F = F * R^3$, complicated products of multiple permutations can be reduced to simpler products.

PERMCALC will compute all these unique products.

```
PERMCALC>I=( )
PERMCALC>R=(0 1 2 3)
PERMCALC>F=(0 1)(2 3)
PERMCALC>close
```

close multiplies every variable by every other variable and keeps a list of all unique permutations. In this case, close generates the other five symmetries. list prints the eight permutations.

The multable command prints a multiplication table of all the symbols. The product A * B is located in row A, column B. For example, R_R (fourth row) times R_F (sixth column) is R_R_F.

```
PERMCALC>multable
```

*	I	R	F	R_R	R_R_R	R_F	R_R_F	R_R_R_F
I	I	R	F	R_R	R_R_R	R_F	R_R_F	R_R_R_F
R	R	R_R	R_F	R_R_R	I	R_R_F	R_R_R_F	F
F	F	R_R_R_F	I	R_R_F	R_F	R_R_R	R_R	R
R_R	R_R	R_R_R	R_R_F	I	R	R_R_R_F	F	R_F
R_R_R	R_R_R	I	R_R_R_F	R	R_R	F	R_F	R_R_F
R_F	R_F	F	R	R_R_R_F	R_R_F	I	R_R_R	R_R
R_R_F	R_R_F	R_F	R_R	F	R_R_R_F	R	I	R_R_R
R_R_R_F	R_R_R_F	R_R_F	R_R_R	R_F	F	R_R	R	I

The powers command of PERMCALC computes and prints the powers A^n of each symbol. powers 8 lists the variables in the subgroup generated by each variable.

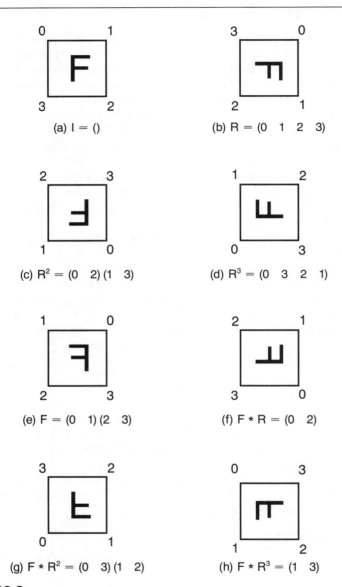

FIGURE 13.2
Symmetries of the square. Each symmetry permutes the four corners of the square. Each of the eight symmetries are shown here. An "F" is shown inside each square to emphasize the effect of each permutation.

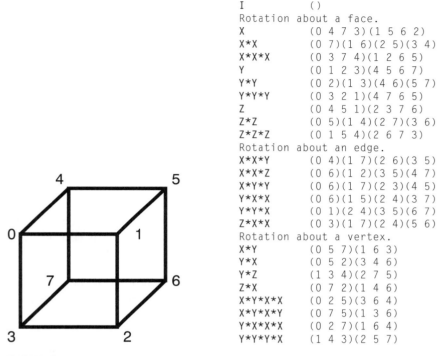

```
I               ()
Rotation about a face.
X               (0 4 7 3)(1 5 6 2)
X*X             (0 7)(1 6)(2 5)(3 4)
X*X*X           (0 3 7 4)(1 2 6 5)
Y               (0 1 2 3)(4 5 6 7)
Y*Y             (0 2)(1 3)(4 6)(5 7)
Y*Y*Y           (0 3 2 1)(4 7 6 5)
Z               (0 4 5 1)(2 3 7 6)
Z*Z             (0 5)(1 4)(2 7)(3 6)
Z*Z*Z           (0 1 5 4)(2 6 7 3)
Rotation about an edge.
X*X*Y           (0 4)(1 7)(2 6)(3 5)
X*X*Z           (0 6)(1 2)(3 5)(4 7)
X*Y*Y           (0 6)(1 7)(2 3)(4 5)
Y*X*X           (0 6)(1 5)(2 4)(3 7)
Y*Y*X           (0 1)(2 4)(3 5)(6 7)
Z*X*X           (0 3)(1 7)(2 4)(5 6)
Rotation about a vertex.
X*Y             (0 5 7)(1 6 3)
Y*X             (0 5 2)(3 4 6)
Y*Z             (1 3 4)(2 7 5)
Z*X             (0 7 2)(1 4 6)
X*Y*X*X         (0 2 5)(3 6 4)
X*Y*X*Y         (0 7 5)(1 3 6)
Y*X*X*X         (0 2 7)(1 6 4)
Y*Y*Y*X         (1 4 3)(2 5 7)
```

FIGURE 13.3
Symmetries of the cube. Each symmetry permutes the eight corners of the
cube. The 24 symmetries have been grouped into those that rotate about a
face, an edge, or a corner.

Symmetries of the Cube

Permutations also generate the symmetries of the cube. In Figure 13.3 the corners of
the cube are labeled 0 through 7. A 90° clockwise rotation of the cube about its right
face (*x*-axis) rearranges the numbers labeling the corners. The permutation X =
(0   4   7   3)(1   5   6   2) describes the relabeling. X is one symmetry of the cube.
Y = (0   1   2   3)(4   5   6   7) is the symmetry that rotates the cube 90° about the
front face (*y*-axis). Z = (0   4   5   1)(2   3   7   6) is the symmetry that rotates 90°
about the top face (*z*-axis).

Multiplying these three basic permutations together in every possible combination gives more permutations and symmetries. Using $X^4 = Y^4 = Z^4 = I$ and Z =
$Y * X * Y^{-1}$, complex products can be reduced to one of 24 distinct permutations.
These 24 permutations are the symmetries of the cube. As a check, there must be exactly 24 distinct permutations because corner 0 can be moved to any one of the eight
corners, and corner 1 can be adjacent to 0 along the *x*-, *y*-, or *z*-axis (8 * 3 = 24).

Start PERMCALC and enter the permutations I, X, Y and Z. close and then list the 24 symmetries of the cube shown in Figure 13.3.

```
PERMCALC>domain I 7
PERMCALC>I=()
PERMCALC>X=(0  4  7  3)(1  5  6  2)
PERMCALC>Y=(0  1  2  3)(4  5  6  7)
PERMCALC>Z=Y*X*power(Y,-1)
PERMCALC>close
```

Adding the "mirror" permutation M = (0 1)(2 3)(4 5)(6 7) generates a larger group with twice as many symmetries (48 permutations). It is not physically possible for us to move a solid cube into this position; but Alice in Wonderland could by taking it "through the looking glass."

Different Representations

There are many different ways to represent a group as permutations. In the example above, we represented the cube's symmetries by permuting its corners. We could also have represented the symmetries by permuting its faces. This would be a little more efficient since there are eight corners and only six faces. Permuting the 12 edges gives a different representation. But all representations have 24 distinct permutations. The smallest representation of this group comes from labeling the cube diagonals (or opposite pairs of vertices) with the numbers 0, 1, 2, and 3.

The size of a representation is not the only consideration. Your choice of representation depends on how you will use the permutations. If you are using permutations to keep track of a particular corner, a representation based on faces will be cumbersome.

Later, in the VLSI design section, we will use the symmetries of the diamond rather than the symmetries of the square. The symmetries of the diamond permute the edges of the square rather than its corners.

Rubik's Cube

I originally started working with the permutation data type during the Rubik's Cube craze. Permutations are the best way—and possibly the only way—to represent Rubik's Cube and operations on it inside a computer. My first implementation was written in Tiny BASIC (a 2K BASIC interpreter for the 8080 processor) in the early 1980s.

Label each facet of Rubik's Cube as shown in Figure 13.4. The elemFormat N command switches PERMCALC to using names rather than numbers for the elements. Each facet must be labeled individually to remember the full state of the cube. The (U8, F2) piece currently has the U8 facet on the up face, and the F2 facet on the front face. But there are permutations where the (U8, F2) cube is in the same position, but the U8 facet is on the front face and the F2 facet is on the up face. This difference is important and the representation must be able to distinguish between them.

Define X, Y and Z as the permutations that turn the entire cube. They are a different representation for the symmetries of the cube; they permute facet labels rather

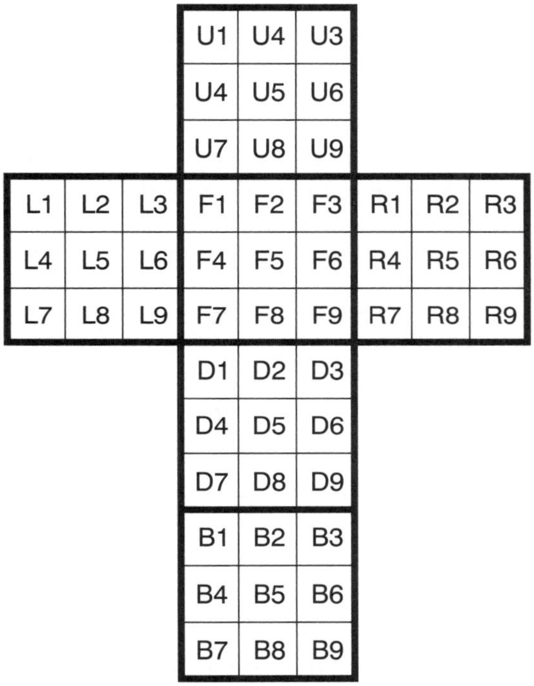

U1	U4	U3
U4	U5	U6
U7	U8	U9

L1	L2	L3	F1	F2	F3	R1	R2	R3
L4	L5	L6	F4	F5	F6	R4	R5	R6
L7	L8	L9	F7	F8	F9	R7	R8	R9

D1	D2	D3
D4	D5	D6
D7	D8	D9
B1	B2	B3
B4	B5	B6
B7	B8	B9

```
elemFormat N
X=(R1 R3 R9 R7)(R2 R6 R8 R4) \
  (L1 L7 L9 L3)(L2 L4 L8 L6) \
  (B1 D1 F1 U1)(B2 D2 F2 U2) \
  (B3 D3 F3 U3)             \
  (B4 D4 F4 U4)(B5 D5 F5 U5) \
  (B6 D6 F6 U6)             \
  (B7 D7 F7 U7)(B8 D8 F8 U8) \
  (B9 D9 F9 U9)             \
Y=(F1 F3 F9 F7)(F2 F6 F8 F4) \
  (B1 B7 B9 B3)(B2 B4 B8 B6) \
  (U1 R3 D9 L7)(U2 R6 D8 L4) \
  (U3 R9 D7 L1)             \
  (U4 R2 D6 L8)(U5 R5 D5 L5) \
  (U6 R8 D4 L2)             \
  (U7 R1 D3 L9)(U8 R4 D2 L6) \
  (U9 R7 D1 L3)
Z=Y*X*Y*Y*Y

F=(F1 F3 F9 F7)(F2 F6 F8 F4) \
  (U7 R1 D3 L9)(U8 R4 D2 L6) \
  (U9 R7 D1 L3)
B=X*X*F*X*X
U=X*X*X*F*X
D=X*F*X*X*X
R=Z*F*Z*Z*Z
L=Z*Z*Z*F*Z

(* squares and inverses *)
F2=F*F
FI=F*F*F
⋮
```

FIGURE 13.4
Rubik's Cube. The six faces of the cube are labeled with U = up, D = down,
L = left, R = right, F = front, B = back. X, Y and Z rotate the entire cube. F
rotates the front face. FI is the inverse of F. F2 is the square of F.

than corner numbers. Working out these permutations by hand is a little tedious. But we need only work out X and Y manually, because from the discussion on cube symmetries, Z can be computed from X and Y as $Z = Y * X * Y^{-1}$. As a check, you might enter these three permutations into PERMCALC and run close. You should still get exactly 24 permutations.

Individual "slices" of Rubik's Cube can be rotated independently while the rest of the cube remains fixed. Let F be the permutation that rotates the nine F-cubes in the front slice 90° clockwise. Define U (up), D (down), L (left), R (right), and B (back) as rotations around the other faces.

Name	Move Sequence	Comment
	Permutation of Facets	
M5	R * U2 * R * FI * D2 * F * RI * U2 * R * FI * D2 * F * RI * RI	twist 2 corner cubes
	(U7 L3 F1) (U9 R1 F3)	
M35	F * UI * FI * R2 * F * DI * F2 * D * F * DI * F2 * D * R2 * U	twist 3 corner cubes
	(U7 F1 L3) (U9 R1 F3) (R9 B3 D9)	
M101	R * B * LI * BI * RI * B * L * BI	interchange 3 corner cubes
	(U3 L3 F3) (U7 U9 B9) (F1 R1 R3)	
M415B	L * F * RI * FI * LI * U2 * R * U * R * UI * R2 * U2 * R	twist 2 edge cubes
	(U6 R2) (U8 F2)	
M530	F * U2 * L2 * D2 * B * D2 * L2 * U2	interchange 3 edge cubes
	(U8 R4 R6) (F2 F6 B6)	

We could work out each of these permutations manually, but there is an easier way. X rotates the D face up to the F face. In this orientation, F rotates the cubes on the current front face (the original D face). X^{-1} rotates the D face back to its original position. So D = X * F * X^{-1}. This is much easier than working out the movement of 21 separate facets. It is also much less error prone. Using different combinations of X, Y, and Z, all the movements of Rubik's Cube are quickly defined. Some simple combinations of these moves are useful enough that new symbols are justified: squares ($F2 = F^2$) and inverses ($FI = F^{-1}$).

We must manually work out the facet permutations for X, Y and F. But all other permutations can be written as products of these. The permutation multiplication routine—not mental gymnastics—builds them. Just as the algebra of numbers helps us solve some problems symbolically, without complex mental arguments, the algebra of permutations help us solve other problems symbolically, with the same economy.

File RUBIK.PER defines permutations X, Y, and F. And it builds Z and the other Rubik's Cube moves.

```
PERMCALC>new
PERMCALC>include rubik.per
```

Do not ask PERMCALC to close these permutations. There are over $4.3 * 10^{19}$ different permutations. You will run out of time, storage, and patience long before close finishes.

With some ingenuity, we can build interesting combinations of moves. The table on page 252 shows five moves, the names given to them by Bandelow (1982), and the resulting permutation. Bandelow also defines moves that twist the middle slices of the cube. MF = Y * F^{-1} * B twists the middle slice adjacent to F. The same technique that computed D from F will compute MB, MU, MD, MR, and ML from MF.

These moves are a few of the moves you might use when building an application to unscramble Rubik's Cube. But a larger library of moves is needed, and the logic to determine when to apply each move (see Bandelow). The solution is too long to include here.

VLSI Design

So far, all examples have been groups with a finite number of permutations. In this example, we combine the finite group GroupD4 (the symmetries of the diamond) and two integers to create a single infinite group.

VLSI (Very Large Scale Integration) chip designs are built by positioning a large number of two-dimensional shapes on different manufacturing levels. A transistor (using MOS technologies) is the intersection of a shape on the diffusion level and a shape on the polysilicon level. The electrical properties of the transistor depend on the size and shape of the intersection. Shapes on the metal level, and polysilicon shapes that do not intersect diffusion shapes, are wires that connect transistors together. Many shapes in a design are rectangles, but more complicated shapes are also common. A wire shape is a sequence of connected line segments that have been fattened to give the wire width. The width and length of a wire determine its capacitance and resistance.

VLSI designs may contain more than a million shapes. It is not practical to design and describe each shape individually. Instead, a small number of shapes are designed and replicated many times. All the shapes for a NAND gate are grouped together in a "cell." When a copy of the NAND is needed, the designer adds another reference to the NAND cell. The reference includes the name of the cell and information on the new orientation and location of the referenced cell.

Cells can be built from other cells. A counter cell is composed of a number of NAND cells plus interconnecting wire shapes. This nesting of cells within cells continues until we reach the cell for the complete chip design.

When a completed chip design is manufactured, all the nested cell references (orientations and locations) are unraveled to find the final coordinates of each shape. The orientation and location of an individual cell reference is an instance of class XfoGroup (Figure 6.2 in Chapter 6) which supports multiplication of cell references (method combine). If a chip contains a reference Ra to a counter cell, and the counter cell contains a reference Rb to a NAND cell, then Ra * Rb is the orientation and location of the NAND cell with respect to the chip cell. Let $<g, x, y>$ describe each cell transformation. First it reorients the shape by group operation g, and then translates the shape by adding (x, y) to all coordinates.

Different sets of group orientations are possible. Most VLSI designs limit themselves to shapes whose edges are parallel to the x- or y-axis. So we will limit orientations to 90° rotations and various flips.

The orientations are described by permutations of the points $pX = (+1, 0)$, $pY = (0, +1)$, $mX = (-1, 0)$, and $mY = (0, -1)$. PERMCALC's close command will generate the eight symmetries of the diamond given the permutations $R = (pX \quad mY \quad mX \quad pY)$ and $F = (pX \quad mX)$. The symmetries of the diamond are the same as the symmetries of the square. But we want to follow the movement of the points $(+1, 0)$, $(0, +1)$, $(-1, 0)$ and $(0, -1)$—the corners of the diamond. The symmetries of the square describe the permutations of the points $(+1, +1)$, $(+1, -1)$, $(-1, -1)$, and $(-1, +1)$. A square-based representation is too awkward for this problem.

GroupD4P is a class that implements the symmetries of the diamond using class Perm. operMul multiplies two permutations, and operInv() computes the inverse. XfoGroup requires these routines be global (not member functions) so it can also support groups that are enumerations. But GroupD4P is more than just a permutation. Its operPoint() method transforms any point on the xy-plane. It fixes the origin and rotates and flips the x- and y-axes.

Class XfoGroup merges a group transformation with a simple translation. It handles the full $<g, x, y>$ transformation. XfoGroup transforms a point p to p' using

$$p' = operPoint(p) + xlate$$

For example, the transformation $<(pX \quad mX), 10, 20>$ means: change the sign of all x-coordinates (interchange $+x$ and $-x$ coordinates), add 10 to x-coordinates and add 20 to y-coordinates. The transformation $<(pX \quad mY \quad mX \quad pY), -17, +32>$ means: rotate the shape 90° clockwise, then subtract 17 from all x-coordinates and add 32 to all y-coordinates. P2BOARD allows GroupD4P as a valid transformation. Permutation $(pX \quad pY)(mX \quad mY)$ flips a region into row-major order.

```
C>p2board "f   r 4 4   p (pX pY)(mX mY)! (0,0)   n 0"
```

The "!" is necessary to end the permutation. Without it, the translation $(0, 0)$ would look like another cycle of the permutation.

Two XfoGroup transformations can be combined into a single XfoGroup transformation. Let $<ga, xa, ya>$ be a transformation to a cell that contains another transformation $<gb, xb, yb>$. This is the same as the single transformation $<gc, xc, yc>$. Combining two XfoGroups a and b to get a new XfoGroup c means c transforms p to p' using

$$p' = b.operPoint(a.operPoint(p) + a.xlate) + b.xlate$$

or writing functions as $(x)f$:

$$p' = ((p)a.operPoint + a.xlate)b.operPoint + b.xlate$$

This formula is easier to work with if you change operPoint() to a matrix gmat. This is always possible since matrices can describe any linear transformation. Another way to say this is: groups can be represented as matrices.

$$p' = (p \times a.gmat + a.xlate) \times b.gmat + b.xlate$$
$$= p \times (a.gmat \times b.gmat) + (a.xlate \times b.gmat + b.xlate)$$

[25]

If *c* is the product of *a* and *b* then

$$c.g = a.g \times b.g$$

$$c.xlate = (a.xlate)b.operPoint + b.xlate$$

Calling a.combine(*b*) changes object *a* to transformation *c*. Transformation *b* is the inverse of *a* when *c* is the identity transformation. So the inverse of *a* is

$$b.g = (a.g)inverse$$

$$b.xlate = -(a.xlate)b.operPoint$$

Calling a.inverse() changes *a* to tranformation *b*.

A production program to manipulate VLSI shapes will perform thousands or millions of transformation multiplications during each run. Since the eight orientations are fixed, a more efficient (and more complex) solution is to convert the GroupD4P class to the enumeration GroupD4. operMul() multiplies two enumerations by looking up the result in its static array. Even though GroupD4 does not directly use permutations, I used PERMCALC to generate the table, and then pasted it into the source code. That is far easier than trying to ensure all 64 entries are correct by hand. The code in operPoint() comes directly from the definition of the permutations. Look at which axis is mapped to pX and pY. In the case for R90 = (pX   mY   mX   pY), mX maps to pY so −*x*In becomes *y*Out, and pY maps to pX so +*y*In becomes *x*Out. Permutation multiplication is now an index of a two-dimensional array.

GroupD4 can also flip a region into row-major order.

```
C>p2board "f   r 4 4    d Diag1 (0,0)   n 0"
```

This example allowed eight different orientations. In other situations, a different set of orientations may be needed. You might want to support rotations but no flipping, or flipping but no rotation. Some memory chips use 60° rotations (the symmetries of a hexagon). You could generalize further and support rotations of 360°/*n*.

GroupD6 is the dihedral group of 6 elements. It rotates, flips, and translates the *u*-, *v*-, and *w*-axes of a hexgrid. GroupD6 is one of the group transformations available in H2Board.

```
C>h2board "f   h 3    d MirU (0,0,0)   n 0"
```

At this point, you may be asking why we have gone to all this trouble when 2×2 matrices would have solved the VLSI problem equally well. In fact, 2×2 matrices are more general since they allow rotation by any angle, not just multiples of 90°. But 2×2 matrices do not account for the translations. The common method of handling translations is to add a "homogeneous" coordinate and use 3×3 matrices (Newman and Sproull, 1973:467). Transformation multiplication and inversion are the normal matrix operations.

But the generality of matrix operations has its price. When transforming a point, XfoGroup <GroupD4> requires one case statement and two adds. 3×3 matrices require nine multiplies, six adds and two divides. When combining two transformations, XfoGroup <GroupD4> requires one table lookup, one case statement and four adds. Matrices require 27 multiplies and 18 adds. Supporting rotations of angles other than 90° requires these be floating point operations.

Possible Improvements

You might add new Perm methods to return "interesting" constant permutations. The deal permutation in the discussion of card decks and the permutation R in the discussion of the round-robin tournament might be good candidates.

If you have to build many enumerations like GroupD4 and GroupD6, it would be worthwhile to add a PERMCALC command that builds the multiplication and inverse tables automatically. This would be particularly true, if you want to build the group of the 24 or 48 (including mirroring) symmetries of the three-dimensional octahedron since those multiplication tables will be very large. You most likely will want the symmetries of the octahedron rather than the symmetries of the cube for the same reason GroupD4P used the symmetries of the diamond rather than the symmetries of the square.

Source Code

File GroupD4P.hpp

```
#ifndef _GROUPD4P_HPP
#define _GROUPD4P_HPP
//***********************************************************************
// TITLE: GroupD4P -- Group operations for dihedral(4)
//
// AUTHOR: Scott N Gerard, Rochester, MN
// LANGUAGE: C++
//
// FUNCTION:
//     The group Dihedral(4):  the group of symmetries of the square.
//     These transformations map the x- and y-axes to themselves in 8
//     different ways.
```

```
//
//          Ident: (x,y) => (+x,+y)    FlipX:  (x,y) => (-x,+y)
//          R90:   (x,y) => (-y,+x)    FlipY:  (x,y) => (+x,-y)
//          R180:  (x,y) => (-x,-y)    Diag1:  (x,y) => (+y,+x)
//          R270:  (x,y) => (+y,-x)    Diag2:  (x,y) => (-y,-x)
//
//      Defines functions for group multiplication and inversion, and
//      for transforming Point2s.
//
// NOTE:
//      This class is specific for Point2 points.
//
// CHANGE LOG:
//      20May93 - Initial coding.  SN Gerard
//****************************************************************************
#include <iostream.h>
#include "Point2.hpp"
#include "Perm.hpp"


//****************************************************************************
// GroupD4P is a permutation of plus-X, minus-X, plus-Y and minus-Y axes.
//****************************************************************************
enum Axes {pX, pY, mX, mY};
static const IdentDSet<Axes> GroupD4PDSet(mY);
typedef Perm<Axes> GroupD4P;

// Declare the 8 elements of D4
const GroupD4P
    IdentP (GroupD4PDSet),
    R90P   (GroupD4PDSet, "(pX mY mX pY)" ),      // two generators
    FlipXP (GroupD4PDSet, "(pX mX)"       ),
    R180P  = R90P * R90P,
    R270P  = R180P * R90P,
    FlipYP = R180P * FlipXP,
    Diag1P = FlipXP * R90P,
    Diag2P = FlipYP * R90P;

Point2 operPoint (const GroupD4P& a, const Point2 p);

GroupD4P operMul (const GroupD4P& a, const GroupD4P& b);
GroupD4P operInv (const GroupD4P& a);

//istream& operator >> (istream& is,       GroupD4P& a);
//ostream& operator << (ostream& os, const GroupD4P a);

#endif
```

File GroupD4P.cpp

```
//****************************************************************************
// TITLE: GroupD4P -- Group operations for dihedral(4)
```

(continued)

File GroupD4P.cpp *(continued)*

```cpp
//
// AUTHOR: Scott N Gerard, Rochester, MN
// LANGUAGE: C++
//
// FUNCTION:
//    The group Dihedral(4):  the group of symmetries of the square.
//    These transformations map the x- and y-axes to themselves in 8
//    different ways.
//
//       Ident: (x,y) => (+x,+y)    FlipX:  (x,y) => (-x,+y)
//       R90:   (x,y) => (-y,+x)    FlipY:  (x,y) => (+x,-y)
//       R180:  (x,y) => (-x,+y)    Diag1:  (x,y) => (+y,+x)
//       R270:  (x,y) => (+y,-x)    Diag2:  (x,y) => (-y,-x)
//
//    Defines functions for group multiplication and inversion, and
//    for transforming Point2s.
//
// NOTE:
//    This class is specific for Point2 points.
//
// CHANGE LOG:
//    20May93 - Initial coding.  SN Gerard
//****************************************************************************
#include <assert.h>
#include "EnumIO.hpp"
#include "Point2.hpp"
#include "GroupD4.hpp"


//****************************************************************************
// transform point
//****************************************************************************
Point2 operPoint (const GroupD4P& a, const Point2 p) {
   int xOut, yOut;

   switch ( a(pX) ) {                // where did (+1,0) end up?
   case pX:  xOut = +p.x();  break;
   case pY:  yOut = +p.x();  break;
   case mX:  xOut = -p.x();  break;
   case mY:  yOut = -p.x();  break;
   };
   switch ( a(pY) ) {                // where did (0,+1) end up ?
   case pX:  xOut = +p.y();  break;
   case pY:  yOut = +p.y();  break;
   case mX:  xOut = -p.y();  break;
   case mY:  yOut = -p.y();  break;
   };
   return Point2( xOut, yOut);
};


//****************************************************************************
// GroupD4 multiplication
//****************************************************************************
```

```
GroupD4P operMul (const GroupD4P& a, const GroupD4P& b)
    { return a * b; }

//*********************************************************************
// GroupD4 inverse
//*********************************************************************
GroupD4P operInv (const GroupD4P& a)
    { return a.inverse(); };


//*********************************************************************
// Axes IO routines
//*********************************************************************
char* AxesNames[] =
    {"pX", "pY", "mX", "mY", ""};

enumIO(Axes,AxesNames);
```

14
Partitions

The VNR Concise Encyclopedia of Mathematics (Gellert, 1975:323) states that partitions and equivalence relations "are found not only in every corner of mathematics, but in almost all the sciences." Whenever a problem talks about elements that are "equal" or "connected," there is a good chance partitions are involved. Finding those partitions, even conceptually, may help you get a hold of the problem. This chapter describes a partition data type for finite partitions you encounter.

A **partition** is a set of elements. But unlike a normal set, the elements of a partition are grouped into **classes.** Every element is in exactly one class. Thus every element is in some class, and the intersection of two different classes is empty. Two elements are said to be **equivalent** if they are in the same class. As an example:

$$partA = (A \equiv B \equiv C \quad D \equiv E \quad F)$$

Partition partA is a partition of the six elements A though F. Equivalence signs "$\equiv$" connect equivalent elements. This partition has three classes: the class of A, B, and C; the class of D and E; and the class of F. The class of F is called a **singleton class** since it contains a single element. Elements A and B are equivalent since they are in the same class. Similarly, $A \equiv C$, $B \equiv C$, and $D \equiv E$. F is not equivalent to any other element. Since A and D are in different classes, they are not equivalent (written $A \not\equiv D$). Similarly, $A \not\equiv F$, $B \not\equiv D$, and so forth. We use "$\equiv$" in text rather than "$=$" because equality asks whether two elements are the same element, and equivalence asks whether two elements share a common property. Since this symbol is not available on most keyboards, equal signs "$=$" are used in programming and input/output. Two elements may be equivalent in one partition but not equivalent in another. When the partition must be specified, write $A \equiv B$ (mod partA), borrowing the notation of modular arithmetic where $1 \equiv 6$ (mod 5), which is a well-known equivalence relation.

The order of elements within a class and the order of classes within the partition is irrelevant. We could also have written *partA* = (*F*   *C* ≡ *A* ≡ *B*   *E* ≡ *D*).

Partition Calculator

PARTCALC is a calculator for partitions. It is based on the calculator in Chapter 9. It provides an interactive platform to access most of the functions available in the C++ Part class. You can use it to experiment with partitions, or you can use it as a work bench for some partition problems. For complicated problems you can either extend PARTCALC (see Chapter 9 for more information on this), or you can write a separate program using the C++ Part class. PARTCALC has a lot of infrastructure, so a separate program will be much smaller.

Start the partition calculator by entering PARTCALC at any DOS command line.

```
C>PARTCALC
```

By default, PARTCALC uses partitions of 25 elements. You can change this with the size command.

```
PARTCALC>size 6
```

The size must be an integer greater than zero. Setting the size to 70,000 will terminate PARTCALC when it tries to allocate its first partition due to lack of memory.[1]

In both PARTCALC and the C++ Part class, equivalent elements are connected with equal signs (=) rather than ≡. Extra spaces are ignored except to separate elements. Partitions are enclosed in parentheses. Note that in PARTCALC, parentheses always signal the beginning of a partition literal, so parentheses cannot be used to group expressions like they do in REALCALC. Square brackets and braces are still available for grouping.

```
PARTCALC>partA = (3=4  0 = 1 =2  5 )
partA=(0=1=2 3=4)
```

PARTCALC uses class Elements (see "Element Class" in Chapter 10), so it supports different formats for elements using command elemFormat. By default, elements are read and written as positive integers.

Equivalence Relations

Partitions are the same as equivalence relations. Knowledge about equivalence relations translates directly into knowledge about partitions. This next section describes the

---

1. The PARTCALC program on the diskette uses the "medium memory model" which only allows 64K for data.

three properties every equivalence relation satisfies. Applications that don't match—
and can't be extended to match—these properties, cannot be modeled as equivalence
relations or as partitions.

First is the concept of a **relation.** A relation R is a set of ordered pairs, x and y,
which satisfy some relationship. We write xRy if x is related to y by relation R. For example, if R is the equality relation "=", we would write the familiar $x = y$. If R is the
relation "is parent of," then xRy means x is the parent of y.

An **equivalence relation** is a relation R that satisfies three properties:

Reflexive   For all elements x, xRx. Every element is related to itself.
Symmetric xRy implies yRx. If x is related to y, then y is related to x.
Transitive xRy and yRz imply xRz. If x is related to y, and y is related to z, then x is
                related to z.

There are many familiar equivalence relations. Each of the following relations is
an equivalence relation. You should satisfy yourself that each is reflexive, symmetric,
and transitive.

1. Fractions: a/b is equivalent to c/d if $a * d = b * c$. This equivalence relation
   is so deeply rooted, some people see ½ and ¼ as identical rather than as distinct yet equivalent.
2. Sex: x has the same sex as y. The sex of an animal might be male or female.
   Or it might be male, female, neutered-male, or neutered-female.
3. Connected regions of a game board: Cell x is connected (equivalent) to cell y
   if movement is possible between the two cells. That is, there is no barrier between the cells.
4. Modular arithmetic: $a \equiv b$ (mod m) if $a - b = k * m$ for some integer k.
5. Parallel lines: line 1 is parallel (equivalent) to line 2.
6. Similar triangles: $\triangle ABC \equiv \triangle DEF$
7. Hexgrid coordinates: coordinate (u, v, w) is equivalent to coordinate $(u + k,
   v + k, w + k)$ for all values of k (see Chapter 8).
8. Group Cosets: Any subgroup H of a group G partitions the elements of G. The
   equivalence classes are the left (or right) cosets of H.
9. Conjugate Group Elements: $g1 \equiv g2$ iff $g1 = h * g2 * h^{-1}$ where $g1$, $g2$, and
   some h are elements of a group G. While not obvious, this means $g1$ and $g2$, as
   permutations, have the same cycle structure. Sometimes equivalence classes
   point out hidden attributes.

More examples are discussed later, but it is also important to look at some examples
that are not equivalence relations and see why.

Connected cells in a board game do not always define an equivalence relation.
Trapdoors that allow travel in only one direction violate the symmetric property.

The "is parent of" relation is not an equivalence relation. It is not reflexive: no one is his own parent. It is not symmetric: a child is not the parent of its parent. And it is not transitive: a grandparent is not the parent of a child. Therefore, we cannot form partitions based on "is parent of." However, we can transform it into a new relation that is an equivalence relation.

To satisfy the reflexive property, every person must be equivalent to himself (xRx). The relation "is parent of, or is self" satisfies the reflexive property.

To satisfy the transitive property, we must add the relations "is grandparent of," "is great grandparent of," and so forth. This "is ancestor of" relation satisfies the transitive property. We simply added all the relations implied by the transitive property and then found a name for the result.

Combining these two ideas gives the relation "is ancestor of, or is self," which is transitive and reflexive but still not symmetric. If xRy, just add yRx and try to name the result. If x is an ancestor of y, then y is a descendant of x. Combining all these ideas gives the relation "is ancestor of, or is self, or is descendant of." Quite a mouthful, but we have finally built an equivalence relation; "is related to" is a simpler name for this relation.

We can transform any relation R that is not an equivalence relation into a new relation S defined by

$$
S = \begin{cases}
xSx & \text{for all } x \\
xSy & \text{if } xRy \text{ or } yRx \\
xSz & \text{if } xSy \text{ and } ySz
\end{cases}
$$

While S is certainly an equivalence relation, it is not the same relation as R. If you are writing an application using S, you may have to add logic to handle the extra relationships that were added to make S an equivalence relation. For example, you may have to filter out the "is self" equivalences. If R is already an equivalence relation, this procedure adds no new equivalences and $S = R$.

Related Relations

The reflexive, symmetric, and transitive properties can be mixed in different ways.

A reflexive and symmetric relation is called a **compatibility relation** (Dorn and Hohn, 1978) or a **similarity relation** (Reisig, 1982). Every equivalence relation is a compatibility relation, but some compatibility relations are not equivalence relations.

A **partial order** is a reflexive, antisymmetric (xRy implies NOT(yRx)), and transitive relation. Partial orders are never equivalence relations.

Equivalent Equivalences

Every partition defines exactly one equivalence relation. The list of all pairs of equivalent elements in a partition defines one equivalence relation. For partA, this list is $A \equiv B$, $A \equiv C$, $B \equiv C$, and $D \equiv E$.

Similarly, every list of equivalent pairs (and the equivalent pairs implied by reflexive, symmetric, and transitive properties) defines one partition. If two elements are equivalent, put them in the same class.

Therefore, every partition is equivalent to an equivalence relation. Think about this statement. Equivalence is both the verb and one of the nouns. Equivalence relations are saying something about themselves. But the statement is more than a tautology. There is real information here. We can divide the set of all concepts into classes. Two concepts are in the same class (equivalent) if every statement about one concept can be rephrased as a statement about the other concept, and the truth of the two statements are the same. Here partition is one concept and equivalence relation (the noun) is another concept. Equivalence (the verb) means the partition and equivalence relation concepts are in the same class. That is, they are the same, or equivalent, concepts. This shows how deeply equivalence relations and partitions are rooted in mathematics.

Whenever we say two things are the "same," or "equal," or "identical" we usually mean they are equivalent under some relation. Equivalence relations hover between the obvious and the subtle.

Matrix Representation

Another way to look at partitions is using a matrix notation. The matrix is square and its rows and columns are labeled with the element names. Entries in the matrix are marked if the row element is equivalent to the column element. Zero, the partition that has no equivalent elements, looks like this:

≡	A	B	C	D	E	F
A	*					
B		*				
C			*			
D				*		
E					*	
F						*

Partition partA above is represented like this:

≡	A	B	C	D	E	F
A	*	*	*			
B	*	*	*			
C	*	*	*			
D				*	*	
E				*	*	
F						*

All elements on the main diagonal are marked because of the reflexive property. The symmetric property of the relation means the matrix is symmetric. Since the matrix must be symmetric, only the upper or lower triangle is really necessary.

The transitive property is a little harder to explain. This table shows the partition (A ≡ B ≡ C E ≡ F) (marked with stars). Adding B ≡ E marks row B, column E (shown with an X). But the transitive property forces other cells to be marked (shown with a T).

≡	A	B	C	D	E	F
A	*	*	*		T	T
B	*	*	*		X	T
C	*	*	*		T	T
D				*		
E	T	X	T		*	*
F	T	T	T		*	*

I find it easier to visualize partitions using the matrix notation. But this requires $Order(n^2)$ units of storage. The partition class stores the same information much more efficiently using only $Order(n)$ units of storage.

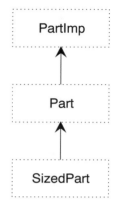

Figure 14.1
Partition classes.

C++ Template Classes

The Part.hpp and Part.cpp files describe the C++ classes related to partitions. Their inheritance is shown in Figure 14.1.

The primary class in user programs is Part. It is a template class with two template parameters. The first template parameter is the "index type" of the partition; the second parameter is the "element type." Unsigned is a common choice for the index type since it allows up to 65535 elements. The element type is used for input and output of elements. The index type must be an integer type with a range large enough to index each element.

The bulk of the code is dependent on just the index type. Class PartImp, with an index template parameter, contains the common code. Class Part is a thin class that tailors PartImp to a specific element type. So if you have multiple partitions with different element types, using the same index type reduces overall code bulk, because only a single, common copy of PartImp must be instantiated.

The simplest way to start your own program is to use unsigned as the element type.

```
#include "Part.hpp"

typedef Part<unsigned, unsigned> Partition;
Partition partA( "(0=1=2 3=4 5)", 6);
```

Using letters for element names as we have in this chapter is easy. Define an enumeration of the letters and use EnumIO (see Chapter 5) to read and write the enumeration on a stream.

```
#include "EnumIO.hpp"
#include "Part.hpp"
```

```
enum  element {A, B, C, D, E, F};
char* elementNames[] = {"A", "B", "C", "D", "E", "F", ""};
enumIO(element,elementNames);

typedef Part<unsigned, element> PartElem;
PartElem partA ("(A=B=C D=E F)", 6); // build partA with a value
```

The second template parameter on Part must be a class that can be converted back and forth to the index type. It must also define $<<$ and $>>$ iostream operators.

The initial value of partA can be specified in the constructor as we have done here. The second parameter on the constructor (6) specifies the number of elements in partA. The value of partA can also be set with an assignment statement.

```
Part<unsigned, element> partA (6);    // construct partA
partA = "(A=B=C D=E F)";              // set value in code body
```

Constructors

Part provides three constructors. The simplest constructor requires the number of elements in the partition. This constructor initializes the partition to zero(). To build a partition *p* of six unsigned integers:

```
Part<unsigned, unsigned>   p(6);
```

Or to build a partition *q* of six enumerated elements:

```
enum  element { A, B, C, D, E, F};
Part<unsigned, element>   q(6);
```

Partitions of characters can be very handy.

```
typedef Part<unsigned,char> charPart;
charPart        cp(256);
```

The second constructor also accepts an initial value. This is more efficient than constructing a partition set to zero() and then assigning it another value later. (See "Partition Literals" on page 268 for details on the string format.)

```
Part<unsigned,unsigned>  p("(0=1=5 2=3=4 6 7=8=9)", 10);
```

The last constructor is the copy constructor to create a copy of an existing partition.

```
Part<unsigned,unsigned>  pCopy(p);
```

The class SizedPart is a derived class of Part. Its constructors build Parts with the specified default size. This is just a convenience, and allows code like this:

```
typedef  SizedPart<unsigned,char,256> sizedCharPart;
sizedCharPart   cp;              // size is not required
```

Assignment

One partition can be assigned to another partition in the obvious way. Partitions can also be assigned a character string.

```
cp = "(1=2=3 4=5=6 7=8=9)";
```

Partition Literals

Partition literals are classic C strings: an array of characters terminated by a null. Equal signs connect equivalent elements. Classes are separated by spaces. The whole thing is enclosed in parentheses. Extra spaces are ignored. Usually, each class is listed in full, but elements can be equivalenced to each other a few at a time.

```
p1 = "(1 = 2=3 4=5=6 7 =8=9)  ";      // complete class listing
p2 = "(1=2 2=3 4=6 7=8 9=7 6=5)";     // same as p1
```

When partitions are output, they are always output as classes, ordered by the smallest element in each class. Singleton classes are suppressed.

Input and Output

The iostream input and output routines convert partitions to and from partition literals.

```
cin >> p;                  // read in a value for p
cout << p;                 // write out p
```

Element Operations

Method setEquiv() makes two elements equivalent to each other. setEquiv() implicitly adds all equivalences implied by the transitive property.

```
Part<unsigned,element>  partA(6);

partA.setEquiv(A,B);
partA.setEquiv(B,C);

partA.setEquiv(D,E);
```

The equiv() method tests whether two elements are equivalent.

```
if (partA.equiv(A,C)) ...      // returns TRUE.
if (partA.equiv(A,D)) ...      // returns FALSE
```

One element of every class is selected to be the **representative** (or rep) of the class. Since every element is in exactly one class, every element has a unique representative. Method rep() returns the representative for any element. Your code should not make assumptions about which element will be the rep for any given class because reps are chosen by an internal algorithm and they usually change after each operation. Reps are useful in algorithm design because two elements are equivalent if and only if (iff) they have the same rep. In fact, this is what equiv() tests.

Partition Operations

Partitions can be added and multiplied.

Partition addition (also called "join" or "union") is defined as $x \equiv y$ (mod partA + partB) iff $x \equiv y$ (mod partA) OR $x \equiv y$ (mod partB). In C++, the + operator adds two partitions.

```
Part<unsigned, element>  partA(6), partB(6), partC(6);

partA = "(A=B=C D=E F)";
partB = "(A=B C=D E F)";
partC = partA + partB;          // partC = (A=B=C=D=E F)
```

$C \equiv D$ (mod partB) merged two classes in partA into a single class. The size of the result (the number of allocated elements) is the maximum of the input sizes.

The same notation is used in PARTCALC.

```
PARTCALC>size 6
PARTCALC>elemFormat n
PARTCALC>partA=(A=B=C D=E F)
partA=(A=B=C D=E)
PARTCALC>partB=(A=B C=D E F)
partB=(A=B C=D)
PARTCALC>partC=partA+partB
partC=(A=B=C=D=E)
```

In matrix notation, addition of two partitions begins as the union of the two matrices; a cell in (partA + partB) is marked if the cell is marked in either partA and partB. Then the cells required by the transitive property are added implicitly. Sophisticated readers may want to prove that (partA + partB) is indeed an equivalence relation.

Partition multiplication (also called "meet" or "intersection") is defined as $x \equiv y$, (mod partA * partB) iff $x \equiv y$ (mod partA) AND $x \equiv y$ (mod partB). In C++, the * operator multiplies two partitions.

```
partD = partA * partB;          // partD = (A=B C D E F)
```

$A \equiv B$ is the only equivalence in both partA and partB. The size of the result is the minimum of the input sizes. Or in PARTCALC,

```
PARTCALC>partD=partA*partB
partD=(A=B)
```

In matrix notation, multiplication is the intersection of the matrices; a cell in (partA * partB) is marked iff the cell is marked in both partA and partB. Again, sophisticated readers may want to prove partA * partB is an equivalence relation.

The "+=" and "*=" operators have the normal semantics.

No Subtraction or Division

There are no subtraction or division operators. Once add has merged two partitions together, the information about the original classes is lost. If C is set equal to A + B, there is no way to recover A given B and C. There are many different A's that give C when added to B.

A	B	C = A + B
(A B = C D = E F)	(A = B C = D E F)	(A = B = C = D = E F)
(A = C B = D = E F)	(A = B C = D E F)	(A = B = C = D = E F)
(A = B = C = D = E F)	(A = B C = D E F)	(A = B = C = D = E F)

Alternatively, we might try to define a subtraction operation using set difference: $x \equiv y \pmod{A - B}$ iff $x \equiv y \pmod{A}$ AND NOT $x \equiv y \pmod{B}$. This relation is symmetric, but it is not reflexive ($x \not\equiv x \pmod{A - B}$), and it is not transitive: $x \equiv y$, $x \equiv z$ and $y \equiv z \pmod{A}$ and $x \equiv z \pmod{B}$ implies $x \equiv y$ and $y \equiv z \pmod{A - B}$ but $x \not\equiv z$ $\pmod{A - B}$. Similarly, there is no division operator that can undo multiplication.

There is, however, method isolate(), which makes one element inequivalent to every other element.

```
partA = "(A=B=C D=E F)";
partA.isolate(B);                // partA=(A=C B D=E F)
```

Or in PARTCALC,

```
PARTCALC>= isolate(partA,B)
(A=C D=E)
```

Special Partitions

There are two special partitions: zero and one. Method zero() returns a partition in which every element is in a separate class. No elements are equivalent (except to themselves). When partitions are declared without a value, they are set to zero. Zero is the identity of addition: adding zero() to any partition doesn't change the partition. Zero is the dominant element of multiplication: multiplying any partition by zero returns zero.

```
myPart partA("(A=B=C D=E F)", 6);
myPart partZero(6);              // = (A B C D E F)

partA += partZero;               // partA unchanged
partA *= partZero;               // partA becomes zero.
```

Method one() returns the partition with all elements in a single class. Every element is equivalent to every other element. One is the identity partition of multiplication and the dominant partition of addition.

```
myPart partA("(A=B=C D=E F)", 6);
myPart partOne(6);              // = (A B C D E F)
partOne.one();                  // = (A=B=C=D=E=F)

partA *= partOne;               // partA unchanged
partA += partOne;               // partA becomes one
```

Method one(n) puts the first n elements ($0..n - 1$) into a single class, and puts all other elements in singleton classes. This is useful when working with small partitions in existing large partition variables.

PARTCALC doesn't have a special zero operator since "()" works as well. It does support one.

```
PARTCALC>partE=one(4)
partE=(A=B=C=D)
```

Comparing Partitions

Two partitions can be compared. Clearly two partitions can be equal. When every pair of equivalent elements in partition A is also in partition B, then A is less than or equal to B (A ≤ B). If B also has equivalent elements that are not in A, then A is strictly less than B (A < B). Two partitions are unordered when A contains equivalent pairs that are not in B, and vice versa. Method compare() returns the partially ordered value between two partitions. The other relational operators (==, <, <=, >, >=, !=) are also defined.

In words, partition A is less than B when it has smaller classes (it also has more classes). Under this definition, zero is the smallest partition: since each element is already in a separate class, no classes can be further divided. Similarly, one is the largest partition.

This gives us a nice mnemonic. Think of the partitions as kind of like real numbers between zero and one. Zero is the smallest partition. One is the largest partition. When two reals are added together, they get closer to one; when two partitions are added together, they get larger classes and also closer to one. When two reals are multiplied, they get closer to zero; when two partitions are multiplied, they get smaller classes and closer to zero.

If A < B, then A is "finer" than B, and B is "coarser" than A. Think of sand and gravel; sand is finer than gravel because the big pieces of gravel have been broken into smaller pieces. In this analogy, coarse gravel is greater than fine sand. One is a single boulder. Zero is fine dust.

Other Methods

Methods rank() and unrank()convert between partitions and integers. Method rank() converts a partition to a unique integer in the range $0..\text{part}(n) - 1$ where $\text{part}(n)$ is the number of partitions of n elements. $\text{rank}(\text{zero}) = 0$ and $\text{rank}(\text{one}(n)) = \text{part}(n) - 1$. unrank() reverses the process by converting an integer back into a partition. The mathematics behind these conversions is quite interesting and is given in "Ranking" on page 278.

```
PARTCALC>rank partA
19
PARTCALC>=unrank(19)
(A=B=C D=E)
```

Method random() returns a random partition. Each partition is equally probable. random(n) returns a random partition of the first n elements. For example, random(5) returns one of the 52 different partitions of the first five elements. Its implementation is covered in "Random Partitions" on page 280.

Method valid() is normally used only by the internal algorithms. It verifies a partition is internally consistent. It should be impossible for clients to ever see valid() fail. But considering the large number of other things that should never happen, valid() is available if needed.

PARTCALC has three table commands:

addtable	Prints the partition addition table.
multable	Prints the partition multiplication table.
comptable	Prints the partition comparison table.

PARTCALC also supports these commands:

partitions	Returns the number of partitions with n elements.
classes	Returns the number of classes in a partition. If classes returns 1, the partition must be one(). If classes returns size, the partition must be zero().

```
PARTCALC>classes partA
3
```

randomDist	randomDist generates many random partitions (with sizes up to 8) and tracks how many times each partition was generated. It then prints the chi-squared statistic for the distribution.
close	Partitions have two operations, so a set of variables can be closed just under addition ("close +"), closed just under multiplication ("close *"), or closed under both ("close +*").

Iterators

There are two iterators for partitions. PartRepIter objects are initialized with a partition, and iterate over the class representatives of the partition. PartElemIter objects are initialized with a PartRepIter, and iterate over all the elements of a single class.

Both iterators have similar methods. Method current() returns the current position of the iterator. operator int() returns zero when the iterator is at its end. Prefix and postfix ++ operators increment the iterator.

These iterators allow you to write doubly nested loops to look at each element of a partition in class order.

```
Part<unsigned, element>        part;
PartRepIter<unsigned, element>  ri;
PartElemIter<unsigned, element> ei;

for (ri = part; ri; ++ri) {
   cout << endl << "Representative = " << ri.current() << "  Elements=";
   for (ei = ri; ei; ++ei) {
      cout << "   " << ei.current();
   };
};
```

After a long series of operations, printing out the class representative is usually sufficient, since all other elements in the class are equivalent to it.

Partition Laws

Partitions do not behave exactly like integers or real numbers. This section lists the laws of partitions and illustrates how partitions behave differently than integers. The laws for addition and multiplication are duals of each other, and are listed together. These laws (Equations [26a–j]) hold for *all* partitions A, B, and C.

Both addition and multiplication have identity and dominant elements. Zero is the identity for addition and the dominant for multiplication. One is the dominant for addition and the identity for addition. There is no dominant for integer addition: that is, $1 + x \neq 1$, in general.

Identity Elements
$$0 + A = A$$
$$1 \times A = A$$
[26a]

Dominant Elements
$$1 + A = 1$$
$$0 \times A = 0$$
[26b]

Partitions don't have inverses:

No inverses

$$no \ A^{-1} \ such \ that \quad \begin{array}{l} A + A^{-1} = 0 \\ A \times A^{-1} = 1 \end{array}$$

[26c]

Every partition has **complements:**

Complements

$$A + A' = 1$$
$$A \times A' = 0$$

[26d]

However, the complement is not always unique. To find one complement of a partition write all the elements in a table, with each class on a separate row. The elements in the columns are the classes of a complement. Changing the order of the elements in the rows gives different complements. For example, the table shows one complement of $(A \equiv B \equiv C \equiv D \quad E \equiv F \equiv G \quad H \equiv I)$ is $(A \equiv E \equiv H \quad B \equiv F \equiv I \quad C \equiv G \quad D)$.

A	B	C	D
E	F	G	
H	I		

Both partitions and integers follow the commutative and associative laws.

Commutative

$$A + B = B + A$$
$$A \times B = B \times A$$

[26e]

Associative

$$A + (B + C) = (A + B) + C$$
$$A \times (B \times C) = (A \times B) \times C$$

[26f]

The next two laws are unique for partitions. The idempotent law says that once you've added A to an expression, adding A again will not change the result. The absorption laws show how A can "trap" and absorb any B.

Idempotent

$$A + A = A$$
$$A \times A = A$$

[26g]

$$A + (A \times B) = A$$

Absorption [26h]

$$A \times (A + B) = A$$

Integers obey the first distributive law but not the second. In general, partitions do *not* obey either distributive law. For instance, A = (1 = 2), B = (1 = 3), and C = (2 = 3) violate both laws. There are however, very important collections of partitions (sets being the best example) that do obey the distributive laws.

$$A \times (B + C) \neq (A \times B) + (A \times C)$$

Not Distributive [26i]

$$A + (B \times C) = (A + B) \times (A + C)$$

Because there are no inverse elements, the cancelation laws do not hold in general. A = 1 violates the first law and A = 0 violates the second.

$$A + B = A + C \;\not\Rightarrow\; B = C$$

No Cancellation [26j]

$$A \times B = A \times C \;\not\Rightarrow\; B = C$$

Implementation

This section describes the internal implementation details, and proves a few key results.

General Implementation

The partition class is an implementation of a well-known algorithm that Knuth (1973a: 353) attributes to M. J. Fischer and B. A. Galler. In that algorithm, a list of equivalent element pairs is input. The algorithm provides an efficient way to determine whether or not two elements are equivalent.

The solution is an array of links (or pointers), one link for every element (see Figure 14.2). The link for an element points to an equivalent element. That element may point off to yet another element, and so on. The array contains a forest of trees. Each tree is a class of the partition, and the root of each tree is the class representative for that class. The shape of the trees is completely irrelevant. The only thing that matters is whether or not two elements are in the same tree.

The partition class uses a special convention for links: a link never points to a higher index. If $\text{link}[i] < i$ then it is a valid pointer to another element. $\text{link}[i] = i$ is interpreted as the "null" link. Since only the tree roots have null links, these are exactly the class representatives. This unusual convention for null was chosen because using null = 0 conflicts with a link to element 0, and null = −1 conflicts with using unsigned integers as the index type.

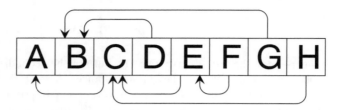

Figure 14.2
Partition Implementation. Partitions contain an array of links. Each element points to an equivalent element. Class representatives link to themselves so their links are not shown. The figure shows the partition (A ≡ C ≡ E ≡ F ≡ H B ≡ D ≡ G).

Method rep() (sometimes called FIND) starts at an element and follows the links until it reaches a null, which is the representative it returns. To speed up future searches, rep() also links the original element directly to the root. This simply changes the shape of the class tree. You can turn off this updating by "freezing" the partition. You freeze a partition with the freeze() method or by placing an exclamation point (!) in the partition literal: "(! 0 = 1   1 = 2   2 = 3)". I invented frozen partitions to simplify testing. They are not normally needed.

The setEquiv method (sometimes called UNION) simply finds the reps of the two elements. If the reps are equal, the two elements are already equivalent and no further work is needed. If the reps are different, one rep (at the higher index) is linked to the other (at the lower index).

Multiplication Implementation

Multiplying C = A ∗ B means looking for all pairs of elements (e, f) that are equivalent in both partitions A and B, and adding (e, f) to C. That is, set $e \equiv f \pmod{C}$ whenever

$$(A.rep(e) = A.rep(f))   AND   (B.rep(e) = B.rep(f))$$

The multiplication algorithm creates the array inx and fills it with element numbers. Then it calls qsort() (the standard C quick sort) to sort the elements in this array based on responses from compRepPair(). Internal function compRepPair() compares two elements e and f by comparing their representatives in partitions A and B. It returns 0 only if both e and f have the same reps in both A and B. The definitions of greater than and less than are not terribly important. Elements that must be setEquiv() in C sort next to each other. After the sort, adjacent elements in inx that compRepPair() says have the same reps in both A and B are setEquiv() in C.

Remember, rep() updates an element to point directly at its class representative (unless the partition is frozen). So although rep() may have to traverse many intermediate links in the beginning of the sort, after just a little while, all elements point directly at their class representative and rep() becomes very fast.

Proof of Compare

To compare two partitions A and B, look for a pair of elements (e, f) that are equivalent in A but not equivalent in B and set flag aSuper = TRUE (A is a superset of B). Similarly, if (e, f) are equivalent in B but not in A, set flag bSuper = TRUE. The four possible states of these two flags determine the partially ordered result: PartLT, PartEQ, PartGT, or PartUN.

The tricky part is computing aSuper and bSuper. Since they are symmetric, we will look only at aSuper, which is equivalent to:

$$aSuper = \exists(e, f) \quad such\ that\ e \equiv f\ (\text{mod } A) \quad and \quad e \not\equiv f\ (\text{mod } B)$$

Changing the $e \equiv f$ (mod A) to a for loop gives the following code:

```
aSuper = FALSE;
for ( ... all (e,f) such that e≡f (mod A) ... )
   if ( e≢f (mod B) ) {
     aSuper = TRUE;
     break;
   };
```

The simplistic solution is a double loop over all pairs of elements that tests every possible pair. This requires $Order(n^2)$ operations. But there is a faster way.

Assume $e \equiv f \equiv g$ (mod A). If $e \not\equiv f$ (mod B), then either $e \not\equiv g$ (mod B) or $f \not\equiv g$ (mod B), or both. g cannot be equivalent to two inequivalent elements (transitive property). Think of the partition as a graph, with the elements as vertices, and equivalent pairs in partition A linked by an edge. In the three-vertex graph of e, f, and g, we do not need to test all three pairs (e, f), (e, g), and (f, g) in the for loop. Testing any two is sufficient. The third edge, which forms a loop in the graph, can be skipped. Using this same argument, all edges that create a loop can be ignored. That is, we only need to check a spanning tree of the equivalent elements in A.

But partitions are implemented as spanning trees. The edges are the links stored in the elem array. So, the for loop needs only to look at the links $(e, f = \text{elem}[e])$. Since a spanning tree of n nodes has $n - 1$ edges, we have reduced the number of tests to $Order(n)$. Adding this all together gives the following simple piece of code:

```
aSuper = FALSE;
for ( ... all elements e ... ) {
   f = A.elem[e];
   if ( !b.equiv(e,f) ) {
     aSuper = TRUE;
     break;
   };
```

Ranking

The number of partitions of n elements, part(n), is a function of the number of partitions of k elements (see Niejenhuis and Wilf, 1975:87–92). part(0) = 1, part(1) = 1, part(2) = 2, part(3) = 5, part(4) = 15, part(5) = 52, and so forth.

$$part(n) = \sum_{k=0}^{n-1} \binom{n-1}{k} part(k) \qquad [27]$$

How can we interpret this formula? Figure 14.3 illustrates the formula for $n = 4$ elements. It shows the 15 partitions of four elements broken down according to the formula. The first column represents the 15 partitions of four elements. Each block in the second column corresponds to one value of k in the sum of Equation [27]. The number in each block is the value of the binomial coefficient, and is the number of copies of part(k) in column 4. For example, the first block is $k = 3$ with one copy of part(3) in column 4. The next block is $k = 2$ with three copies of part(2). Everything so far (except for ordering) comes straight from the equation. The next-to-last column shows the rank() value for the partition listed in the last column.

The unrank algorithm starts with all elements "free" or unassigned to any class. Then it picks a free element and builds its class. Although it doesn't matter too much which element is chosen, it always picks the largest free element. For partitions of four elements the largest free element is 3. After removing the largest element, there are $n - 1$ free elements. There is only one way to make element 3 a singleton class (block with $k = 3$). This leaves part(3) different ways to partition the three remaining free elements. Element 3 can be part of a two-element class in $3 = \binom{3}{2}$ different ways (block with $k = 2$); it can be equivalent to element 0, 1, or 2. The remaining two free elements can be partitioned in part(2) distinct ways. Similarly, element 3 can be part of a three-element class in $3 = \binom{3}{1}$ distinct ways. The remaining element can be partitioned in part(1) ways.

Rather than picking which elements will be equivalent to element 3, the algorithm selects the elements that will remain free. This is done by numbering the $\binom{n-1}{k}$ copies of part(k) using the binomial number system with nome = k. (The nome is the number of binomials in the sum. See "Binomial Number System" in Chapter 3 for more details.) The cogets (the numbers on the top of the binomial coefficient) in the expansion are the elements that remain free. For example, look at the second block ($k = 2$) in column 2. The three sub-blocks are numbered 0, 1, and 2 and these values are expressed as the sum of $k = 2$ (the nome) binomial coefficients. The sub-block for 0 has cogets 0 and 1, so elements 0 and 1 remain free, and 2 is set equivalent to 3. The sub-block for 1 shows that elements 2 and 0 remain free. The last sub-block for $k = 2$ leaves elements 2 and 1 free.

part(n)	$\binom{n-1}{k}$	binomial numbering	part(k)	rank	partition
part(4) = 15	$1 = \binom{3}{3}$	$0 = \binom{2}{3} + \binom{1}{2} + \binom{0}{1}$	part(3) = 5	0	0 1 2 3
				1	0 = 1 2 3
				2	0 1 = 2 3
				3	1 0 = 2 3
				4	0 = 1 = 2 3
	$3 = \binom{3}{2}$	$0 = \binom{1}{2} + \binom{0}{1}$	part(2) = 2	5	0 1 2 = 3
				6	0 = 1 2 = 3
		$1 = \binom{2}{2} + \binom{0}{1}$	part(2) = 2	7	0 2 1 = 3
				8	0 = 2 1 = 3
		$2 = \binom{2}{2} + \binom{1}{1}$	part(2) = 2	9	1 2 0 = 3
				10	1 = 2 0 = 3
	$3 = \binom{3}{1}$	$0 = \binom{0}{1}$	part(1) = 1	11	0 1 = 2 = 3
		$1 = \binom{1}{1}$	part(1) = 1	12	1 0 = 2 = 3
		$2 = \binom{2}{1}$	part(1) = 1	13	2 0 = 1 = 3
	$1 = \binom{3}{0}$	0	part(0) = 1	14	0 = 1 = 2 = 3

FIGURE 14.3
Partition ranking.

unrank() reduces the rank value in column 5 using Equation [27] until it finds the correct value of k. Then the remainder is converted to the binomial number system, giving the list of free elements. All the other elements are setEquiv() to the largest element. This leaves a reduced problem of unranking a partition of k elements. The process repeats with $n = k$ of a reduced table. Note that at each new stage, the free elements are effectively renumbered to the integers 0 through $k - 1$. Method rank() is simply the opposite of unrank().

By assigning low ranks to high values of k, the zero() partition has a rank of 0, and one() has a rank of part(n) $- 1$. Adding large-numbered, singleton classes to the end of a partition does not change its rank value. Therefore, you can store partitions with n elements inside a partition variable that has room for more than n elements without changing their rank values.

The rank() and unrank() methods are limited by the precision of the long integer array that stores the rank number. With a 31-bit longs, their limit is a maximum of 15 elements.

Random Partitions

One way to generate random partitions of elements $0..n - 1$ is to generate a random integer and use unrank() to convert it to a partition. The resulting partition is as random as the initial integer. But this method has the same limitation as unrank(): it works only for partitions of 15 elements or less.

Niejenhuis and Wilf (1975) give an algorithm for generating random partitions that does not suffer from this limitation. (Although they do not directly address ranking and unranking, the ranking algorithms in the previous section were adapted from their work.) I have found a modification of their random algorithm that is faster. The algorithm must randomly select k of the $n - 1$ free elements at each stage. They call a routine to do this once per stage. To handle the general case, their algorithm sorts the k elements (to prevent duplicates). My improvement is to generate a random permutation once at the beginning, and then select elements $k..n - 1$ at each stage. Duplicate elements are automatically prevented. By definition, a permutation contains each element exactly once.

1. Set result = zero().
2. Generate a random *permutation* perm of elements 0 through $n - 1$.
3. Set $m = n$.
4. Select $0 \leq k < m$ according to the probability of k in Equation [27].
5. Set perm(k) $\equiv$ perm($k + 1$) $\equiv \cdots \equiv$ perm($m - 1$) in result. Elements perm(0) through perm($k - 1$) remain free.
6. If $k = 0$ then return result. Else set $m = k$ and go to 4.

This algorithm is simple to implement, but does it produce some partitions more frequently than others? The next section shows that each partition is equally likely.

Step 4 produces a decreasing sequence of k's.

$$n = k_0 > k_1 > k_2 > \cdots > k_t = 0$$

Let $j_i = k_{i-1} - k_i$, so that $k_i = j_{i+1} + j_{i+2} + \cdots + j_t$, and $n = j_1 + j_2 + \cdots + j_t$. The j_i are the number of equivalent elements in step 5. That is, the ith class has exactly j_i elements.

The order of the j_i is not always important. Let $(c_1, s_1; c_2, s_2; \cdots; c_d, s_d)$ represent all orderings of the j_i that have c_i occurrences of $s_i = j_i$ elements. So $(c_i, s_i) = (1, 3; 2, 1)$ represents one class of size 3 and two classes of size 1, or $(3, 1, 1)$, $(1, 3, 1)$ and $(1, 1, 3)$. Since the j_i are the class sizes for a partition, every partition implies a specific set of (c_i, s_i). Each element is in exactly one class, therefore:

$$n = c_1 s_1 + c_2 s_2 + \cdots + c_d s_d \qquad [28]$$

Figure 14.4 illustrates how the algorithm works. It makes two basic decisions. First, it randomly orders the elements by picking a random permutation (step 2). This selects one column in the table. Second, it randomly selects a sequence of k_i—and therefore j_i— that specify how those elements are combined into classes (step 4). This selects one row in the table. Step 5 converts the j_i into the pattern shown in the table.

The probability of generating a k is (from Equation [27])

$$Prob(k) = \frac{part(k)}{part(n)} \binom{n-1}{k} \qquad [29]$$

The probability of selecting a row in Figure 14.4 is the probability of generating its sequence of k_i.

$$
\begin{aligned}
Prob_{row}(j_1, \ldots, j_t) &= \frac{part(k_1)}{part(n)} \binom{n-1}{k_1} \frac{part(k_2)}{part(k_1)} \binom{k_1 - 1}{k_2} \\
&\quad \times \cdots \frac{part(k_t)}{part(k_{t-1})} \binom{k_{t-1} - 1}{k_t} \frac{part(0)}{part(k_t)} \binom{k_t - 1}{0} \\
&= \frac{1}{part(n)} \binom{n-1}{k_1} \binom{k_1 - 1}{k_2} \cdots \binom{k_{t-1} - 1}{k_t} \\
&= \frac{1}{part(n)} \binom{n}{k_1} \frac{n - k_1}{n} \binom{k_1}{k_2} \frac{k_1 - k_2}{k_1} \cdots \binom{k_{t-1}}{k_t} \frac{k_{t-1} - k_1}{k_{t-1}}
\end{aligned}
$$

Since the k_i fully determine the j_i, this can be simplified to

$$Prob_{row}(j_1, \ldots, j_t) = \frac{1}{part(n)} \frac{n!}{k_1! \, j_1!} \frac{j_1}{k_0} \frac{k_1!}{k_2! \, j_2!} \frac{j_2}{k_1} \cdots \frac{k_{t-1}!}{k_t! \, j_t!} \frac{j_t}{k_{t-1}}$$

Prob	j_i	pattern	All permutations of 4 elements (6 of 24 columns)					
1/15	1,1,1,1	x_1 x_2 x_3 x_4	0 1 2 3	0 1 3 2	0 2 1 3	0 2 3 1	0 3 1 2	0 3 2 1
1/15	1,1,2	$x_1=x_2$ x_3 x_4	0=1 2 3	0=1 3 2	0=2 1 3	0=2 3 1	0=3 1 2	0=3 2 1
2/15	1,2,1	x_1 $x_2=x_3$ x_4	0 1=2 3	0 1=3 2	0 2=1 3	0 2=3 1	0 3=1 2	0 3=2 1
3/15	2,1,1	x_1 x_2 $x_3=x_4$	0 1 2=3	0 1 3=2	0 2 1=3	0 2 3=1	0 3 1=2	0 3 2=1
3/15	2,2	$x_1=x_2$ $x_3=x_4$	0=1 2=3	0=1 3=2	0=2 1=3	0=2 3=1	0=3 1=2	0=3 2=1
1/15	1,3	$x_1=x_2=x_3$ x_4	0=1=2 3	0=1=3 2	0=2=1 3	0=2=3 1	0=3=1 2	0=3=2 1
3/15	3,1	x_1 $x_2=x_3=x_4$	0 1=2=3	0 1=3=2	0 2=1=3	0 2=3=1	0 3=1=2	0 3=2=1
1/15	4	$x_1=x_2=x_3=x_4$	0=1=2=3	0=1=3=2	0=2=1=3	0=2=3=1	0=3=1=2	0=3=2=1

FIGURE 14.4
Selecting random partitions. The first column is $Prob_{row}(j_1, j_2, \ldots, j_t)$, the probability of selecting the row. The j_i column shows the sizes of each class. The pattern column shows which elements will be made equivalent. The remaining columns show the partition generated by each permutation. (Due to size limitations, only six columns are shown. The full table has 24 columns.)

$$Prob_{row}(j_1, \ldots, j_t) = \frac{1}{part(n)} \frac{n!}{j_1! j_2! \ldots j_t!} \frac{j_1}{k_0} \frac{j_2}{k_1} \ldots \frac{j_t}{k_{t-1}} \quad [30]$$

For example, assume the algorithm generates $n = k_0 = 4$, $k_1 = 2$, $k_2 = 1$ and $k_3 = 0$. Then $j_1 = 2, j_2 = 1$ and $j_3 = 1$. The probability of generating the row with $j_i = (2, 1, 1)$ is

$$Prob_{row}(2, 1, 1) = \frac{1}{part(4)} \frac{4!}{2! 1! 1!} \frac{2}{4} \frac{1}{2} \frac{1}{1} = \frac{3}{15}$$

Since the order of elements within a class and the order of the classes are irrelevant in the permutation, each partition may appear multiple times in each row (for example, $(0 = 1 \quad 2 = 3)$ is the same partition as $(3 = 2 \quad 1 = 0)$). A class with j_i elements is generated in $j_i!$ different ways. A partition that has c_i classes of size s_i can be generated in $c_i!$ different ways by interchanging classes of size s_i. So, if the class sizes of a partition match the row, the fraction of the $n!$ permutations that produce the partition is

$$Prob_{col}(partition\ p\ in\ one\ row) = \frac{j_1!\,j_2!\ldots j_t!\,c_1!\,c_2!\ldots c_d!}{n!} \qquad [31]$$

What is the probability of partition $(0 = 1\quad 2\quad 3)$ appearing in a row? There is one class of size 2 $(c_1, s_1) = (1, 2)$ and two classes of size 1 $(c_2, s_2) = (2, 1)$. So its probability is

$$Prob_{col}(0 = 1\quad 2\quad 3) = \frac{2!\,1!\quad 1!\,2!}{4!} = \frac{1}{6}$$

That is, the four partitions $(0 = 1\quad 2\quad 3)$, $(0 = 1\quad 3\quad 2)$, $(1 = 0\quad 2\quad 3)$, and $(1 = 0\quad 3\quad 2)$ out of the 24 partitions in the row are the same partition.

Rows with $(j_1, j_2, \ldots, j_t)$ only generate partitions with class sizes j_i. So, the probability of selecting a specific partition p is the sum, over all rows that produce p, of the row probability times the column probability; that is, Equation [30] times Equation [31] summed over all j_i coefficients in Equation [30].

$$Prob(p) = \sum_{(c_i,\,s_i)} Prob_{row}(j_1 \ldots j_t)\, Prob_{col}(p)$$

$$= \frac{c_1!\,c_2!\ldots c_d!}{part(n)} \sum_{(c_i,\,s_i)} \frac{j_1}{k_0}\frac{j_2}{k_1}\cdots\frac{j_t}{k_{t-1}} \qquad [32]$$

If partitions are to be equally likely, we must have the following.

THEOREM:

$$\frac{1}{c_1!\,c_2!\ldots c_d!} = \sum_{(c_i,s_i)} \frac{j_1}{k_0}\frac{j_2}{k_1}\cdots\frac{j_t}{k_{t-1}} \qquad [33]$$

PROOF: The proof is by induction on the number of j_i.

When there is just one j, then $n = k_0 = j_1$ and $(c_1, s_1) = (1, j)$. Both sides of Equation [33] evaluate to 1.

When there are multiple j_i, the terms in the sum can be grouped by their value of j_1, which takes on each of the values s_i.

$$\sum_{(c_1, s_1; \ldots; c_d, s_d)} = \frac{s_1}{n} \sum_{(c_1 - 1, s_1; c_2\, s_2; \ldots; c_d, s_d)} + \frac{s_2}{n} \sum_{(c_1\, s_1; c_2-1, s_2; \ldots; c_d, s_d)} + \cdots + \frac{s_d}{n} \sum_{(c_1, s_1; c_2, s_2; \ldots; c_d-1, s_d)}$$

$$[34]$$

Assuming the theorem holds for smaller number of j_i, replace the sums on the right-hand side of Equation [34].

$$\sum_{(c_1, s_1; \ldots; c_d, s_d)} = \frac{s_1}{n(c_1 - 1)! \, c_2! \ldots c_d!} + \frac{s_2}{nc_1!(c_2 - 1)! \ldots c_d!} + \cdots + \frac{s_d}{nc_1! \, c_2! \ldots (c_d - 1)!}$$

$$= \frac{c_1 s_1 + c_2 s_2 + \cdots + c_d s_d}{nc_1! \, c_2! \ldots c_d!}$$

The numerator is just n (Equation [28]), which proves the result.

$$\sum_{(c_1, s_1; \ldots; c_n, s_d)} = \frac{1}{c_1! \, c_2! \ldots c_d!} \qquad \text{[35]} \; \blacksquare$$

Combining Equations [32] and [35] shows each partition is equally likely.

$$Prob(p) = \frac{1}{part(n)} \qquad \text{[36]}$$

This routine is faster than the ranking or unranking routines because the selection of free elements is done by the random permutation routine. It does this by selecting n random integers and interchanging elements without any testing. unrank() uses numToCogets(), which linearly searches for each of k_i cogets of the binomial representation for each iteration of the loop.

Is it possible to use this faster algorithm in the ranking routines? Probably not. To generate all partitions of n elements we need a value between 0 and $n! - 1$ to generate the random partition, plus more bits to select the j_i values. But this is more than the number of partitions. For example, there are five distinct partitions of three elements, but there are six (=3!) different permutations. We apparently need more bits than are available to unrank().

The random() algorithm is also not limited by the precision of a long integer. The random permutation is generated from n independent random values in the range $0..n$. The only limit comes in selecting the random values of k using Equation [29]. This calculation uses double floats and overflows on partitions(219).

Possible Extensions

Add a class count to the PartImp member data. Only repi() and setEquivi() need to be modified to update this value.

It is easy to write a method similar to compare(A, B) that returns three partitions: the (e, f) pairs found only in A, the (e, f) pairs found only in B, and the (e, f) pairs found in both A and B. This decomposition is not unique.

Depending on the application, you might need more random selection methods beyond the equiprobable partitions of Equation [36]. For example:

- Return a random class.
- Return a random class where the probability of selecting a class is proportional to its size (easy).
- Return a random element of class i.

It might be more appropriate to print out "frozen" partitions as pairs of equivalent elements.

Source Code

File Part.hpp

```cpp
#ifndef _PART_HPP
#define _PART_HPP
//********************************************************************
// TITLE: Part  --  partition operations
//
// AUTHOR: Scott N Gerard, Rochester, MN
// LANGUAGE: C++
//
// FUNCTION:
//    A partition P of elements in E is a set of classes such that every
//    element e in E is in exactly one class.  If two elements e and f
//    are in the same class of partition P, they are "equivalent".
//
//    In a partition P, if e is equivalent to f, and e is equivalent to
//    g, then e is also equivalent to g.
//
//    Every class has one favored element called its "representative".
//    Class representatives are chosen by an internal algorithm, and in
//    general, change each time the partition changes.
//
//    PartRepIter iterates over class representatives of a partition.
//    PartElemIter iterates over the elements of a single class.
//
// CHANGE LOG:
//    28Jun91 - Initial coding.  Modify module Perm. SN Gerard
//    12Apr92 - Convert from Modula-2 to C++.  SN Gerard
//    01Nov92 - Split element and index types.  SN Gerard
//********************************************************************
```

(continued)

File Part.hpp   *(continued)*

```cpp
#include <iostream.h>

#include "Bool.hpp"
#include "PartCompare.hpp"

//***********************************************************************
// Return the number of distinct partitions of n elements.
//***********************************************************************
double partitions (int n);

//***********************************************************************
// PartImp:   Partition Base Implementation
//
// The base routines to work with partitions.  PartImp partitions
// elements of the template index class Inx.  Inx must be an integer
// type.  If Inx is unsigned short, PartImp supports up to 65535
// elements.
//***********************************************************************

template<class Inx>                      // type of array index
class PartImp {

    typedef PartImp<Inx> ThisClass;

public:
    //*******************************************************************
    // Constructors and destructor (size must be >= 1)
    //*******************************************************************
    PartImp(const Inx size);
    PartImp(const char* string, const Inx size);
    PartImp(const PartImp& p);

    ~PartImp();

    //*******************************************************************
    // Assignment operators
    //*******************************************************************
    PartImp& operator = (const PartImp& b);     // set from other part
    PartImp& operator = (const char*);          // set from string

    //*******************************************************************
    // Convert a string to a partition.  Return TRUE if conversion was ok
    //*******************************************************************
    virtual BOOL parseString (const char *s);

    //*******************************************************************
    // The following methods end with the letter 'i' to signify that they
    // take Inx values.  Class Part contains versions without the 'i'
    // that take Elem values.
    //*******************************************************************
```

```
//*******************************************************************
// Every class in a partition has one element that is the
// representative of the class.  The representative for a class can
// change every time the partition is changed.
//*******************************************************************
virtual Inx repi (const Inx a) const;


//*******************************************************************
// Add "element a is equivalent to element b".  That is, merge the
// classes for elements a and b.
//*******************************************************************
virtual PartImp& setEquivi (const Inx a, const Inx b);


//*******************************************************************
// Are two elements in a partition equivalent?
//*******************************************************************
virtual BOOL equivi (const Inx a, const Inx b) const
    { return BOOL( repi(a) == repi(b) ); };


//*******************************************************************
// Make element a not equivalent to any other element.  This is,
// put a in a separate class.
//*******************************************************************
virtual PartImp& isolatei (const Inx a);


//*******************************************************************
// Return the size of the partition.
//*******************************************************************
virtual Inx size () const  { return siz; };


//*******************************************************************
// Return the number of classes in the partition.
//*******************************************************************
virtual Inx classes () const;


//*******************************************************************
// Special partitions.
//
// "zero"   is the partition with every element in a separate class.
// "one"    is the partition with just one class.
// "random" is a random partition.  Each partition is equally likely.
//*******************************************************************
virtual PartImp& zero ();
virtual PartImp& one (Inx n);
virtual PartImp& one ()              { return one(siz);    };
virtual PartImp& random (Inx n);
virtual PartImp& random ()           { return random(siz); };


//*******************************************************************
// Compare two partitions.   Partitions are partially ordered.
//*******************************************************************
friend PartCompare compare (const ThisClass& a, const ThisClass& b);
```
(continued)

File Part.hpp *(continued)*

```cpp
    friend BOOL operator == (const ThisClass&a, const ThisClass& b)
       { return BOOL( compare(a,b) == PartEQ);  };
    friend BOOL operator != (const ThisClass&a, const ThisClass& b)
       { return BOOL( compare(a,b) != PartEQ);  };
    friend BOOL operator <  (const ThisClass&a, const ThisClass& b)
       { return BOOL( compare(a,b) == PartLT); };
    friend BOOL operator <= (const ThisClass&a, const ThisClass& b)
       { return BOOL( compare(a,b) <= PartEQ);  };
    friend BOOL operator > (const ThisClass&a, const ThisClass& b)
       { return BOOL( compare(a,b) == PartGT); };
    friend BOOL operator >= (const ThisClass&a, const ThisClass& b) {
       PartComp comp = compare(a,b);
       return BOOL( (comp == PartEQ) || (comp == PartGT) );
    };

    //**********************************************************************
    // Add (also called join and or least upper bound) two partitions.
    // This is the transitive union of the two partitions.
    //**********************************************************************
           ThisClass& operator += (const ThisClass& b);
    friend ThisClass  operator +  (const ThisClass&a, const ThisClass& b);

    //**********************************************************************
    // Multiply (also called meet or greatest lower bound ) two
    // partitions together.  This is the intersection of two partitions.
    //**********************************************************************
           ThisClass& operator *= (const ThisClass& b);
    friend ThisClass  operator *  (const ThisClass& a, const ThisClass& b);

    //**********************************************************************
    // Compute a hash value for a partition.
    //**********************************************************************
    virtual Inx hash () const;

    //**********************************************************************
    // Return the rank of partition p. Each partition returns a unique
    // value in the range [0.. n-1] where n is the number of partitions
    // of size().  This value can be used to convert partitions to an
    // array index.
    //**********************************************************************
    virtual long rank () const;

    //**********************************************************************
    // Given a value in the range [0..n] (as returned by rank()),
    // return the corresponding partition.
    //**********************************************************************
    virtual ThisClass& unrank (long n);

    //**********************************************************************
    // IO operations using external format of a list of elements connected
    // by equal signs.  For example, "(a=b=c d=e=f f=g h=h=i)".
```

```
      // elements connected by = are "equivalent" to each other.
      //    - '()' is the zero partition.
      //    - elements names can be repeated in a class
      //    - if an element appears in two separate classes lists, the
      //        classes are merged into a single class.
      //    - for testing purposes, adding a '!' inside the parentheses
      //        "freezes" the partition.  rep() does not update the internal
      //        structure of frozen partitions.
      //*******************************************************************
      friend ostream& operator << (ostream&, const ThisClass&);
      friend istream& operator >> (istream&,       ThisClass&);


      //*******************************************************************
      // Virtual functions used for reading/writing elements.  These are
      // usually redefined in class Part<Inx,Elem>.
      //*******************************************************************
      virtual void writeElement (ostream& os, const Inx a) const;
      virtual Inx   readElement (istream& is) const;


      //*******************************************************************
      // For testing purposes, a partition can be "frozen".  rep() does
      // not change the internal structure of frozen partitions.
      // These routines are not used in normal operation.
      //*******************************************************************
      virtual void freeze(BOOL f)            { frozen = f; };
      virtual BOOL isFrozen()                { return frozen; };


      //*******************************************************************
      // Consistency checkers.
      //*******************************************************************
      virtual BOOL validInx (const Inx i) const;   // is i in range?
      virtual BOOL valid () const;                 // is partition valid?

   protected:
      //*********************************************************************
      // Store the number of elements in the partition for range checking.
      // Also store a pointer to an array of elements.
      //*********************************************************************
      Inx  siz;                              // size of elem.  Must be >=1.
      Inx* elem;                             // array of elements
      BOOL frozen;                           // can rep() change partition?

      // Pointers to the partitions in the multiplication operation.
      // These variables are needed to communicate between operator* and
      // compRepPair().
      static const ThisClass* aMulOperand;
      static const ThisClass* bMulOperand;
      static int compRepPair (const Inx* e, const Inx* f);

      void newPart (Inx size);        // allocate storage
   };
```

(continued)

File Part.hpp *(continued)*

```cpp
//*********************************************************************
// Part:  partitions of a user-defined element type Elem.
//
// Inx must be an integer type.
// Class Elem must support
//    Elem(Inx)         - constructor from Inx
//    operator Inx()    - conversion to Inx
//    operator >>       - read from istream
//    operator <<       - write to ostream
//
//*********************************************************************

template <class Inx, class Elem>
class Part: public PartImp<Inx> {

    typedef PartImp<Inx> BaseClass;
    typedef Part<Inx,Elem> ThisClass;

public:
    //*****************************************************************
    // Constructors with a default size
    //*****************************************************************
    Part(const Inx size): PartImp<Inx>(size) {};
    Part(const char* string, const Inx size) :PartImp<Inx>(size) {
        // can't use PartImp(string,size) constructor because
        // PartImp::readElement will be used rather than Part::readElement.
        *this = string;             // can't us
    };

    Part(const PartImp<Inx>& p): PartImp<Inx>(p) {};

    // default destructor

    //*****************************************************************
    // Assignment operators
    //*****************************************************************
    ThisClass& operator = (const ThisClass& b)
        { this->BaseClass::operator = (b); return *this; };
    ThisClass& operator = (const char* s)
        { this->BaseClass::operator= (s); return *this; };

    //*****************************************************************
    // Functions that work with the element type.
    //*****************************************************************
    virtual Elem rep (const Elem& a) const
        { return Elem( BaseClass::repi( Inx(a))); };

    virtual ThisClass& setEquiv (const Elem& a, const Elem& b) {
        BaseClass::setEquivi( Inx(a), Inx(b) );
        return *this;
    };
```

```
     virtual BOOL equiv (const Elem& a, const Elem& b) const
        { return BaseClass::equivi(Inx(a),Inx(b) ); };

     virtual ThisClass& isolate (const Elem& a) {
        BaseClass::isolatei(Inx(a));
        return *this;
     };

     //********************************************************************
     // Functions that work with the element type.
     //********************************************************************
     virtual void writeElement (ostream& os, const Inx a) const
        { os << Elem(a); };                   // convert Inx to Elem and write
     virtual Inx readElement (istream& is) const {
        Elem e;
        is >> e;                              // read in data of type Elem
        return Inx(e);                        // convert Elem to Inx
     };

     friend ThisClass  operator + (const ThisClass&a, const ThisClass& b)
        { return Part<Inx,Elem>( operator + (BaseClass(a),BaseClass(b)) ); };

     friend ThisClass operator * (const ThisClass& a, const ThisClass& b)
        { return Part<Inx,Elem>( operator * (BaseClass(a),BaseClass(b)) ); };

     friend class PartRepIter<Inx,Elem>;  // class (rep) iterator
     friend class PartElemIter<Inx,Elem>; // elements within a class

};

//**********************************************************************
//
// SizedPart, a derived class of Part, has a default size on its
// constructors.
//
//
// This template class extends Part with a constructor that has a
// default size.  This is a separate class to avoid duplicating all the
// Part code for each different default size.
//**********************************************************************

template<class Inx, class Elem, unsigned DefaultSize>
class SizedPart: public Part<Inx, Elem> {
public:
     //********************************************************************
     // Constructors.  Override Part constructors with a default size.
     //********************************************************************
     SizedPart(const unsigned sx=DefaultSize)
        : Part<Inx,Elem>(sx) {};
     SizedPart(const char* string, const unsigned sx=DefaultSize)
        : Part<Inx,Elem>(string, sx)   {};
     SizedPart(const SizedPart& s)
        : Part<Inx,Elem>(s) {};
```

File Part.hpp *(continued)*

```
   SizedPart& operator = (const SizedPart& s) {
      (Part<Inx,Elem>&) *this = (Part<Inx,Elem>&) s;
      return *this;
   };
};

//*************************************************************************
//
//                              Iterators
//
//*************************************************************************

template<class Inx, class Elem> class PartElemIter;

//*************************************************************************
//
// PartRepIter: Iterate over all class representatives of a partition.
//
//*************************************************************************

template<class Inx, class Elem>
class PartRepIter {
public:
   PartRepIter();
   PartRepIter(const Part<Inx,Elem>&);

   // use default copy constructor
   PartRepIter& operator = (const Part<Inx,Elem>& p);

   // use default assignment
   // use default destructor

   Elem operator ++ ();
   Elem operator ++ (int);
   Elem current () const        { return Elem(cur); };
   operator int ()              { return BOOL( cur < partp->siz ); };
   void restart ()              { cur = 0; };

   friend class PartElemIter<Inx,Elem>;

protected:
   const Part<Inx,Elem>* partp;          // pointer to partition
   Inx   cur;                            // current element
};


//*************************************************************************
//
// PartElemIter: Iterate over all elements in a single class of a
// partition.
//
//*************************************************************************
```

```
template<class Inx, class Elem>
class PartElemIter {

public:
    PartElemIter();                         // no assigned class yet
    PartElemIter(const PartRepIter<Inx,Elem>& r);
                                            // for all elems in class of r
    PartElemIter(const Part<Inx,Elem>& p, const Elem& e);
                                            // for all elems in class of e

    // use default copy constructor
    PartElemIter& operator = (const PartRepIter<Inx,Elem>& );

    // use default assignment
    // use default destructor

    Elem operator ++ ();
    Elem operator ++ (int);
    Elem current () const       { return Elem(cur); };
    operator int ()             { return BOOL( cur < partp->siz ); };
    void restart ()             { cur = rep; };

protected:
    const Part<Inx,Elem>* partp;        // pointer to partition
    Inx   rep;                          // representative
    Inx   cur;                          // current element
};

#endif
```

15

Partition Applications

The following sections show partitions in use. Most readers will only be interested in a subset of the applications. Read those that interest you and skip the rest.

Kinds of Examples

Equivalence relations usually follow one of a small number of patterns. These patterns are defined using one or more functions $f()$.

Same Attribute

$f()$ maps each element to an attribute of that element. Two elements are equivalent if they have the same value of the attribute.

$$f: \text{element} \mapsto \text{value}. \qquad f(x) = f(y) \text{ implies } x \equiv y$$

This is the most obvious type of partitioning. The classes are easily named by the attribute values. For example, students are partitioned by their current grade level; students are equivalent if they are in the same grade in school. All the first graders are in one class, all the second graders are in another class, and so forth. The classes may be more permanent than the current attributes. Next year, all the first graders will still be in the same class, but that class will then be called second grade. This permanence is more pronounced when we refer to them as the class of 2004 (the year they graduate from high school).

Sometimes the attribute is continuous rather than discrete. Defining two people as equivalent only when they are exactly the same height creates an infinite number of classes. It would be difficult to find two equivalent people. A better definition is: two people being equivalent if they are *about* the same height. But be careful. Calling people equivalent if the difference in their heights is one inch or less is *not* an equivalence relation. Suppose Andy is 5 feet 7 inches tall, Bob is 5 feet 8 inches, and Craig is 5 feet 9 inches. Andy is equivalent to Bob, and Bob is equivalent to Craig, but Andy is *not* equivalent to Craig, violating the transitive property. The solution is to divide the attribute range into "bins" or classes:

- 5 feet 7 inches $\leq$ height $<$ 5 feet 8 inch
- 5 feet 8 inches $\leq$ height $<$ 5 feet 9 inches
- 5 feet 9 inches $\leq$ height $<$ 5 feet 10 inches

None of the people are equivalent with these bins.

Step Functions

$f()$ transforms—or steps—from one element (x) to another element (y).

$$f: \text{element} \mapsto \text{element}. \qquad f(x) = y \text{ implies } x \equiv y$$

In a graph, edges "step" from one node to an adjacent node. Therefore, the two nodes are connected (or equivalent).

Stepping functions are the heart of one major use for partitions: connection. They compute connected regions of a game board, and connected components of a graph. Step functions are also used in "Polya's Example" on page 308.

As a final example, let $fp(a/b) = (p*a)/(p*b)$, where p is a prime number, be an infinite set of step functions. The $fp()$ generate the equivalence relation of the rational numbers. The equivalence classes of rational numbers can be named with a ratio value. But the idea of a ratio is not explicit in the definition of equivalence. Perhaps ratios were discovered as important, yet hidden, properties of rational numbers.

Parallel Equivalence

Step functions can create equivalence relations in another way.

$$f: \text{element} \mapsto \text{element}. \qquad x \equiv y \text{ implies } f(x) \equiv f(y)$$

$f()$ is a step function. It doesn't create the initial set of equivalent pairs $x \equiv y$. These come from somewhere else. $f()$ just takes those initial equivalent pairs and extends them to a "parallel" set of equivalent elements. Also note that x is not necessarily equivalent to $f(x)$. Finite state machines make heavy use of parallel equivalence (see "Finite State Machines" on page 301).

Connection

Partitions model *connections*. They are very efficient at representing connection over any number of edges, but that efficiency comes by ignoring the details of the path. If your application always works with paths, then partitions are probably not appropriate. But there are many cases where the path is unimportant, or is important only some of the time. Many of the examples in this chapter involve connection. They explore vertices connected by edges, people connected by kinship, and colored bracelets connected by permutations.

To ensure a pressurized system is air- or watertight, you pressurize the container and see if the pressure bleeds off. If you are building containers that usually pass this test, this test will quickly tell you of success or failure. You only have to look for leaks in systems that fail. This example shows the difference between connection and paths. First the primary goal is not to find a path; the question is "Is there a leak?" rather than "Where is the leak?" Second, the length of the path is unimportant; a nearby leak is no more important than a leak far away—a leak is a leak.

Pressure is the equivalence relation.[1] It is clearly reflexive. It is symmetric since pressure P at one point means adjacent points also have pressure P. And in a static system, it is transitive; pressure does not drop as you move along a pipe. In fact, you're testing whether the inside of the system is equivalent to the outside.

This same metaphor applies equally well to checking electrical circuits for shorts with pressure replaced by voltage. Primarily, you want to know whether the power lead is equivalent in voltage to the ground lead. Only if this fails will you have to find the short.

Connected Components of a Graph

An undirected graph is a collection of vertices and a collection of edges that connect two vertices. A connected component of a graph is the set of vertices that are connected by zero or more edges. "is connected to" is an equivalence relation in an undirected graph. It is reflexive: every element is connected to itself using zero edges. It is symmetric: the graph has undirected edges. And it is transitive: if x is connected to y (by n edges), and y is connected to z (by m edges), then x is connected to z (by $n + m$ edges).

The procedure for computing the connected components in an undirected graph is straightforward. Start with the zero partition (no vertices currently connected).

```
Part<unsigned,vertice>  components(n);   // initialized to zero()

for ( ... all edges ... ) {
    vertice f = edge.from();    // from endpoint
    vertice t = edge.to();      // to endpoint
    components.equiv(f, t);
};
// the classes of components are the connected components
```

---

1. Gravity is a small part of the equivalence since pressure increases with depth.

Kruskal's Spanning Tree

The idea of connected components can be extended to compute a minimal spanning tree in a connected graph. A spanning tree of a graph is a tree (no loops) that connects all the vertices. If each edge has a weight, we might be interested in the spanning tree with the smallest total weight. Kruskal's algorithm provides the answer. The edges are sorted into increasing order of weight. The next smallest weight edge is added if it will not cause a loop. This continues until all vertices are connected.

How do we know if an edge will cause a loop without searching through the entire graph? Use partitions. Create a partition of vertices. If two vertices are connected by the spanning tree, they will be equivalent. Otherwise, they are not yet connected.

```
Part<unsigned,vertice>  components(n);    // initialized to zero()
unsigned        totalWeight = 0;          // sum of weights

for (... all edges ...) {                 // from smallest to largest
   vertice f = edge.from();               // from endpoint of edge
   vertice t = edge.to();                 // to endpoint of edge
   if (!components.equiv(f,t)) {
      // f and t not yet in the same component.
      // edge won't create loop
      totalWeight += edge.weight();
      components.setEquiv(f, t);
      ... add (f,t) to spanning tree ...
      if (components.classes() == 1)
         break;                           // all vertices are in tree
   };
};
```

Note that this algorithm does not need to know the path between the end-points of an edge. It just needs to know whether or not a path exists. Partitions answer this question quickly and without extra work. A solution based on walking around the connected components to find an explicit path would be wasteful.

Connected Regions of a Game Board

Connection also applies to game boards. Define the step functions north(x), east(x), south(x) and west(x). If a game piece sitting at cell x can move north, then $x \equiv$ north(x). If movement is symmetric, south(x) and west(x) are redundant. By transitivity, $x \equiv$ north(x) and $x \equiv$ east(x) imply north(x) $\equiv$ east(x). This makes x equivalent to every other cell that can be reached by any sequence of moves. The classes of the partition are the connected regions of the board. There is no move that will connect any cell in one class with any cell in another class.

In some games, there are different types of moves: driving, flying, sailing, and so on. Each type of move generates one partition: the cells connected by driving alone is one partition called drive; the cells connected by flying alone is another partition called fly; and so on. Partition addition merges these two partitions (drive + fly) to get the cells that are connected when both driving and flying. drive + fly + sail is the connected components reachable by any of the three methods of transportation.

Connected People over Time

The genes in the nucleus of every human cell are a blending of the genetic material from the mother and father. Every cell also contains mitochondria that convert chemical energy into a usable form. The mitochondrial genes are distinct from the nuclear genes. They are copied strictly from the mother. Using samples of mitochondrial genes from people all over the world, some scientists (Wilson and Cann, 1992) believe they can identify a unique female—they naturally call her Eve—from which all mitochondrial genes, and all humans, descended.

If true, the partition of all humans, living or dead, under the "is related to" equivalence relation would be a single class. Not a very interesting exercise. Instead, we might parameterize the "is parent of" relation according to the time of conception.

Define two step functions father(x, t) and mother(x, t). father(x, t) returns the biological father of person x when t equals the time of conception. If t is not the time of x's conception, father(x, t) does not return any thing. mother(x, t) returns x's biological mother at the same time. The partition of people related since 1900 might be called the clans of the twentieth century.

$$20th\, Century\, Clans = \sum_{1900\, \leq\, t} x \equiv father(x, t) \equiv mother(x, t)$$

Connected Continents

Partitions can determine the possibility of animal migrations. Divide the face of the earth—land and water—into sections. Assign each section a wet/dry attribute at each point in time. Make two sections equivalent if they are adjacent and have the same wet/dry attribute. These equivalences change over time because sea and lake levels have changed through history. Call the two partitions wet(time) and dry(time).

Modern humans first appeared in southern Africa around 100,000 years ago. As glaciers advanced and held more water, sea level dropped. The exposed land connected some regions that were previously unconnected. It is safe to assume that land animals were able to migrate in both directions (symmetric) between these two previously disconnected land masses.

The Bering Strait is the most popular example of this. When the sea level drops 100 meters below its current level, as it did during the various Wisconsin glacier advances, a land bridge called Beringia connects Siberia with Alaska (Hammond, 1988:68–71). Humans in North and South America are thought to have originally migrated from Asia over the Beringia land bridge.

More than 10,000 years ago, the Sunda shelf under parts of the South China Sea was exposed connecting the Phillipines, Borneo, Celebes, Java, and Sumatra to the IndoChina mainland (Vietnam, Cambodia, Malaya, etc). Humans in China would have had easy access to these islands by walking over the Sunda shelf.

The Sahul shelf connects Australia with New Guinea. But there is no connection between the Sunda and Sahul shelves. Some scientists believe humans must have had seagoing crafts to cross the 60 kilometers of open sea between them, but there is no archaeological evidence of this. The effects of seagoing crafts can be captured by partitions. Let sail(dist) be the equivalence relation that connects two land masses if they are less than dist kilometers apart. Sailing is certainly reflexive and symmetric. It is also essentially transitive since humans would be able to make multiple hops, resting on intermediate islands, to cross larger distances. The sum dry(time) + sail(dist) is a new equivalence relation that more closely captures the possibilities of human migration.

The wet partition captures the connected bodies of water used for aquatic migration. All of the world's oceans and seas are connected together. However, the Atlantic and Pacific oceans are only connected below South America and Africa, and above North America and Asia. Aquatic life that only survives in the warm waters around the equator would not be able to migrate from the Atlantic to the Pacific. So define a climate(temp) relation that connects parts of the ocean that have temperatures in a suitable range. Aquatic life can migrate only when a route is available (wet) and when they can survive the trip (climate). The real connected regions are wet(t) * climate(temp).

Perhaps someday, future archaeologists will use an equivalence relation like sail(dist) with distances of 60 light-years to chart the dispersal of mankind throughout the galaxy.

FORTRAN EQUIVALENCE

This is one of the classic applications of partitions and equivalence relations. The FORTRAN EQUIVALENCE statement specifies that two variables should overlap in storage. Assume the following equivalence of simple variables.

```
INTEGER A, B, C, D, E, F, G, H, I
EQUIVALENCE (A, B), (D, G), (H, G), (C, I), (G, H)
```

First, the FORTRAN compiler must compute the equivalence classes. To do this, start with the zero() partition, and add each pair of equivalent elements. The equivalence relation is "is allocated the same word of storage." The resulting partition is (A = B C = I D = G = H E F). Finally, storage is allocated for each of the five equivalence classes. Knuth(1973a:360, exercise 11) shows how EQUIVALENCE processing can be extended to handle arrays.

Sets as Partitions

A great many problems are nicely solved with sets. But unlike Pascal and Modula-2, neither C nor C++ support a set type. We could write a set data type (which isn't a bad idea), but we can use partitions if sets aren't available.

Partitions are more flexible than sets. Partitions can represent every set, but there are partitions that are not sets. This is particularly useful when partitions are needed anyway. Using partitions to represent sets is similar to using floating point numbers to represent integers.

In a set, every element is either IN or OUT of the set. We will add another element called IN to the partition. Every element in the set is made equivalent to IN. Every other element must be in a singleton class. Then partition addition is the same as set union and partition multiplication is the same as set intersection. For example:

```
enum elem {IN, A, B, C, D, E, F};
Part<unsigned, elem> setA(7), setB(7);

setA = "(IN=A=B=C=D)";          // A, B, C and D are in setA
setB = "(IN=C=D=E=F)";          // C, D, E and F are in setB

cout << setA + setB;            // = (IN=A=B=C=D=E=F)
cout << setA * setB;            // = (IN=C=D)
```

The restriction that OUT elements must be singleton classes is important, as the following example shows:

```
setA = "(IN=A B=C=D)";          // set = A (incorrect)
setB = "(IN=B A=C=D)";          // set = B (incorrect)

cout << setA + setB;            // = (IN=A=B=C=D); should be (IN=A=B)
cout << setA * setB;            // = (IN A B C=D); should be zero
```

In the sum, the problem is that IN ≡ A (mod setA) and A ≡ C (mod setB). Therefore IN ≡ C (mod setA + setB) by transitivity. But C is not in either set. When OUT elements are not equivalent to any other elements, transitivity cannot cause any problems. The product of two elements is correct, but the example shows equivalent OUT elements are not cleaned up. This will cause errors in future additions.

Pin Swapping

The design of VLSI (Very Large Scale Integration) chips begins with logical design: the selection of individual logic blocks (NANDs, NORs, etc.) and their logical interconnection. Then physical design assigns locations on the silicon wafer to the logic blocks and the interconnections. The major phases of physical design are:

placement   Assign locations to each logic block outline.
wiring   Route the interconnections as stick figures.
shapes   Convert block outlines and stick-figure interconnections to rectangles.

The placement phase tries to put connected blocks close to each other. But every block is connected, directly or indirectly, to every other block, so placement must make many compromises. There may be many logic blocks that compute the same logic value. This usually happens when logic is paralleled to reduce the electrical load on any one block. Pin swapping tries to exploit this flexibility in the logical design to improve the physical wiring.

Pin swapping interchanges two pins between equivalent wiring nets to reduce the amount of wire interconnection. Swaps can be made between equivalent pins, where equivalence is defined in the following way:

1. Every pin is equivalent to itself.
2. Two input pins are equivalent if they are connected by wires to equivalent output pins. But the input pins are not equivalent to the output pin (parallel equivalence).
3. Two output pins are equivalent if they are computed by equivalent logic driven by equivalent inputs. That is, if $ox = fx(ix1,\ldots,ixn)$ and $oy = fy(iy1, ,iyn)$, and $fx \equiv fy$, $ix1 \equiv iy1, \ldots, ixn \equiv iyn$, then $ox \equiv oy$ (parallel equivalence again). Usually $fx \equiv fy$ only when they are exactly the same function (NAND, NOR, etc.). But stating the problem as equivalent functions handles the case where some logic blocks compute multiple functions. For example, a driver cleans up and repowers a signal. It is implemented as two inverters. The internal, inverted signal can also be provided as an output. There is no reason blocks requiring the inverted signal cannot be driven from the internal output. An adder block that outputs the exclusive-OR of its inputs is another example.

These three points propagate equivalence throughout all the pins. First make every pin equivalent to itself—the zero partition. Then step 2 equivalences all the receiving, block input pins of each net to each other since they are driven by the same output. Step 3 walks these equivalences through the logic blocks to generate more equivalent output pins. Repeating steps 2 and 3 steps equivalences throughout the network.

This particular equivalence relation does not handle every type of equivalence we might think of. For example, it does not handle the case of double inversion. Even though a signal passing though two inverter blocks is the same logical signal, the pins before the inverters are not equivalent to the pins after the inverters. However, we may want to exclude double inversion since the pins would not have equivalent electrical delays.

Double inversion is just a special case of logic blocks generating the same logical function in different ways. For example, using two OR blocks to compute (*a* OR *b*) OR *c* is different than using two OR blocks to compute *a* OR (*b* OR *c*) by our definition of equivalence. The only way to handle general logical equivalence is to assign each pin (or net) with the boolean expression it computes. Then two pins are equivalent if they have the same expression. This form of equivalence, while it more closely corresponds to our intuitive notion of equivalence, requires much more computing power and will not lead to substantially more equivalent pins in practice. And since this intuitive equivalence relation does not account for block delays, it may be the wrong relation to use.

Finite State Machines

In this section we use partitions to reduce a finite state machine (FSM) to an equivalent FSM with the minimum number of states (see "Finite State Machines" in

Chapter 11). Since an FSM implementation requires hardware or software resources for every state, reducing the number of states reduces the cost. This is one of the classic applications of partitions.

State minimization is sometimes done by starting with a partition of large classes and then refining or splitting the classes. Here we will start with partitions of small classes and then merge them together into larger classes.

Let P be a partition of the states S of a finite state machine M. Build a new FSM M′ with one state for each class of P where

$$next'(rep(s), x) = rep(next(s, x))$$

$$out'(rep(s)) = out(s)$$

[37]

$rep(s)$ is the class representative for the class of P that contains s. next′() is the state transition function for FSM M′ that maps each class of P to another class of P. out′() produces output for M′ based on the current class of P. That is, if next$(s,x) = t$ in M, then next′$(rep(s),x) = $ rep(t) in M′. next′() and out′() are only well-defined functions if all the elements in each class of P agree on their definition. The problem is to find partitions P of the states S that make next′() and out′() well-defined.

When is next′() well-defined? Assume $s \equiv t \pmod P$ where s and t are states of M. M can have different values of next() for s and t. But since s and t are in the same state of M′ (same class of P), M′ cannot distinguish between these states and cannot use that information to affect its decision on the next state. If M′ cannot distinguish s and t, then it cannot distinguish them after it reads a 0. So, $s \equiv t$ implies next$(s,0) \equiv$ next$(t,0)$. If this were not true, then M′ would have two transitions out of the combined state $s \equiv t$ labeled 0: one going to rep(next$(s,0)$) and one going to rep(next$(t,0)$). next′() is well-defined only if these two states are the same state in M′ for all input symbols x.

$$s \equiv t \,(\bmod P) \qquad implies \qquad next(s,x) \equiv next(t,x)\,(\bmod P) \qquad [38]$$

Partitions that satisfy Equation [38] are called **closed partitions** (Dorn and Hohn, 1978:292). Every closed partition generates an FSM M′ with a well-defined next′().

A **basic partition** P_{st} is defined as $s \equiv t$ plus all equivalences implied by Equation [38]. Therefore, next$(s, 0) \equiv$ next$(t, 0)$ and next$(s, 1) \equiv$ next$(t, 1)$ are in P_{st}. We can't stop after just one input. If next$(s, 0) \equiv$ next$(t, 0)$, applying Equation [38] again implies next$(s, 00)^2 \equiv$ next$(t, 00)$. Continuing gives the partition

$$P_{st} = (s \equiv t \quad next(s, 0) \equiv next(t, 0) \quad next(s, 1) \equiv next(t, 1)$$

$$next(s, 00) \equiv next(t, 00) \quad next(s, 01) \equiv next(t, 01)$$

$$next(s, 10) \equiv next(t, 10) \quad next(s, 11) \equiv next(t, 11)$$

$$next(s, 000) \equiv next(t, 000) \; \ldots)$$

[39]

---

2. next(s, xy) means next(next$(s, x), y)$.

State s	next(s, 0)	next(s, 1)	out(s)
A	E	B	0
B	C	F	1
C	D	A	0
D	E	B	0
E	C	F	1
F	A	D	1

FIGURE 15.1
Finite state machine M1.

As an example, Figure 15.1 shows FSM M1. The basic partition P_{AD} contains A ≡ D. A ≡ D implies next(A, 0) ≡ next(D, 0), or E ≡ E. Function next(*, 1) implies B ≡ B. Since no new equivalent pairs were added, there is no need to check any further. The basic partition P_{AD} = (A ≡ D   E ≡ E   B ≡ B). We could build an FSM from the partition P_{AD} = (A ≡ D   B   C   E   F) because its next() function maps classes to classes.

The basic partition P_{CF} starts with C ≡ F, and next(*, 0) adds D ≡ A, next(*, 1) adds A ≡ D, next(*, 00) adds E ≡ E, and so forth. The result is the partition P_{CF} = (C ≡ F   D ≡ A   A ≡ D   E ≡ E . . .) or (A ≡ D   C ≡ F).

The terms for next(s, 0x) ≡ next(t, 0x) are contained in $P_{next(s, 0), next(t, 0)}$. So Equation [39] can be rewritten as

$$P_{st} = (s \equiv t) + P_{next(s, 0), next(t, 0)} + P_{next(s, 1), next(t, 1)} \qquad [40]$$

Using the facts $P_{st} = P_{ts}$ and $P_{ss} = $ zero() reduces the number of basic partitions we have to compute.

We are going to compute the basic partitions for all pairs of states. Writing Equation [40] for each pair of states gives a set of simultaneous partition equations. We will solve these equations iteratively using

$$P_{st} = P_{st} + (s \equiv t) + P_{next(s, 0), next(t, 0)} + P_{next(s, 1), next(t, 1)} \qquad [41]$$

First, set every basic partition $P_{st} = $ zero(). Then iteratively reevaluate the equations from [41] until the basic partitions stop changing. This procedure works because partition addition is idempotent (Equation [26g]). Once a partition has been added to basic partition, adding in the same partition again doesn't change the result. Figure 15.2 shows the partition equations and basic partitions for FSM M1.

	B	**C**	**D**
A	AB = AB + (A = B) + CE + BF AB = (A = B = C = D = E = F)	AC = AC + (A = C) + DE + AB AC = (A = B = C = D = E = F	AD = AD + (A = D) AD = (A = D)
B		BC = BC + (B = C) + CD + AF BC = (A = B = C = D = E = F)	BD = BD + (B = D) + CE + BF BD = (A = B = C = D = E = F)
C			CD = CD + (C = D) + DE + AB CD = (A = B = C = D = E = F)
D			
E			

	E	**F**
A	AE = AE + (A = E) + CE + BF AE = (A = B = C = D = E = F)	AF = AF + (A = F) + AE + BD AF = (A = B = C = D = E = F)
B	BE = BE + (B = E) BE = (B = E)	BF = BF + (B = F) + AC + DF BF = (A = B = C = D = E = F)
C	CE = CE + (C = E) + CD + AF CE = (A = B = C = D = E = F)	CF = CF + (C = F) + AD + AD CF = (A = D C = F)
D	DE = DE + (D = E) + CE + BF DE = (A = B = C = D = E = F)	DF = DF + (D = F) + AE + BD DF = (A = B = C = D = E = F)
E		EF = EF + (E = F) + AC + DF EF = (A = B = C = D = E = F)

FIGURE 15.2
Basic partitions for M1. The first row of each cell is the equation for a basic partition. The second row is the value of the basic partition.

Writing out the simultaneous partition equations is not difficult, but it is tedious—even for a moderate number of states. Program FSMPART on the diskette automates this task. Its input is a file with one state per line. The first column is the state name. The remaining columns are the values of next() for the different input symbols. The input file for FSM M1 is shown in Figure 15.3 and is included on the diskette.

```
C>FSMPART m1.fsm m1.peq
```

```
// FSMPART input file for FSM M1
A E B
B C F
C D A
D E B
E C F
F A D
```

FIGURE 15.3
File m1.fsm. Input file for FSMPART to generate simultaneous partition equations for FSM M1.

This command creates the simultaneous partition equations shown in Figure 15.4 in output file m1.peq. This file can be included directly by PARTCALC. The includeChg command reads the file repeatedly until the partition values stop changing.

```
PARTCALC>includeChg m1.peq
⋮
PARTCALC>list
```

The list shows all the basic partitions for the machine.

Dorn and Hohn (1978) show that adding or multiplying any two closed partitions together produces another closed partition. They also show that every closed partition is the sum of basic partitions. So every closed partition is a basic partition, or the sum of basic partitions. PARTCALC's close + command looks at all pairs of variables x and y.

```
size 6
elemFormat n
elemName A B C D E F
//
AB=AB+(A=B)+CE+BF
AC=AC+(A=C)+DE+AB
AD=AD+(A=D)
AE=AE+(A=E)+CE+BF
AF=AF+(A=F)+AE+BD
//
BC=BC+(B=C)+CD+AF
BD=BD+(B=D)+CE+BF
BE=BE+(B=E)
BF=BF+(B=F)+AC+DF
//
CD=CD+(C=D)+DE+AB
CE=CE+(C=E)+CD+AF
CF=CF+(C=F)+AD+AD
//
DE=DE+(D=E)+CE+BF
DF=DF+(D=F)+AE+BD
//
EF=EF+(E=F)+AC+DF
```

FIGURE 15.4
File m1.peq. Simultaneous partition equations for M1 as generated by FSMPART. This file is ready for input to PARTCALC.

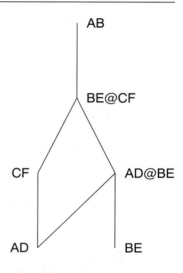

FIGURE 15.5
Hasse diagram of closed partitions.

If no existing partition has the value $x + y$, a new variable, named $x @ y$ ("@" for addition), is created. In this case, `close` adds variables BE@CF and AD@BE.[3]

```
PARTCALC>close +
PARTCALC>listValue
```

The `listValue` command lists the variables by value. It shows there are six distinct closed partitions.

```
AB=(A=B=C=D=E=F)
AD=(A=D)
BE=(B=E)
CF=(A=D C=F)
AD@BE=(A=D B=E)
BE@CF=(A=D B=E C=F)
```

The `hasse` command in PARTCALC prints the information necessary to construct a **Hasse diagram** (pronounced hah'-suh). It lists all pairs of variables $x < y$ where there is no distinct variable z such that $x < z < y$. This means that x is "just less than" y since there is no z between them. This is sometimes called the covering relation. It also lists duplicate variables (same value as another variable) that are the same point in the Hasse diagram. Figure 15.5 shows the Hasse diagram for the closed partitions of machine M1.

---

3. Command `close*` adds new products, named $x\#y$ ("#" for multiplication), for missing products $x * y$.

State s	next(s, 0)	next(s, 1)	out(s)
A = D	B = E	B = E	0
B = E	C	F	1
C	A = D	A = D	0
F	A = D	A = D	1

FIGURE 15.6
FSM M1min. The minimal
FSM for machine M1.

Different, well-defined FSMs can be built from each of these six partitions. But so far we have ignored the out() function. This omission is most obvious because $P_{AB} =$ (A = B = C = D = E = F = G) = one() is a closed partition. P_{AB} produces an FSM that has a single state. This machine cannot possibly generate the correct output.

The states of M′ must also generate the same output as M. out′() is well-defined only when all states of M in the same class of P generate the same output. This leads to a new partition P_{out}.

$$P_{out} = (s \equiv t) \qquad if \qquad out(s) = out(t)$$

Suppose we try to build a new FSM using some partition P. If $P \leq P_{out}$ then P is a refinement of P_{out} and each class of P is completely contained in a class of P_{out}. Since each class of P_{out} has the same value of out(), each class of P will have the same value of out′(). Partitions with this property are called **output-consistent.** Any FSM built from a partition that is both closed and output-consistent (next′() and out′() of Equation [37] are well-defined) is equivalent to the original FSM.

For M1, $P_{out} = (A \equiv C \equiv D\ B \equiv E \equiv F)$. The only closed and output-consistent partitions for M1 are

```
AD=(A=D)
BE=(B=E)
AD@BE=(A=D  B=E)
```

Clearly, the partition with the smallest number of classes generates the smallest machine. Partition (A $\equiv$ D   B $\equiv$ E   C   F) has the fewest classes, and produces M1min (Figure 15.6), the minimal FSM equivalent to M1 (Figure 15.1).

Partitions can extract more information from an FSM. Define

$$P_{in} = (next(s, x) \equiv next(s, y))$$

for all states s in S and all inputs x and y in I. P_{in} describes how an FSM moves between states regardless of the input sequence. Again, suppose we want to build an FSM using some partition P. If $P \geq P_{in}$ then P is coarser than P_{in} and the classes of P are mergers of the classes in P_{in}. Partitions with this property are **input-consistent.** Dorn calls partitions that are both closed and input-consistent **input-independent.** For example, an FSM that oscillates between 0 and 1—regardless of input—has an input consistent partition. In FSM M1,

$$P_{in} = (E \equiv B \quad C \equiv F \quad D \equiv A \quad E \equiv B \quad C \equiv F \quad A \equiv D)$$

$$= (A \equiv D \quad B \equiv E \quad C \equiv F)$$

M1 does not have any closed, input- and output-consistent partitions. Its output is dependent on the input. However, if M1 were changed so out(F) = 0, then P_{out} = $(A \equiv D \equiv C \equiv F \quad B \equiv E)$ and $P = (A \equiv C \quad B \equiv E \quad C \equiv F)$ is a closed, input- and output-consistent partition. The machine generated by this partition outputs the repeating pattern 010010010010... regardless of the input. Similarly, changing M1 so that out(C) = 1 produces a machine that outputs the repeating pattern 011011011011....

Rather than simply reducing the number of states in an FSM, FSMs can be decomposed into two or more different machines that together perform the same function. Both parallel and serial decompositions are possible. An FSM with two closed partitions P1 $*$ P2 = 0 can be decomposed into two parallel FSMs, one FSM built from P1 and the other built from P2. See Dorn and Hohn (1978) for a good writeup.

Polya's Example

Much of computer science involves counting and enumerating. In this section, we look at a method for dealing with problems that have unusual constraints. But these problems are not uncommon.

How many different bracelets of five beads can be made from black (B) and white (W) beads? Two bracelets are the same (equivalent) if they look the same after any number of flips and rotations. For example, "WBBBB" is the same as "BWBBB." The common methods of counting do not work because they cannot handle flipping and rotating. Spend a few minutes working on this problem. Or if you'd like a more challenging problem, find the number of distinct five-bead bracelets made with three colors.

This is not an isolated problem. There are other examples. How many ways are there to paint the faces of a cube using two colors? Or from computer science, how many distinct boolean functions have three inputs? Or from chemistry, how many distinct chemical compounds can be made with H– and CH$_3$ radicals attached to the six slots of a benzene ring? (See Figure 15.7.)

Each of these problems requires a kind of mental gymnastics that would be hard to program. Any such program seems to be far too specialized to qualify for inclusion in a general purpose library. However, each of these problems is related and can be solved with the same general purpose machinery.

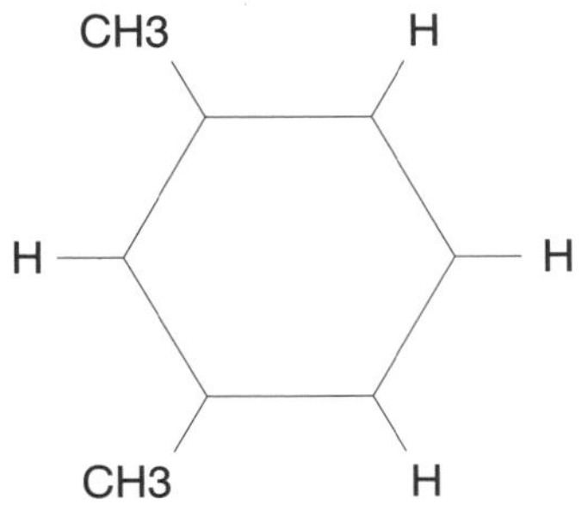

FIGURE 15.7
Benzene ring. A benzene ring is six carbon atoms arranged in a hexagon or ring. This benzene ring has four H— and two CH_3— radicals attached to its six slots.

Each of these problems has the same structure: there is an object with s slots or positions, and each slot can be painted one of c colors. (In the bracelet problem, there are five slots and two colors.) Without any rotation or flipping, there are c^s different paintings. But some of these c^s paintings are equivalent. In the bead problem, rotating a bracelet painting one fifth of a turn is not a different painting. Similarly, flipping a bracelet painting over is the same painting. How can we formalize these notions?

Permutations perfectly describe rotations and flipping (see Chapter 12). If the slots of the five beads are numbered one through five (see Figure 15.8), rotation of the bracelet is the slot-to-slot permutation R = (1 2 3 4 5), and flipping is the slot-to-slot permutation F = (1)(2 5)(3 4). These two permutations generate G, the group of all possible movements of the bracelet. R^2 is a rotation of two fifths of a complete turn, F * R is a flip followed by a rotation. G contains 10 different movements.

A **painting** is a mapping from slots to colors. A painting is easily represented as a FunDRng function (see "FunDRng Class" in Chapter 10). The function [B, B, B, B, B] paints each bead (slot) black. [B, W, B, W, W] paints the first and third beads black and the rest white.

Since every permutation is also a FunDRng, we can combine movements and paintings using function composition. Multiplication of a slot-to-slot function (the permutation) and a slot-to-color function (the painting) gives a different slot-to-color painting. This new painting is the result of permuting the slots. Permuting the slots[4] of painting P1 by rotation R gives a new painting P2 = R * P1 that is equivalent to P1. Similarly, P3 = F * P1 is equivalent to P1. In other words, P1 ≡ P2 ≡ P3 under the step functions of G. Therefore P1 ≡ g * P1 where g is any of the 10 movements in group G.

The number of distinct paintings is the number of painting equivalence classes. If we can find the equivalence classes, we have solved the problem.

---

4. R permutes the slots, not the colors. That is, R relabels the slots with new numbers, and then uses those numbers to assign colors. So R * P1 looks like the colors have been rotated by R^{-1}. To permute the colors, use R^{-1} * P1. Since every rotation is in the group generated by R and F, this distinction will not change the final result.

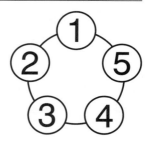

FIGURE 15.8
Bracelet with five beads (slots).

Polya and Redfield developed a beautiful theory (based on conjugacy classes in the group of permutations) to count the number of equivalent classes (see Dorn and Hohn, 1978:242). I strongly encourage readers who enjoyed the group theoretic aspects of permutations to see one of the references on this topic. The answer is not obvious, but is the simple evaluation of a polynomial. However, the construction of the polynomial is heavily dependent on the group of permutations and its representation in slots. For example, the polynomial for coloring the faces of a cube is very different than the polynomial for coloring the edges of a cube. Any library class based on this method would require a lot of sophistication from its users.

There is a further result (the Redfield-Polya Theorem) that breaks the total count into the number of equivalent classes that use the same number of colors. For example, it counts the number of paintings that are all white, the number that have two white beads and three black beads, and so on.

But any application that needs to know the number of distinct paintings will most likely also need a representative of each painting. For this reason, and because of the sophistication needed to use Polya's theory, I have chosen a more brute force approach. It requires modest amounts of information from the user, and provides a representative for every painting.

Algorithm 1

1. Allocate a partition of c^s elements. Each element corresponds to one painting.
2. For each generator g of the group G, and for each painting p of the partition, set $p \equiv g * p$.

We need to loop only over the generators of the group (not every element in the group) since $p \equiv g * p$ and $(g * p) \equiv g * (g * p)$ imply $p \equiv g^2 * p$. One of these equivalences is computed processing painting p, the other processing painting $(g * p)$. The group generators are step functions that "connect" paintings together, much like cells of a game board are connected.

Alternatively, depending on the problem, we could use:

Algorithm 2

1. Allocate a partition of c^s elements. Each element corresponds to one painting.
2. For every element g of the group (not just the generators), and every class representative p in the painting partition, set $p \equiv g * p$.

We need to loop only over class representatives. If r is the representative for p then there is some $g1$ such that $g1 * r = p$. Also, if $q \equiv p$ there is a $g2$ such that $q = g2 * p$. Then $q = g2 * p = g2 * (g1 * r) = (g2 * g1) * r = g3 * r$ where $g3 = g2 * g1$. So $q = g3 * r$ and $q \equiv r$.

The choice between Algorithms 1 and 2 depends on the number of group generators versus the number of class representatives as the computation proceeds. Algorithm 2 loops over all group elements. This can be quite large in general. For example, the Manthieu group M_{11} has three generators, but 7920 group elements (Coxeter and Maser, 1980:99–100). Class Polya uses Algorithm 1 since it does not require the computation or storage of all the group elements.

Note that any algorithm that loops over just the generators of the group and just the class representatives of the partition will not generate all equivalences. For example, assume R is a rotation of four slots (1 2 3 4) and p is some painting. The four paintings that should be equivalent are ($p \equiv R * p \equiv R^2 * p \equiv R^3 * p$). The first iteration with p (the rep of the first singleton class) and R (the only generator) produces $p \equiv R * p$. The next rep is $R^2 * p$, which produces $R^2 * p \equiv R^3 * p$ giving the partition ($p \equiv R * p$ $R^2 * p \equiv R^3 * p$). The product of R with either rep p or $R^2 * p$ produces no new equivalences. This algorithm is flawed.

The basic algorithm can be pushed another step. Above, we used slot-to-slot permutations to define equivalence. We can also make two paintings equivalent using color-to-color permutations. That is $p1 \equiv p2$ when $p1 * h \equiv p2$ and h is a generator of a color permutation group H. In the bead problem, if $h = $ (W B) then WWWWW $\equiv$ BBBBB, and WWWBB $\equiv$ BBBWW by h, and BBBWW $\equiv$ WWBBB by rotation. In other words, we don't care about the actual colors, just the pattern of same and different colors.

Polya Class
Polya's class interface is a straightforward implementation of algorithm 1.

1. Determine the number of slots and build a DSet for the slots. Determine the number of colors and build a DSet for the colors.

   In the bracelet example, there are five slots numbered 1..5, and two colors named black (B) and white (W).
2. Construct a Polya object passing it the DSets for the slots and colors.

   The constructor allocates a partition of c^s elements and initializes the partition to zero(). Every partition element is a painting that is a FunDRng function from s slots to c colors.
3. Determine the generators of G, the group of slot-to-slot permutations. G defines which paintings are equivalent. Add each generator g of G to the object.

Every painting p in the partition is composed (premultiplied) by g and $p \equiv g * p$. Remember, you only need to add the group generators, not every element of the group. However, adding extra group elements will not change the final result.

In the bracelet example, R = (1   2   3   4   5) and F = (1) (2   5) (3   4) generate the motions of the bracelet.

4. Determine the generators H, the group of color-to-color permutations. Add each generator h of H to the object.

Every painting p in the partition is composed (postmultiplied) by h and $p \equiv p * h$.

5. After all generators are added, you can iterate over the class reps to get representative paintings.

POLYAT provides a simple shell for using the Polya class. For the five-bead, two-color problem with no color-to-color equivalences, the input looks like this:

```
C>polyat
Slot domain (first last): 1 5
Color domain (first last): 1 2
Slot permutations separated by ',' and ended with '.'
(1 2 3 4 5),(1)(2 5)(3 4).
Color permutations separated by ',' and ended with '.'
().
0=List representatives; 1=list class contents:0
1: [1 1 1 1 1]
2: [2 1 1 1 1]
3: [2 2 1 1 1]
4: [2 1 2 1 1]
5: [2 2 2 1 1]
6: [2 2 1 2 1]
7: [2 2 2 2 1]
8: [2 2 2 2 2]
```

The identity color-to-color permutation was specified because you must specify at least one permutation. It does not generate any equivalences. Figure 15.9 shows the eight distinct bracelets.

You can easily rerun the bracelet problem again with the color-to-color permutation (1   2). It results in four classes with representatives (a)–(d) in Figure 15.9.

Distinct Circuits

POLYAT also computes the number of distinct boolean circuits of n inputs. There are 2^{2^n} different possible circuits with n inputs; an exponentially growing number. If you were a business person charged with building, or even maintaining an inventory of all these distinct (inequivalent) parts, you would look for some way to reduce that number. The number of distinct circuits can be reduced using Polya's theory. The "slots" in this problem are the circuit input patterns and the "colors" are the circuit outputs 0 and 1.

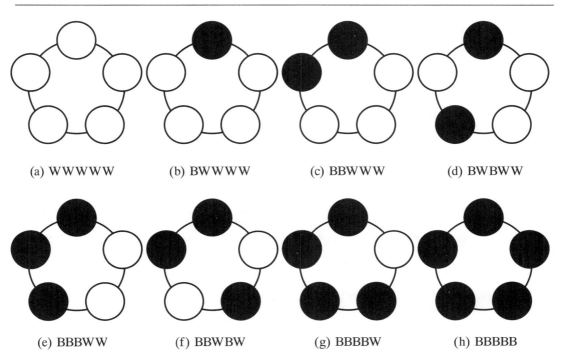

FIGURE 15.9
Distinct bracelets. Representatives of the distinct bracelets made from five beads of two colors. The captions name each painting. They name the colors as they appear around the bracelet. For example, WBWBB means "white, black, white, black, black."

As an example, we will look at circuits with three inputs. Every three-input circuit can receive $2^3 = 8$ input patterns, and it maps each of those eight input patterns to a 0 or 1 output. So each circuit is a function (FunDRng) from the domain [0..7] to the range [0..1]. Figure 15.10 shows a cube where the x-, y- and z-axes correspond to the three input bits, and the cube's verticies represent each of the eight possible input patterns (slots).

The circuit user can easily swap input signals between input pins. Swapping input pins creates a permutation of the input patterns (slots), which is the same as a permutation of the cube verticies (a symmetry of the cube). Swapping input pins 1 and 2 creates a slot-to-slot permutation that changes 010 into 100, and changes 011 into 101. All other verticies map to themselves (e.g., 110 does not change when the first two 1's are interchanged). The slot-to-slot permutation Swap12 = (010 100)(011 101) creates an equivalence between input patterns and therefore an equivalence between circuits.

Permutating the input pins by (1   2   3) creates the slot-to-slot permutation Rotate123 = (001   100   010)(011   101   110). Permutations Swap12 and Rotate123

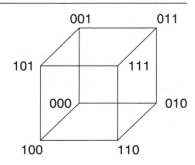

FIGURE 15.10
Pattern of three input bits. Three input bits form eight patterns that are arranged as the verticies of a cube.

generate the group of all six possible permutations of three items.[5] Therefore, these two permutations are the ones we need to give to POLYAT. POLYAT does not support user-defined names like 010 or 110, so these binary patterns have been converted to decimal numbers.

```
C>polyat
Slot domain (first last):0 7
Color domain (first last):1 2
Slot permutations separated by ',' and ended with '.'
(2 4)(3 5), (1 4 2)(3 5 6).
Color permutations separated by ',' and ended with '.'
().
0=List representatives; 1=list class contents:0
1: [1 1 1 1 1 1 1 1]
2: [2 1 1 1 1 1 1 1]
...
79: [1 2 2 2 2 2 2 2]
81: [2 2 2 2 2 2 2 2]
```

Allowing input pin swapping reduced the number of distinct circuits from 256 to 80.

The circuit user can also easily invert any input signal. Inverting input signal 1 converts 000 to 100, 001 to 101, and so forth. Inv1 = (000   100)(001   101)(010   110) (011   111) is a slot-to-slot permutation. We also want to allow inversion of pin 2. But this is just the permutation Inv2 = Swap12^{-1} * Inv1 * Swap12, and therefore is not a generator of the larger group. Similarly, inversion of pin3 is a combination of other permutations. You can verify that these three permutations are indeed generators by entering them into PERMCALC and running close.

The circuit user can invert the output as well as inverting inputs. This gives a permutation of the output value and is the color-to-color permutation InvOut = (1   2).

---

5. The is the symmetric group S_3.

```
C>polyat
Slot domain (first last):0 7
Color domain (first last):1 2
Slot permutations separated by ',' and ended with '.'
(2 4)(3 5), (1 4 2)(3 5 6), (0 4)(1 5)(2 6)(3 7).
Color permutations separated by ',' and ended with '.'
(1 2).
0=List representatives; 1=list class contents:0
 1: [1 1 1 1 1 1 1 1]
 2: [2 1 1 1 1 1 1 1]
 3: [2 2 1 1 1 1 1 1]
 4: [1 2 2 1 1 1 1 1]
 5: [2 2 2 1 1 1 1 1]
 6: [2 2 2 2 1 1 1 1]
 7: [1 2 2 1 2 1 1 1]
 8: [2 2 2 1 2 1 1 1]
 9: [1 1 1 2 2 1 1 1]
10: [2 1 1 2 2 1 1 1]
11: [2 2 1 2 2 1 1 1]
12: [1 2 2 2 2 1 1 1]
13: [1 1 2 2 2 2 1 1]
14: [2 1 1 2 1 2 2 1]
```

With inversions of inputs and outputs, there are now only 14 distinct circuits. Quite a reduction from the original 256.

Try computing the number of distinct circuits with two inputs. Theoretically, POLYTA will solve the problem with four inputs. But that requires a partition with $2^{2^4} = 65536$ elements and each element must be at least two bytes. But the 8086 family of processors impose a hard limit of 64K per segment. POLYAT should handle the four-input case on a different processor.

This section was built by combining many existing pieces. It used Functions (FunDRngs), Permutations, and Partitions. And it solves a class of problems that are not handled by most existing approaches.

Source Code

File Polya.hpp

```cpp
#ifndef _POLYA_HPP
#define _POLYA_HPP
//*********************************************************************
// TITLE: Polya -- Polya's theory of enumeration
//
// PROGRAMMER: Scott N Gerard
// LANGUAGE: C++
```

(continued)

File Polya.hpp *(continued)*

```
//
// FUNCTION:
//
//     Inx must be an integer type large enough to hold 0..slots*colors-1.
//
// CHANGE LOG:
//     01May93 - Initial coding.  SN Gerard
//****************************************************************************
#include <assert.h>
#include <math.h>
#include "Part.hpp"
#include "Perm.hpp"

template <class Inx, class Slot, class Color> class PolyaRepIter;
template <class Inx, class Slot, class Color> class PolyaElemIter;

template<class Inx, class Slot, class Color>
class Polya {

public:
    typedef FunDRng<Slot,Color> Painting;
    typedef Perm<Slot>          SlotPerm;
    typedef Perm<Color>         ColorPerm;
    typedef Part<Inx,Inx>       Partition;

protected:
    DSet<Slot>*   slotDSet;
    DSet<Color>*  colorDSet;
    Inx           slots;        // number of slots
    Inx           colors;       // number of colors

    Partition*    equiv;        // partition of equivalent paintings

    friend class PolyaRepIter<Inx,Slot,Color>;
    friend class PolyaElemIter<Inx,Slot,Color>;

public:
    Polya(DSet<Slot>& slotdset, DSet<Color>& colordset);
    virtual ~Polya();

    //****************************************************************************
    // slot-to-slot equivalence generator.
    //****************************************************************************
    void slotGen (const SlotPerm& generator);

    //****************************************************************************
    // color-to-color equivalence generator.
    //****************************************************************************
    void colorGen (const ColorPerm& generator);
};
```

```
//*******************************************************************
//
//                              Iterators
//
//*******************************************************************


//*******************************************************************
// PolyaRepIter: Iterate over all class representatives of a partition.
//*******************************************************************
template <class Inx, class Slot, class Color>
class PolyaRepIter: public PartRepIter<Inx,Inx> {

    typedef PartRepIter<Inx,Inx>  BaseClass;
    typedef Polya<Inx,Slot,Color> RefClass;
    typedef RefClass::Painting     Painting;
    typedef RefClass::Partition    Partition;

public:
    PolyaRepIter();
    PolyaRepIter(const Polya<Inx,Slot,Color>& p);

    Painting operator ++ ();
    Painting operator ++ (int i);

    Painting current () const
        { return currentPainting; };

    void restart();

    friend class PolyaElemIter<Inx,Slot,Color>;

private:
    const RefClass* polya;         // pointer to iteratee
    Painting  currentPainting;     // cache current painting
};

//*******************************************************************
// PolyaElemIter: Iterate over all elements in a single class of a
// partition.
//*******************************************************************
template<class Inx, class Slot, class Color>
class PolyaElemIter: public PartElemIter<Inx,Inx> {

    typedef PartElemIter<Inx,Inx>  BaseClass;
    typedef Polya<Inx,Slot,Color>  RefClass;
    typedef RefClass::Painting      Painting;
    typedef RefClass::Partition     Partition;

public:
    PolyaElemIter(): PartElemIter<Inx,Inx>() {};
    PolyaElemIter(const PolyaRepIter<Inx,Slot,Color>& r);
```

(continued)

File Polya.hpp *(continued)*

```
    // for all elems in class of e
    PolyaElemIter(const Polya<Inx,Slot,Color>& p, const Painting& e)
       :PartElemIter<Inx,Inx>(* p.equiv, e.rank()) {};

    Painting operator ++ ();
    Painting operator ++ (int i);

    Painting current () const
       { return currentPainting; };

    void restart();

private:
    const RefClass* polya;        // pointer to iteratee
    Painting  currentPainting;    // cache current painting
};


#endif
```

File Polya.cpp

```
//****************************************************************************
// TITLE: Polya -- Polya's theory of enumeration
//
// PROGRAMMER: Scott N Gerard
// LANGUAGE: C++
//
// FUNCTION:
//
//    Inx must be an integer type large enough to hold 0..slots*colors-1.
//
// CHANGE LOG:
//    01May93 - Initial coding.  SN Gerard
//****************************************************************************
#include <assert.h>
#include <math.h>

#include "Part.cpp"
#include "Polya.hpp"


//****************************************************************************
// Constructor
//****************************************************************************
template <class Inx, class Slot, class Color>
Polya<Inx,Slot,Color>::Polya(DSet<Slot>& slotdset, DSet<Color>& colordset)
   :slotDSet(&slotdset), colorDSet(&colordset),
    slots(slotdset.count()), colors(colordset.count()),
    equiv( new Partition(pow(colors,slots)) )
    {};
```

```
//***************************************************************************
// Destructor
//***************************************************************************
template <class Inx, class Slot, class Color>
Polya<Inx,Slot,Color>::~Polya()
   { delete equiv; };


//***************************************************************************
// slot-to-slot equivalence generator
//***************************************************************************
template <class Inx, class Slot, class Color>
void Polya<Inx,Slot,Color>::slotGen
   (const /*SlotPerm*/ Perm<Slot>& generator)
{
   if ( generator.isIdent() )                 // ignore request
      return;

   /*Painting*/ FunDRng<Slot,Color> initPainting (*slotDSet,*colorDSet);
   /*Painting*/ FunDRng<Slot,Color> newPainting  (*slotDSet,*colorDSet);

   for (Inx i = 0; i < equiv->size(); ++i) {
      initPainting.unrank(i);
      // newPainting = generator * initPainting.   pre-multiplication
      compose( (Painting&)generator, initPainting, newPainting);
      Inx newI = newPainting.rank();
      equiv->setEquiv(i, newI);
   };
};


//***************************************************************************
// color-to-color equivalence generator
//***************************************************************************
template <class Inx, class Slot, class Color>
void Polya<Inx,Slot,Color>::colorGen
   (const /*ColorPerm*/ Perm<Color>& generator)
{
   if ( generator.isIdent() )                 // ignore request
      return;
   /*Painting*/ FunDRng<Slot,Color> initPainting(*slotDSet,*colorDSet);
   /*Painting*/ FunDRng<Slot,Color> newPainting (*slotDSet,*colorDSet);

   for (Inx i = 0; i < equiv->size(); ++i) {
      initPainting.unrank(i);
      // newPainting = initPainting * generator.   post-multiplication
      compose( initPainting, (Painting&)generator, newPainting);
      Inx newI = newPainting.rank();
      equiv->setEquiv(i, newI);
   };
};
```

(continued)

File Polya.cpp *(continued)*

```
//**************************************************************************
//
//                              Iterators
//
//**************************************************************************


//**************************************************************************
// PolyaRepIter: Iterate over all class representatives of a partition.
//**************************************************************************
template <class Inx, class Slot, class Color>
PolyaRepIter<Inx,Slot,Color>::PolyaRepIter()
    :PartRepIter<Inx,Inx>(), polya(0), currentPainting() {};

template <class Inx, class Slot, class Color>
PolyaRepIter<Inx,Slot,Color>::PolyaRepIter(const Polya<Inx,Slot,Color>& p)
    :PartRepIter<Inx,Inx>( (const Partition&) *p.equiv ),
    polya(&p),
    currentPainting(* p.slotDSet, * p.colorDSet) {};

template <class Inx, class Slot, class Color>
/*Painting*/
FunDRng<Slot,Color> PolyaRepIter<Inx,Slot,Color>::operator ++ () {
    BaseClass::operator++();
    if ( *this )                      // if cur is valid
        currentPainting.unrank(cur);
    return currentPainting;
};

template <class Inx, class Slot, class Color>
/*Painting*/
FunDRng<Slot,Color> PolyaRepIter<Inx,Slot,Color>::operator ++ (int i) {
    BaseClass::operator++(i);
    if ( *this )                      // if cur is valid
        currentPainting.unrank(cur);
    return currentPainting;
};

template <class Inx, class Slot, class Color>
void PolyaRepIter<Inx,Slot,Color>::restart() {
    BaseClass::restart();
    currentPainting.unrank(cur);
};

//**************************************************************************
// PolyaElemIter: Iterate over all elements in a single class of a
// partition.
//**************************************************************************
template<class Inx, class Slot, class Color>
PolyaElemIter<Inx,Slot,Color>::PolyaElemIter
    (const PolyaRepIter<Inx,Slot,Color>& r)
    :PartElemIter<Inx,Inx>(r), //  (const Partition&) *r.polya->equiv ),
```

```
      polya(r.polya),
      currentPainting(* r.polya->slotDSet, * r.polya->colorDSet)
      { currentPainting.unrank(cur); };

template<class Inx, class Slot, class Color>
/*Painting*/
FunDRng<Slot,Color> PolyaElemIter<Inx,Slot,Color>::operator ++ () {
   BaseClass::operator++();
   if ( *this )                        // if cur is valid
      currentPainting.unrank(cur);
   return currentPainting;
};

template<class Inx, class Slot, class Color>
/*Painting*/
FunDRng<Slot,Color> PolyaElemIter<Inx,Slot,Color>::operator ++ (int i) {
   BaseClass::operator++(i);
   if ( *this )                        // if cur is valid
      currentPainting.unrank(cur);
   return currentPainting;
};

template<class Inx, class Slot, class Color>
void PolyaElemIter<Inx,Slot,Color>::restart() {
   BaseClass::restart();
   currentPainting.unrank(cur);
};
```

File PolyaT.cpp

```
// Test Polya object

#include <new.h>
#include <iostream.h>
#include <strstream.h>
#include <iomanip.h>

#include "Polya.hpp"

// types for Polya object
typedef unsigned long Inx;
typedef unsigned Slots;
typedef unsigned Colors;

#include "Polya.cpp"
#include "Perm.cpp"
#include "SimpHasher.cpp"

//******************************************************************
// memory allocation error handler
//******************************************************************
```

(continued)

File PolyaT.cpp *(continued)*

```cpp
void newErrorHandler() {
   cout << "Could not allocate memory\n";
   exit(EXIT_FAILURE);
};

void main() {
   set_new_handler(newErrorHandler);
   unsigned first, last;

   cout << "Slot domain (first last):";
   cin  >> first >> last;
   ShiftDSet<Slots>  slotDSet(first,last);

   cout << "Color domain (first last):";
   cin  >> first >> last;
   ShiftDSet<Colors> colorDSet(first,last);

   Perm<Slots>                slotPerm(slotDSet);
   Perm<Colors>               colorPerm(colorDSet);
   Polya<Inx,Slots,Colors>    polya(slotDSet,colorDSet);

   char ch;
   cout << "Slot permutations separated by ',' and ended with '.'\n";
   do {
      cin >> slotPerm;
      polya.slotGen(slotPerm);
      cin >> ch;
   } while ( ch != '.');

   cout << "Color permutations separated by ',' and ended with '.'\n";
   do {
      cin >> colorPerm;
      polya.colorGen(colorPerm);
      cin >> ch;
   } while ( ch != '.' );

   int classContents;
   cout << "0=List representatives; 1=list class contents:";
   cin >> classContents;

   // print out the representatives
   unsigned i=0;
   for (PolyaRepIter<Inx,Slots,Colors> ri=polya; ri; ++ri) {
      cout << ++i << ": " << ri.current() << endl;
      if ( classContents ) {
         for (PolyaElemIter<Inx,Slots,Colors> ei=ri; ei; ++ei) {
            cout << "           " << ei.current() << endl;
         };
      };
   };
};
```

BIBLIOGRAPHY

Bandelow, C. 1982. *Inside Rubik's Cube and Beyond.* Boston: Birkhauser.

Beasley, J. D. 1990. *The Mathematics of Games.* New York: Oxford.

Booch, G. September 1992a. "The Booch Method: Notation, Part I." *Computer Language.* Vol. 9, No. 9, pp. 47–70.

———. October 1992b. "The Booch Method: Notation, Part II." *Computer Language.* Vol. 9, No. 10, pp. 36–55.

Coplien, J. O. 1992. *Advanced C++: Programming Styles and Idioms.* Reading, MA: Addison-Wesley.

Coxeter, H. S. M.; Maser, W. O. J. 1980. *Generators and Relations for Discrete Groups,* 4th ed. Berlin: Springer-Verlag.

Dorn, L. L.; Hohn, F. E. 1978. *Applied Modern Algebra.* New York: Macmillan.

Fraleigh, J. B. 1976. *A First Course in Abstract Algebra.* Reading, MA: Addison-Wesley.

Furtado, A. L. September 1987. "Generalized Set Comparison." *SIGPLAN Notices.* Vol. 19, No. 9, pp. 12–15.

Gellert, W., et al., ed. 1975. *The VNR Concise Encyclopedia of Mathematics,* 2nd ed. New York: VNR.

Gimpel, J. F. 1976. *Algorithms in Snobol4.* New York: Wiley.

Hammond Inc. 1988. "Past Worlds: The Times Atlas of Archaeology." Maplewood, NJ: Hammond.

The Institute of Electrical and Electronics Engineers, Inc. 1981. "A Proposed Standard for Binary Floating-Point Arithmetic." Draft 8.0 of *IEEE Task* P754. Los Alamitos, CA: Computer reprint.

Ives, F. M. 1976. "Permutation Enumeration: Four New Permutation Algorithms." *Communications of the ACM.* Vol. 19, No. 2, pp. 68–72.

Knuth, D. E. 1973a. *The Art of Computer Programming,* 2nd ed. Vol. 1. Reading, MA: Addison-Wesley.

———. 1968b. *The Art of Computer Programming.* Vol. 2. Reading, MA: Addison-Wesley.

———. 1973c. *The Art of Computer Programming.* Vol. 3. Reading, MA: Addison-Wesley.

Kolman, B. 1976. *Introductory Linear Algebra with Applications.* New York: Macmillan.

Kraitchik, M. 1953. *Mathematical Recreations.* New York: Dover.

Lidl, R.; Pilz, G. 1984. *Applied Abstract Algebra.* New York: Springer-Verlag.

Lippman, S. B. 1989. *C++ Primer.* Reading, MA: Addison-Wesley.

Meyers, S. 1992. *Effective C++: 50 Specific Ways to Improve Your Programs and Designs.* Reading, MA: Addison-Wesley.

Newman, W. M.; Sproull, R. F. 1973. *Principles of Interactive Computer Graphics.* New York: McGraw-Hill.

Niejenhuis, A.; Wilf, H. S. 1975. *Combinatorial Algorithms.* New York: Academic Press.

Reisig, W. 1982. *Petri Nets, An Introduction.* Berlin: Springer-Verlag. Translated.

Sadie, S., ed. 1980. "Change ringing." *The New Grove Dictionary of Music and Musicians.* London: Macmillan.

Sakkinen, M. August 1987. "Comparison as a Value-yielding Operation." *SIGPLAN Notices.* Vol. 22, No. 8, pp. 105–110.

Sayers, D. L. 1962. *The Nine Tailers.* London: Harcourt, Brace.

Scott, D. S.; Iyengar, S. S. 1986. "TID—A Translation Invariant Data Structure for Storing Images." *CACM.* Vol. 29, No. 5, p. 418.

Sebesta, R. W.; Taylor, M. A. December 1985. "Minimal Perfect Hash Functions for Reserved Word Lists." *SIGPLAN Notices.* Vol. 20, No. 12, pp. 47–53.

Sedgewick, R. 1984. *Algorithms.* Reading, MA: Addison-Wesley. Reprinted with corrections.

Stroustrup, B. 1991. *The C++ Programming Language,* 2nd ed. Reading, MA: Addison-Wesley.
Wilson, A. C.; Cann, R. L. April 1992. "The Recent African Genesis of Humans." *Scientific American,* pp. 68–73.

INDEX